Federated Learning for of Vehicles: IoV Image Processing, Vision and Intelligent Systems

(Volume 3)

Federated Learning Based Intelligent Systems to Handle Issues and Challenges in IoVs
(Part 1)

Edited by

Shelly Gupta
CSE (AI) Department
KIET Group of Institutions, U.P.,
Delhi-NCR Ghaziabad, India

Puneet Garg
Department of CSE-AI
KIET Group of Institutions, Ghaziabad, U.P., India

Jyoti Agarwal
CSE Department
Graphics Era University (Deemed to be), India

Hardeo Kumar Thakur
School of Computer Science Engineering and Technology
(SCSET)
Bennett University, Greater Noida
U.P., India

&

Satya Prakash Yadav
School of Computer Science Engineering and Technology
(SCSET)
Bennett University, Greater Noida
U.P., India

Federated Learning for Internet of Vehicles: IoV Image Processing, Vision and Intelligent Systems

(Volume 3)

Federated Learning Based Intelligent Systems to Handle Issues and Challenges in IoVs

(Part 1)

Editors: Shelly Gupta, Puneet Garg, Jyoti Agarwal, Hardeo Kumar Thakur & Satya Prakash Yadav

ISBN (Online): 978-981-5313-02-4

ISBN (Print): 978-981-5313-03-1

ISBN (Paperback): 978-981-5313-04-8

©2024, Bentham Books imprint.

Published by Bentham Science Publishers Pte. Ltd. Singapore. All Rights Reserved.

First published in 2024.

need for a court order if at any point you breach any terms of this License Agreement. In no event will any delay or failure by Bentham Science Publishers in enforcing your compliance with this License Agreement constitute a waiver of any of its rights.

3. You acknowledge that you have read this License Agreement, and agree to be bound by its terms and conditions. To the extent that any other terms and conditions presented on any website of Bentham Science Publishers conflict with, or are inconsistent with, the terms and conditions set out in this License Agreement, you acknowledge that the terms and conditions set out in this License Agreement shall prevail.

Bentham Science Publishers Ltd.
Executive Suite Y - 2
PO Box 7917, Saif Zone
Sharjah, U.A.E.
Email: subscriptions@benthamscience.net

BENTHAM SCIENCE

CONTENTS

PREFACE

In an era where the Internet of Vehicles (IoVs) is altering our transportation environment, the demand for intelligent systems capable of effectively processing and analysing massive volumes of data has never been more. The convergence of IoVs with powerful machine learning algorithms has opened up new opportunities to improve road safety, efficiency, and user experience. However, this rapid evolution presents its own set of obstacles, ranging from data privacy concerns to the intricacies of real-time decision-making.

By examining the cutting-edge federated learning paradigm, this book, Federated Learning Based Intelligent Systems to Handle Issues and Challenges in IoVs, aims to answer these urgent problems. Federated learning, in contrast to conventional centralized methods, permits decentralized data processing, allowing cars to jointly learn from local data while maintaining privacy. This approach not only reduces the hazards connected with data exchange, but it also improves the adaptability of intelligent systems under a variety of driving situations.

We explore the major issues that IoVs are now confronting throughout this work, such as data heterogeneity, network latency, and the requirement for strong security measures. Each chapter mixes theoretical ideas with practical examples, showing how federated learning can be used to develop resilient, intelligent systems that can thrive in the dynamic environment of connected automobiles.

We encourage you to consider the revolutionary possibilities of these technologies as you set out on this journey through the nexus of federated learning and IoVs. Our hope is that this book will not only be a valuable resource for researchers and practitioners, but will also stimulate more innovation in the sector, paving the way for smarter, safer transportation systems.

We are grateful to the authors, scholars, and practitioners who have contributed their skills to this work. We are building the foundation for a time when intelligent technologies prioritize privacy and safety over transportation.

Shelly Gupta
CSE (AI) Department
KIET Group of Institutions, U.P.,
Delhi-NCR Ghaziabad, India

Puneet Garg
Department of CSE-AI
KIET Group of Institutions, Ghaziabad, U.P., India

Jyoti Agarwal
CSE Department
Graphics Era University(Deemed to be), India

Hardeo Kumar Thakur
School of Computer Science Engineering and Technology (SCSET)
Bennett University, Greater Noida
U.P., India

&

Satya Prakash Yadav
School of Computer Science Engineering and Technology (SCSET)
Bennett University, Greater Noida
U.P., India

List of Contributors

Apurva Jain	Dr. Akhilesh Das Gupta Institute of Technology & Management, New Delhi, India
Achal Kaushik	Bhagwan Parshuram Institute of Technology, GGSIPU, New Delhi, India
Anurag Gupta	CSE AI Department, KIET Group of Institutions, Ghaziabad, India
Anjali Chauhan	CSE AI Department, KIET Group of Institutions, Ghaziabad, India
Arvind Panwar	School of Computing Science and Engineering, Galgotias University, Greater Noida, India
Gopal Krishna	Uttaranchal Institute of Technology, Uttaranchal University, Dehradun, India
Gaurav Singh Negi	Uttaranchal Institute of Technology, Uttaranchal University, Dehradun, India
Jyoti Agarwal	Graphic Era University, Dehradun, India
Jitendra Kumar Gupta	Uttaranchal Institute of Technology, Uttaranchal University, Dehradun, India Department of Computer Science & Engineering, Dr. BR Ambedkar National Institute of Technology, Jalandhar, India
Jyoti Parashar	Dr. Akhilesh Das Gupta Institute of Technology & Management, New Delhi, India
Kapil Kumar Sharma	Department of MCA, IMS Engineering College, Ghaziabad, India School of Computer Science and Application, IIMT University, Meerut, India
Lokesh Meena	Dr. Akhilesh Das Gupta Institute of Technology & Management, New Delhi, India
Manish Kumar	School of Computing Science and Engineering, Galgotias University, Greater Noida, India
Neha Sharma	USICT, GGSIPU, New Delhi, India Bharati Vidyapeeth College of Engineering, Paschim Vihar, New Delhi, India
Nisar Ahmad Malik	Govt Degree College Kulgam, J&K, India
Prachi Dahiya	Department of CSE, Delhi Technological University, Delhi, India
Priyanka Gaba	School of Computer Science Engineering and Technology, Bennett University, Greater Noida, India
Soumya Sharma	Bhagwan Parshuram Institute of Technology, GGSIPU, New Delhi, India
Umang Kant	Department of CSE-AIML, KIET Group of Institutions, Ghaziabad, UP, India
Urvashi Sugandh	School of Computing Science and Engineering, Galgotias University, Greater Noida, India
Vishal Gupta	NSUT East Campus (Formerly AIACT&R), New Delhi, India
Virendra Singh Kushwah	VIT Bhopal University, Sehore, India

CHAPTER 1

Technologies to Solve the Routing Issues in IoVs

Anurag Gupta[1] and **Anjali Chauhan**[1,*]

[1] *CSE AI Department, KIET Group of Institutions, Ghaziabad, India*

Abstract: This book chapter explores the challenges and technologies involved in solving routing issues in the context of the Internet of Vehicles (IoV). The IoV represents a dynamic and complex network environment that connects vehicles, infrastructure, and various other entities. Efficient routing is crucial for timely and reliable information exchange in such networks. The chapter begins by discussing the unique challenges associated with routing in IoV, such as frequent topology changes, limited bandwidth, and high vehicle mobility. It emphasizes the need for robust and efficient routing protocols to ensure seamless data delivery in vehicular networks. Next, the chapter provides a comprehensive review of existing routing techniques and protocols designed specifically for IoV. It covers geographic routing, cluster-based routing, and hybrid routing approaches, examining their strengths, limitations, and applicability to different IoV scenarios. The chapter also discusses the importance of considering quality-of-service (QoS) metrics, such as latency, reliability, and energy efficiency, when designing routing solutions for IoV. Furthermore, the chapter explores advanced technologies that can enhance routing performance in IoV. It delves into the integration of IoV with cloud computing, edge computing, and the Internet of Things (IoT). These technologies offer additional computational resources, data storage capabilities, and real-time data processing at the network edge, leading to improved routing efficiency and reduced latency. The chapter also highlights the role of artificial intelligence (AI) and machine learning (ML) techniques in addressing routing challenges in IoV. It explores how AI and ML algorithms can analyze and predict vehicular mobility patterns, optimize routing decisions, and mitigate network congestion. The chapter emphasizes the potential of AI and ML to adaptively optimize routing strategies based on real-time network conditions. Finally, the chapter concludes by discussing open research challenges and future directions for solving routing issues in IoV. It identifies areas such as intelligent routing protocols, energy-efficient routing schemes, and security mechanisms as critical research domains. The chapter underscores the importance of ongoing research and development to ensure the efficient and secure operation of IoV routing. Overall, this book chapter provides a comprehensive overview of the technologies proposed to address routing issues in the IoV. It serves as a valuable resource for researchers, practitioners, and policymakers working in the field of vehicular networking, offering insights into the challenges, solutions, and future directions for efficient and reliable routing in IoV environments.

---

* **Corresponding author Anjali Chauhan:** CSE AI Department, KIET Group of Institutions, Ghaziabad, India; E-mail: anjisingh.chauhan@gmail.com

Shelly Gupta, Puneet Garg, Jyoti Agarwal, Hardeo Kumar Thakur & Satya Prakash Yadav (Eds.)

Keywords: Machine learning, Anomaly detection, Artificial intelligence, Federated learning, Internet of vehicles, Routing protocols.

INTRODUCTION TO ROUTING ISSUES IN IOV

Routing plays an important role when we implement communication between the Internet of Vehicles. While the network of the Internet of Vehicles provides a real-time information on the road and the information of the vehicles, it becomes necessary to understand IOT, IoV, and Intelligent IoV Systems. Hence, further in this section, we understand these concepts well [1].

Overview of IoV and Related Concepts

The world we live in today is becoming increasingly connected, transforming the way we interact with our surroundings and each other. At the heart of this digital revolution lies the Internet of Things (IoT), a groundbreaking concept that has the potential to revolutionize various aspects of our lives. The IoT refers to a vast network of interconnected devices, objects, and systems, all equipped with sensors, software, and connectivity, enabling them to collect, exchange, and analyze data [2].

One of the most useful applications of IoT is the Internet of Vehicles [2]. The automotive industry is undergoing a profound transformation, fueled by technological advancements and the growing interconnectedness of our world. At the forefront of this revolution is the concept of the Internet of Vehicles (IoV), an innovative paradigm that combines transportation and information technologies to create a smart, efficient, and interconnected vehicular ecosystem [3]. The IoV leverages the power of the Internet of Things (IoT) to connect vehicles, infrastructure, and passengers, enabling seamless communication, data sharing, and intelligent decision-making. In this chapter, we will explore the fascinating realm of the Internet of Vehicles, uncovering its principles, applications, and the transformative impact it holds for transportation systems of the future. In order to maintain an efficient system for IoVs, we needed to build an Intelligent Internet of Vehicles. The concept of the Intelligent Internet of Vehicles (IoV) takes the interconnectedness of vehicles to a whole new level by incorporating advanced technologies and intelligent systems. By leveraging the power of artificial intelligence (AI), machine learning, and data analytics, the IoV transforms vehicles into intelligent entities capable of making autonomous decisions, adapting to changing conditions, and providing personalized services. Intelligent IoV systems can analyze vast amounts of data collected from various sources, such as sensors, cameras, and infrastructure, to make informed decisions about navigation, traffic management, and safety. With AI algorithms continuously learning from real-time data, vehicles become more efficient, responsive, and capable of communicating and collaborating with each other and the surrounding environment [4]. The Intelligent IoV holds immense potential in revolutionizing transportation, offering optimized routes, predictive maintenance, intelligent parking solutions, and enhanced safety features. By embracing intelligence, the IoV promises to reshape the way we travel, making our journeys more efficient, convenient, and enjoyable.

Importance of Efficient Routing in IoV

Efficient routing is of paramount importance in the Internet of Vehicles (IoVs) as it directly impacts the overall performance, safety, and reliability of vehicular networks. The IoVs ecosystem encompasses a vast network of interconnected vehicles, infrastructure, and various smart devices, all of which rely on effective routing to enable seamless communication and efficient data exchange. This section explores the significance of efficient routing in IoVs, highlighting its various benefits and implications [5].

Enhancing Traffic Management and Congestion Control

Efficient routing algorithms and protocols play a crucial role in managing traffic flow and alleviating congestion in IoVs. By intelligently directing vehicles through optimal routes, traffic congestion can be minimized, leading to improved overall traffic efficiency and reduced travel time. Effective routing enables traffic management systems to dynamically adapt and reroute vehicles based on real-time traffic conditions, ensuring smooth traffic flow and minimizing bottlenecks [6].

Enabling Vehicular Services and Applications

IoVs offer a plethora of services and applications to enhance the driving experience and provide value-added functionalities. Efficient routing is crucial for enabling these services, such as location-based services, navigation systems, infotainment, and vehicle-to-vehicle (V2V) or vehicle-to-infrastructure (V2I) communication. Routing algorithms ensure that the relevant data is efficiently delivered to the intended recipients, enabling a wide range of IoVs applications to function optimally [7].

Optimizing Resource Utilization and Energy Efficiency

Efficient routing algorithms contribute to optimizing resource utilization and energy efficiency in IoVs. By dynamically determining the most energy-efficient routes and minimizing unnecessary vehicle movement, routing protocols can help reduce fuel consumption and minimize carbon emissions. Furthermore, intelligent routing decisions can optimize the utilization of available network resources, such as bandwidth and computing resources, leading to improved network efficiency and performance [8].

Enabling Scalability and Seamless Mobility

As the number of connected vehicles and devices in IoVs continues to grow, the routing infrastructure needs to be scalable and capable of handling the increasing traffic. Efficient routing algorithms and protocols provide the necessary scalability to accommodate the expanding network, ensuring seamless connectivity and communication between vehicles. This scalability allows IoVs to support a wide range of applications, services, and devices without compromising network performance. In Fig. (**1**), we can see how IoVs connect over the Internet [9].

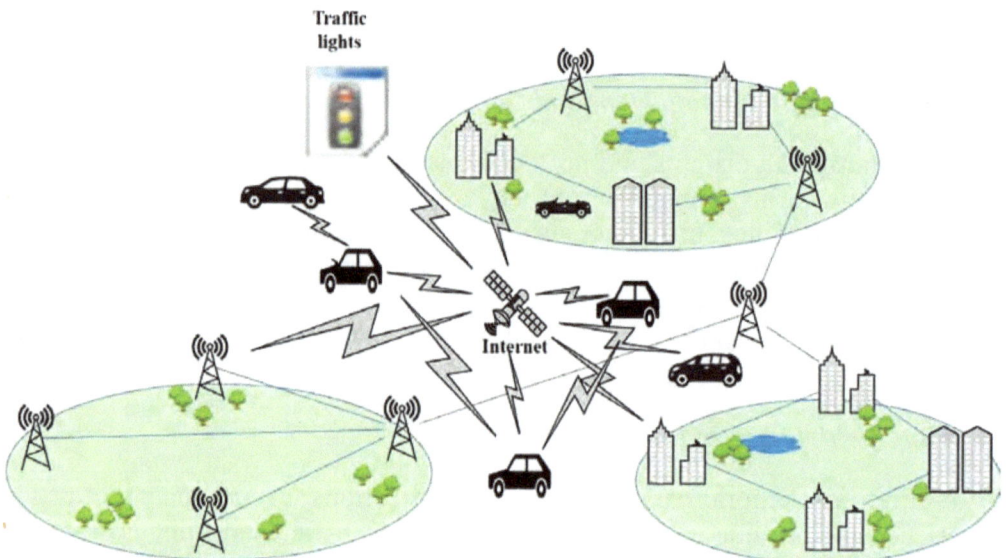

Fig. (1). IoV communication.

Hence, it is quite evident that an efficient routing is vital for the successful operation of IoVs. It enhances traffic management, facilitates real-time communication for safety applications, enables various vehicular services, optimizes resource utilization, and ensures scalability and seamless mobility [10]. By adopting advanced routing technologies and protocols, the challenges and limitations associated with routing in IoVs can be addressed, leading to a more efficient, secure, and reliable vehicular network.

Historical Details about IoV and its Evolution Over Time

The Internet of Vehicles (IoV) has emerged as a groundbreaking concept that revolutionizes how we interact with and navigate the modern transportation landscape. In this chapter, we embark on a historical journey through the evolution of IoV, focusing on its transformative impact on routing efficiency [11]. We will also delve into specific examples and real-world scenarios where efficient routing has made a significant impact and explore the persistent challenges and innovative solutions that have arisen along the way.

Early Pioneers and Visionaries

The roots of IoV can be traced back to the visionary ideas of pioneers who recognized the potential of connected vehicles. In the late 20th century, researchers and inventors like Victor Szebehely envisioned the integration of technology into vehicles to improve safety and efficiency [12]. Although rudimentary, these early concepts laid the groundwork for IoV's development.

Emergence of Vehicular Ad-Hoc Networks (VANETs)

The true catalyst for IoV's evolution was the emergence of Vehicular Ad-Hoc Networks (VANETs) in the early 2000s. VANETs represented a pivotal shift by enabling vehicles to communicate with each other and with roadside infrastructure [13]. One of the most notable examples of VANET's impact on routing efficiency is its application in Intelligent Transportation Systems (ITS) on highways. Case study: The development of adaptive traffic management systems, such as the one implemented on the I-95 highway in the United States, showcased how real-time data from connected vehicles could be used to optimize traffic flow and reroute vehicles to reduce congestion.

Connectivity Beyond VANETs

As IoV continued to evolve, it expanded beyond the confines of VANETs. The introduction of cellular connectivity, exemplified by the deployment of 4G and later 5G networks, played a pivotal role in IoV's growth. This shift allowed vehicles to access the internet directly, facilitating cloud-based routing solutions. Case study: Ride-sharing services like Uber and Lyft rely heavily on real-time routing algorithms that leverage cellular connectivity to match passengers with nearby drivers, optimizing routes for efficiency [14].

Challenges and Issues in Routing

Despite the remarkable progress, IoV has encountered several significant challenges in routing:

Dynamic Network Topology

IoV networks are highly dynamic, with vehicles constantly entering and leaving the network. Traditional routing protocols struggle to adapt to this ever-changing topology.

Data Privacy and Security

Routing sensitive data in IoV, such as location information, raises concerns about privacy and security. Protecting this data while ensuring efficient routing is a complex task.

Scalability

As the number of connected vehicles grows, routing solutions must scale to handle the increasing data volume and network size.

Case Study

Tesla's Autopilot system uses edge computing to process sensor data and make split-second routing decisions for safe autonomous driving.

Challenges and Issues in Routing for IoV

Despite the potential benefits and advancements in routing technologies, the Internet of Vehicles (IoVs) face several challenges and issues that need to be addressed for efficient and reliable routing. This section explores the key challenges and issues associated with routing in IoVs, highlighting the complexities and potential limitations [14].

Highly Dynamic and Heterogeneous Network Topology

IoVs consist of a highly dynamic and heterogeneous network topology, with vehicles constantly moving, joining, and leaving the network. This dynamic nature poses challenges for routing protocols as they need to adapt and quickly establish routes based on the changing network conditions [15]. The varying communication ranges, network densities, and different vehicle types further complicate the routing process, requiring robust and adaptive routing algorithms.

Scalability and Network Management

The scalability of routing solutions is a significant challenge in IoVs due to the large number of connected vehicles and devices. As the network expands, routing protocols must handle the increased traffic and efficiently manage network resources [16]. The design of scalable routing algorithms that can handle the growing network size while maintaining low latency and high throughput is a complex task. Additionally, network management becomes challenging, requiring mechanisms to monitor and maintain the network's health, update routing information, and handle failures or disruptions.

Quality of Service (QoS) and Resource Constraints

Routing in IoVs must consider the Quality of Service (QoS) requirements of different applications and services. Applications such as real-time video streaming, autonomous driving, and safety-critical communications demand low latency, high reliability, and bandwidth guarantees [17]. However, the limited available network resources, including bandwidth, computing power, and energy, pose constraints on routing decisions. Balancing QoS requirements with resource constraints is a significant challenge that requires intelligent routing algorithms and efficient resource management techniques.

Security and Privacy Concerns

IoVs are susceptible to various security and privacy threats, and routing plays a crucial role in ensuring secure and private communication. Routing protocols must protect against attacks such as malicious data injection, spoofing, and denial-of-service attacks [18]. Additionally, privacy concerns arise due to the collection and dissemination of sensitive location and behavior data. Ensuring secure and privacy-preserving routing is a significant challenge that requires robust authentication, encryption, and anonymization techniques.

Interoperability and Standardization

IoVs involve multiple stakeholders, including vehicle manufacturers, infrastructure providers, and communication service providers [19]. The lack of standardized protocols and interoperability among different IoV components poses challenges for seamless routing. Different vehicle types, communication technologies, and infrastructure variations require standardized protocols and interfaces to ensure interoperability. Standardization efforts are necessary to enable efficient routing and smooth integration of different IoVs components.

Real-Time Data and Traffic Management

Routing decisions in IoVs heavily rely on real-time data, including traffic conditions, vehicle speeds, and environmental factors [20]. The timely collection and dissemination of accurate data pose challenges due to communication delays, network congestion, and data quality issues. Additionally, efficient traffic management and congestion control demand real-time updates and dynamic routing decisions. Developing robust data collection mechanisms, traffic prediction algorithms, and intelligent traffic management systems is crucial for addressing these challenges.

Addressing these challenges and issues requires interdisciplinary research efforts, involving computer scientists, engineers, transportation experts, and policymakers. By developing innovative routing algorithms, incorporating machine learning and artificial intelligence techniques, and establishing standardized protocols, the routing issues in IoVs can be effectively mitigated, leading to a more efficient and reliable Internet of Vehicles ecosystem [21].

TRADITIONAL ROUTING PROTOCOLS IN IOV

In the realm of the Internet of Vehicles (IoVs), traditional routing protocols have played a significant role in establishing communication paths and facilitating data exchange between vehicles and infrastructure. These routing protocols, designed for ad hoc and mobile networks, have been adapted and employed in IoVs to address the unique challenges posed by vehicular environments. This section explores some of the traditional routing protocols commonly used in IoVs and discusses their characteristics, advantages, and limitations [22]. Fig. (**2**) represents all the routing protocols used in IoV in brief.

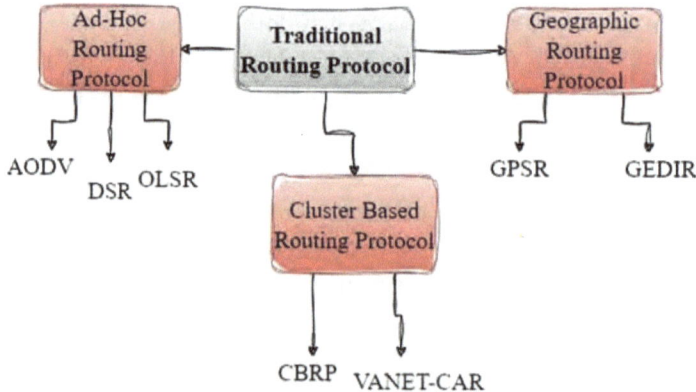

Fig. (2). Routing protocols for IoVs.

Ad Hoc Routing Protocols

Ad hoc routing protocols are widely utilized in IoVs to enable communication between vehicles in the absence of a fixed infrastructure [23]. These protocols establish and maintain dynamic routes by leveraging the collaboration of neighboring vehicles.

Key Ad Hoc Routing Protocols Used In IoVs Include

Ad hoc On-Demand Distance Vector (AODV)

AODV is a reactive routing protocol that establishes routes only when needed. It utilizes route discovery and maintenance mechanisms to establish communication paths between vehicles dynamically. AODV is known for its low routing overhead and quick route establishment. However, it may incur higher latency for establishing new routes, especially in large-scale networks [24].

Dynamic Source Routing (DSR)

DSR is another reactive routing protocol that relies on source routing. In DSR, each packet carries a list of nodes (hops) that the packet should traverse to reach its destination. DSR allows for efficient route caching, reducing routing overhead. However, maintaining and updating route caches can be challenging in highly dynamic vehicular environments.

Optimized Link State Routing (OLSR)

OLSR is a proactive routing protocol that builds and maintains a network-wide topology by periodically exchanging link state information between vehicles. OLSR minimizes route discovery latency as routes are pre-established, making it suitable for IoVs with frequent data exchange. However, the overhead associated with frequent control message exchange may impact network scalability.

Geographic Routing Protocols

Geographic routing protocols exploit the geographical information of vehicles to make routing decisions. These protocols utilize location-based routing mechanisms to forward packets toward the destination based on the vehicle's geographic coordinates. Some notable geographic routing protocols used in IoVs are:

Greedy Perimeter Stateless Routing (GPSR)

GPSR is a popular geographic routing protocol that employs a greedy forwarding mechanism. It selects the neighbor closest to the destination to forward packets. In case of obstacles or local minima, GPSR utilizes perimeter routing by forwarding packets around the obstacle [25]. GPSR offers low routing overhead and is well-suited for large-scale vehicular networks. However, its performance may be affected by signal interference and dynamic network topology changes.

Geographic Distance Routing (GEDIR)

GEDIR is a distance-based geographic routing protocol that selects the next hop based on the geographic distance to the destination [26]. It aims to minimize the total distance traveled by packets, thereby reducing energy consumption and delay. GEDIR provides efficient routing in IoVs with static or semi-static traffic patterns. However, it may encounter challenges in highly dynamic scenarios with rapid vehicle movements.

Cluster-Based Routing Protocols

Cluster-based routing protocols divide the vehicular network into clusters, with each cluster having a designated cluster head responsible for managing intra-cluster and inter-cluster communications [27]. This approach helps in reducing routing overhead and improves scalability. Notable cluster-based routing protocols in IoVs include:

Cluster-Based Routing Protocol (CBRP)

CBRP creates clusters dynamically and selects cluster heads based on parameters like connectivity and residual energy. Cluster heads perform routing tasks and facilitate communication within and between clusters. CBRP provides efficient routing and reduces the number of control messages. However, cluster formation and maintenance overhead can impact scalability in large-scale IoVs.

Vehicular Ad Hoc Network Clustering and Routing (VANET-CAR)

VANET-CAR is a cluster-based routing protocol designed specifically for vehicular networks. It employs a centralized approach to form clusters and assign cluster heads. VANET-CAR offers efficient routing and enables scalable communication in IoVs. However, the centralized nature may introduce a single point of failure and require additional management overhead.

While traditional routing protocols have been employed in IoVs, they may face challenges when applied to highly dynamic and resource-constrained vehicular environments. As IoVs evolve and new requirements emerge, there is a need for advanced and tailored routing protocols that address the specific challenges of vehicular networks, such as real-time traffic information, energy efficiency, and security [28].

Various research works have been carried out already that compare and analyze the various characteristics of these protocols. Researchers in [29 - 31] have very efficiently compared and explained these protocols.

INTELLIGENT TRANSPORT SYSTEM (ITS) FOR IMPROVED ROUTING

Intelligent Transportation Systems (ITS) have revolutionized the way transportation systems operate, aiming to enhance safety, efficiency, and sustainability. Within the realm of the Internet of Vehicles (IoVs), ITS plays a crucial role in improving routing by leveraging advanced technologies and intelligent algorithms [32]. This chapter focuses on the application of ITS for improved routing in IoVs, exploring various components, techniques, and benefits associated with intelligent routing systems.

ITS and Its Role in IoV

Intelligent Transportation Systems (ITS) have become a significant part of IoVs. ITS combines advanced technologies, data analytics, and communication systems to enhance transportation efficiency, safety, and sustainability. In the context of IoVs, ITS serves as a foundation for intelligent routing, enabling seamless communication, data exchange, and decision-making among vehicles, infrastructure, and other stakeholders [33]. The roles of ITS in IoVs can be discussed further:

Data Collection and Sharing

ITS facilitates the collection of real-time data from various sources, including vehicle sensors, roadside infrastructure, and external data providers. This data includes traffic conditions, road hazards, weather information, and vehicle status. ITS enables the sharing of this data among vehicles and infrastructure, creating a dynamic and comprehensive information network for routing decisions.

Real-Time Traffic Monitoring and Prediction

ITS leverages data analytics and machine learning techniques to monitor and predict traffic conditions in real time. By analyzing traffic flow, congestion patterns, and historical data, ITS systems can provide accurate traffic predictions. This information is vital for intelligent routing decisions, as vehicles can dynamically adapt their routes to avoid congestion and select the most efficient paths.

Dynamic Route Guidance and Navigation

ITS provides dynamic route guidance and navigation services to vehicles in IoVs. By integrating real-time traffic information, road conditions, and user preferences, ITS algorithms can recommend optimal routes to drivers. These systems continuously update routes based on changing traffic conditions, incidents, and user inputs, ensuring efficient and stress-free navigation.

Incident Detection and Emergency Services

ITS enables the detection and reporting of incidents such as accidents, road closures, or adverse weather conditions. Through vehicle-to-vehicle (V2V) and vehicle-to-infrastructure (V2I) communication, ITS systems can quickly disseminate incident information to nearby vehicles, alerting them to potential dangers. Furthermore, ITS facilitates emergency services by guiding emergency vehicles to incidents through optimized routes, minimizing response times.

Energy Efficiency and Sustainability

ITS promotes energy-efficient driving and eco-friendly routing. By considering vehicle characteristics, traffic conditions, and environmental factors, ITS algorithms can suggest routes that minimize fuel consumption and emissions. Eco-routing techniques optimize routes based on energy-efficiency metrics, contributing to environmental sustainability and reducing the carbon footprint of IoVs.

Overall, ITS serves as an enabler for intelligent routing in IoVs by leveraging advanced technologies, data analytics, and communication systems. By collecting and sharing real-time data, predicting traffic conditions, providing dynamic route guidance, and promoting energy efficiency, ITS enhances the performance, safety, and sustainability of IoVs, creating a more connected and intelligent transportation ecosystem.

Components of ITS

Intelligent Transportation Systems (ITS) comprise various components that work together to improve transportation efficiency, safety, and sustainability. These components encompass hardware, software, communication systems, and data analytics capabilities. Fig. (**3**) represents the communication among the components of ITS [34]. The key components of ITS are:

Sensors and Detectors

Sensors and detectors are crucial components of ITS, which collect real-time data about the transportation environment. These include:

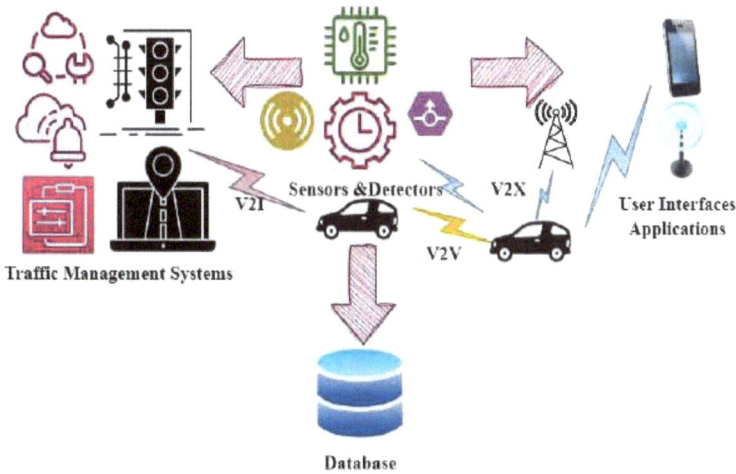

Fig. (3). Intelligent transport system for improved routing.

Vehicle Sensors

Sensors installed within vehicles capture data such as speed, acceleration, GPS location, fuel consumption, and vehicle diagnostics.

Roadside Sensors

Roadside sensors monitor traffic flow, vehicle presence, and environmental conditions. They can include technologies like loop detectors, video cameras, radar, and LiDAR.

Environmental Sensors

These sensors measure factors like temperature, humidity, air quality, and visibility to provide contextual information for transportation systems.

Communication Systems

Communication systems enable the exchange of data and information between vehicles, infrastructure, and other ITS components. Key communication systems in ITS include:

Vehicle-to-Vehicle (V2V) Communication

V2V communication enables vehicles to exchange information, such as speed, location, and safety-related data, to support cooperative applications like collision avoidance and traffic coordination.

Vehicle-to-Infrastructure (V2I) Communication

V2I communication allows vehicles to communicate with roadside infrastructure, including traffic signal systems, toll booths, and parking facilities. This enables real-time data exchange and coordination between vehicles and infrastructure.

Vehicle-to-Everything (V2X) Communication

V2X communication refers to the broader concept of vehicles communicating with various entities, including other vehicles, infrastructure, pedestrians, and cyclists. It encompasses both V2V and V2I communication, as well as Vehicle-to-Pedestrian (V2P) and Vehicle-to-Network (V2N) communication.

Data Collection and Analytics

ITS relies on data collection and analytics to extract meaningful insights and support decision-making processes. This includes:

Data Collection

ITS collects and integrates data from various sources, such as vehicle sensors, roadside sensors, and external data providers. This data includes traffic flow, weather conditions, incidents, and other relevant information.

Data Analytics

ITS employs advanced data analytics techniques, including machine learning and artificial intelligence, to process and analyze collected data. This enables traffic prediction, incident detection, route optimization, and other intelligent functionalities.

Control and Management Systems

Control and management systems in ITS provide centralized or distributed control over transportation operations. These systems include:

Traffic Management Systems

Traffic management systems monitor and control traffic flow by dynamically adjusting signal timings, managing lane closures, and providing real-time traffic information to drivers.

Incident Management Systems

Incident management systems detect and respond to incidents, such as accidents or road hazards. They facilitate coordination between emergency services, provide incident notifications, and support incident clearance operations.

Fleet Management Systems

Fleet management systems are utilized by transportation companies to monitor and optimize the operations of their vehicle fleets. These systems provide functionalities such as tracking, scheduling, routing, and fuel management.

User Interfaces and Applications

User interfaces and applications in ITS provide the means for users to interact with the system and access relevant information. These include:

Navigation Systems

Navigation systems offer route guidance, turn-by-turn directions, and real-time traffic updates to drivers, helping them navigate efficiently and avoid congestion.

Traveler Information Systems

Traveler information systems provide real-time information about traffic conditions, incidents, road closures, and alternative routes to assist travelers in making informed decisions.

Mobile Applications

Mobile applications enable users to access ITS services and information through their smartphones or other mobile devices. These applications may include features like journey planning, ride-sharing, and multimodal trip booking.

These components of ITS work in synergy to create an intelligent and connected transportation ecosystem. By collecting, analyzing, and utilizing real-time data, communicating effectively, and implementing intelligent control systems, ITS aims to improve transportation efficiency, safety, and sustainability for both drivers and the overall transportation network [35].

V2X Communication for Routing Optimization

Intelligent transportation systems rely on efficient routing optimization to enhance the performance and safety of transportation networks. One of the key technologies driving this optimization is Vehicle-to-Everything (V2X) communication. V2X communication enables vehicles to exchange real-time information with other vehicles, infrastructure, and network systems, resulting in improved routing decisions and overall system efficiency [36].

V2X communication plays a pivotal role in routing optimization by facilitating the exchange of valuable traffic-related data among vehicles and infrastructure. Through V2V communication, vehicles can share information about their current positions, speed, and acceleration. This real-time data empowers routing algorithms to make informed decisions based on actual traffic conditions, allowing for dynamic route adjustments to avoid congestion and optimize travel times [37].

In addition to V2V communication, V2X encompasses V2I and V2N communication, expanding the scope of data exchange beyond vehicle-to-vehicle interactions. V2I communication enables vehicles to communicate with roadside infrastructure, such as traffic signal systems, toll booths, and parking facilities. By accessing real-time traffic signal timings and infrastructure information, routing algorithms can make intelligent decisions to optimize routes, minimize delays at intersections, and enhance traffic flow efficiency.

V2X communication also leverages vehicle-to-network (V2N) connectivity, allowing vehicles to access centralized traffic management systems and data repositories. By tapping into these resources, vehicles can receive up-to-date information about traffic conditions, road incidents, and alternative routes. This data empowers routing algorithms to dynamically adapt and optimize routes based on real-time traffic information, ensuring efficient navigation and minimizing travel time.

Moreover, V2X communication facilitates cooperative behavior among vehicles, leading to enhanced routing optimization. Vehicles can exchange data regarding their intended routes, lane changes, and traffic maneuvers through V2V communication. This cooperative approach enables routing algorithms to consider the collective traffic information and make routing decisions that benefit the overall system efficiency. Cooperative merging, lane selection, and traffic flow coordination are achieved through this collaborative effort, resulting in smoother traffic operations and reduced congestion [38].

Safety is another critical aspect of V2X communication for routing optimization. By exchanging real-time information about hazardous conditions, such as accidents, roadwork, and adverse weather, vehicles can proactively adapt their routes to avoid potential dangers. Routing algorithms can incorporate this safety information to steer vehicles away from high-risk areas, ensuring safer journeys for all road users.

Furthermore, V2X communication enables eco-routing, promoting sustainability in transportation systems. Vehicles can receive environmental data, such as air quality information and emission levels, through V2X connections. By integrating this data into routing algorithms, eco-routing strategies can be employed to suggest routes that minimize fuel consumption and emissions, contributing to greener transportation and reduced environmental impact.

To fully realize the potential of V2X communication for routing optimization, several challenges need to be addressed. Standardization of communication protocols is crucial to ensure interoperability and seamless data exchange among vehicles and infrastructure from different manufacturers and service providers. Additionally, robust security measures must be in place to protect the integrity and privacy of the exchanged data, safeguarding against unauthorized access and misuse [39].

In Table **1**, we have compared various V2X categories that have been used in recent times. The comparison consists of features like latency, data rate, and reliability which can help a user to choose which V2X technology is to be used.

Table 1. Analysis of Existing V2X Communications.

Sr. No.	V2X Category	Communication Type	Latency	Data Rate	Reliability
1.	Safety and traffic Efficiency [10]	V2V, V2P	100ms	Not a concern	Not yet explicated
2.	Autonomous driving [11]	V2N, V2N, V2I	1 ms	10 Mbps	99.99%
3.	Vehicular Internet and Infotainment [12]	V2N	100 ms	0.5 mbps	Not a concern
4.	Remote diagnostics and management [13]	V2I, V2N	Not a concern	Not a concern	Not a concern

V2X communication is a transformative technology that significantly contributes to routing optimization in intelligent transportation systems. By facilitating real-time data exchange, cooperative behavior, and enhanced safety considerations, V2X communication empowers routing algorithms to make intelligent decisions, optimize routes, and improve the overall transportation system efficiency. With continued advancements and widespread adoption, V2X communication will continue to play a pivotal role in shaping the future of routing optimization in intelligent transportation systems [40].

Benefits of Intelligent Routing

Intelligent routing is a critical component in the field of transportation and plays a pivotal role in optimizing the efficiency, safety, and reliability of routing decisions. By leveraging advanced technologies and data analysis techniques, intelligent routing algorithms can make informed decisions in real-time, adapting to changing traffic conditions, minimizing congestion, and enhancing overall transportation system performance [15].

Multi-Criteria Optimization

Intelligent routing algorithms consider multiple criteria when determining the best route. Beyond simply minimizing travel distance or time, these algorithms take into account various factors such as road conditions, traffic congestion, fuel efficiency, and user preferences. By incorporating these criteria into the routing decision-making process, intelligent routing systems can generate personalized routes that cater to the specific needs and preferences of individual drivers. This approach ensures a more customized and optimized routing experience for users, leading to improved satisfaction and efficiency [41].

Dynamic Route Guidance

Intelligent routing systems provide dynamic route guidance to drivers based on real-time traffic information. Through connected vehicle technology and V2X communication, vehicles can receive updates on traffic conditions, incidents, and alternative routes in real time. Intelligent routing algorithms analyze this information and generate route guidance that considers the current traffic situation. By dynamically adjusting routes to avoid congested areas or accidents, these systems help drivers navigate efficiently and minimize travel delays [42].

Adaptive Traffic Signal Control

Intelligent routing algorithms often work in conjunction with adaptive traffic signal control systems. By utilizing real-time traffic data and advanced algorithms, these systems adjust the timing of traffic signals at intersections to optimize traffic flow. Intelligent routing algorithms take advantage of this adaptive signal control to identify the most efficient path, considering the expected signal timings. By synchronizing traffic signal patterns with routing decisions, intelligent routing algorithms can minimize stops, reduce delays, and improve overall traffic efficiency [43].

Consideration of Dynamic Factors

Intelligent routing algorithms are designed to consider dynamic factors that impact routing decisions. These factors include real-time incidents, road closures, weather conditions, and special events. By continuously monitoring and analyzing these dynamic factors, intelligent routing systems can quickly identify disruptions and reconfigure routes accordingly. This adaptability ensures that drivers are guided along the most suitable and efficient paths, even in the presence of unforeseen circumstances.

Integration with Connected Infrastructure

Intelligent routing systems can leverage connected infrastructure to enhance their capabilities. By integrating with centralized traffic management systems, traffic information centers, and data repositories, these systems can access comprehensive and up-to-date information on road conditions, traffic patterns, and incident alerts. This integration enables intelligent routing algorithms to make more informed and accurate routing decisions, improving overall system efficiency and user experience.

Therefore, it was concluded that intelligent routing plays a vital role in optimizing transportation systems by utilizing advanced technologies and data analysis techniques. By considering real-time traffic information, personal preferences, and dynamic factors, intelligent routing algorithms can generate efficient and personalized routes. With the integration of connected infrastructure and adaptive traffic control systems, intelligent routing continues to evolve, paving the way for improved traffic management, reduced congestion, and enhanced overall transportation system performance.

Challenges Associated with the Deployment and Integration Of Intelligent Routing Systems

Deploying and integrating intelligent routing systems, especially in the context of the Internet of Vehicles (IoV), comes with several limitations and challenges that need to be carefully considered:

Scalability

Challenge

As the number of connected vehicles and devices in the IoV ecosystem increases, scalability becomes a significant challenge. Routing systems must efficiently handle a large volume of data and devices while maintaining low-latency communication.

Solution

Implementing scalable routing algorithms and distributed systems that can adapt to growing networks is crucial. Techniques like edge computing can help offload processing tasks from centralized servers, improving scalability.

Cost

Challenge

Developing and deploying intelligent routing systems can be costly. This includes the cost of infrastructure, hardware, software development, maintenance, and ongoing operational expenses.

Solution

Cost-effective solutions may involve open-source software, partnerships with industry stakeholders, and the utilization of existing infrastructure where possible. Governments and private enterprises can collaborate to share the financial burden of large-scale IoV deployments.

Infrastructure Requirements

Challenge

Intelligent routing systems often require significant infrastructure upgrades and installations. This includes the deployment of roadside sensors, communication equipment, and edge computing nodes.

Solution

Careful planning and phased deployment can help manage infrastructure requirements. Governments and municipalities can invest in infrastructure upgrades gradually, prioritizing areas with the most significant traffic challenges and potential benefits.

Privacy and Security

Challenge

Routing systems in IoV collect and transmit sensitive data, including location information. Ensuring the privacy and security of this data is paramount, as it can be vulnerable to cyberattacks and misuse.

Solution

Implement robust encryption, authentication, and access control mechanisms to protect data. Compliance with data protection regulations and standards is essential, and constant monitoring for security threats is crucial.

Interoperability

Challenge

IoV ecosystems involve various stakeholders, including vehicle manufacturers, infrastructure providers, and service operators. Ensuring interoperability among different systems and devices can be challenging.

Solution

Develop and adhere to standardized communication protocols and data formats to facilitate interoperability. Industry-wide collaboration and adherence to open standards can help mitigate interoperability issues.

Data Quality and Reliability

Challenge

The quality and reliability of data collected and used for routing can vary due to factors like GPS accuracy, sensor malfunctions, or communication issues.

Solution

Implement redundancy and error-checking mechanisms to ensure data quality and reliability. Continuous monitoring and maintenance of data sources can help mitigate these challenges.

Intelligent Route Planning and Navigation

Intelligent route planning and navigation systems have revolutionized the way people travel by providing efficient and optimized routes to their destinations.

These systems utilize advanced technologies and algorithms to analyze various factors and generate personalized navigation guidance. This section explores the concept of intelligent route planning and navigation, highlighting its benefits and key components [44].

Understanding Intelligent Route Planning and Navigation

Intelligent route planning and navigation systems use a combination of data analysis techniques, real-time information, and algorithms to generate optimized routes. These systems go beyond basic point-to-point navigation and consider factors such as traffic conditions, road network topology, user preferences, and real-time incidents. By leveraging this information, intelligent systems can generate routes that minimize travel time, avoid congestion, and provide an overall better user experience.

Real-Time Traffic and Incident Monitoring

A crucial aspect of intelligent route planning and navigation is the ability to monitor real-time traffic conditions and incidents. These systems collect data from various sources, including sensors, GPS devices, and connected vehicles, to gather information about traffic flow, congestion, and accidents. By analyzing this data in real-time, intelligent systems can provide accurate and up-to-date information to users, enabling them to choose the most optimal routes based on current traffic conditions.

Data Analytics and Machine Learning

Intelligent route planning and navigation systems rely on advanced data analytics techniques and machine learning algorithms to process and analyze vast amounts of data. These algorithms can identify traffic patterns, predict congestion, and make informed routing decisions based on historical and real-time data. By continuously learning and adapting, intelligent systems can improve their route planning accuracy and efficiency over time, providing users with more reliable and optimal routes [45].

Personalized Preferences and User Feedback

Intelligent route planning and navigation systems take into account individual user preferences to generate personalized routes. Users can input their preferred route types, such as avoiding toll roads or highways, prioritizing scenic routes, or selecting the fastest path. Additionally, these systems can consider user feedback and historical data to further customize routing recommendations. By incorporating personalization, intelligent systems cater to the specific needs and preferences of each user, enhancing their navigation experience.

Multi-Modal and Multi-Criteria Routing

Intelligent route planning and navigation systems support multi-modal and multi-criteria routing, considering various transportation modes and criteria. They can incorporate information about public transportation options, such as buses, trains, and subways, allowing users to seamlessly switch between different modes of transport during their journey. Furthermore, these systems can optimize routes based on multiple criteria, such as minimizing travel time, reducing fuel consumption, or prioritizing eco-friendly options. This flexibility enables users to choose the most suitable routes based on their preferences and specific requirements.

As a final point, intelligent route planning and navigation systems have transformed the way people navigate through their daily journeys. By leveraging real-time data, advanced analytics, and machine learning algorithms, these systems provide optimized routes that minimize travel time, avoid congestion, and cater to individual preferences. With their ability to adapt to changing conditions and integrate with connected infrastructure, intelligent route planning and navigation systems continue to improve transportation efficiency, enhance user experiences, and contribute to the development of smarter cities [46].

Case Studies of Successful Implementations of Intelligent Transport Systems for Improved Routing in IoV

Waze: Crowdsourced Real-Time Navigation

Waze is a popular navigation app that relies on crowdsourced data from millions of users to provide real-time traffic information and routing recommendations. It collects data from smartphones, including GPS location and speed, to analyze traffic patterns. By aggregating this data, Waze offers dynamic routing suggestions to users, helping them avoid traffic jams and accidents. Waze is a prime example of how ITS and IoV can harness the power of crowd intelligence to optimize routing.

V2I Communication in Ann Arbor, Michigan

The U.S. Department of Transportation (USDOT) conducted a large-scale IoV pilot project in Ann Arbor, Michigan, to study the benefits of Vehicle-to-Infrastructure (V2I) communication. Over 2,800 vehicles were equipped with V2I technology that allowed them to communicate with roadside infrastructure. The project demonstrated how vehicles could receive real-time traffic signal information and adjust their speed to reduce fuel consumption and improve traffic flow. This example showcases the potential of V2I communication in routing optimization and traffic management.

Singapore's Electronic Road Pricing (ERP) System

Singapore's ERP system is a pioneering example of a dynamic toll collection system that uses IoV technologies to manage congestion and optimize routing. The system employs gantries equipped with RFID and GPS technology to track vehicles and charge tolls based on traffic conditions and congestion pricing. This not only generates revenue for road maintenance but also encourages drivers to choose alternative routes during peak hours, thus alleviating traffic congestion in specific areas.

Smart Intersection Management in Los Angeles

Los Angeles deployed a smart intersection management system that uses IoV technologies to improve traffic flow and reduce accidents. Cameras and sensors at intersections monitor vehicle and pedestrian movements. The system can adjust traffic signal timings in real-time to optimize vehicle flow and reduce congestion. This implementation demonstrates the potential of ITS in urban environments to enhance routing and improve overall traffic efficiency.

Cooperative Adaptive Cruise Control (CACC) on I-80 in Wyoming

In Wyoming, the I-80 corridor is equipped with a Cooperative Adaptive Cruise Control (CACC) system. Trucks equipped with CACC technology communicate with each other and follow at a safe distance, optimizing traffic flow and reducing fuel consumption. This IoV implementation showcases the use of vehicle-to-vehicle (V2V) communication to enhance routing and traffic management, especially in long-haul trucking scenarios.

CLOUD COMPUTING AND FOG COMPUTING IN IOV ROUTING

Cloud computing and fog computing have become a major field to work on IoV. To understand more about cloud computing and fog computing for IoV, we shall go through further sections.

Overview of Cloud Computing and Fog Computing

Cloud computing and fog computing are two prominent paradigms in the realm of distributed computing. Both approaches provide computational resources and services, but they differ in terms of their architecture, proximity to end-users, and data processing capabilities. This section provides an overview of cloud computing and fog computing, highlighting their key characteristics and differences [47].

Cloud Computing

Cloud computing refers to the delivery of computing resources, including servers, storage, databases, and software applications, over the Internet. In a cloud computing model, these resources are centrally managed and accessed by users on-demand, typically through a pay-per-use pricing model. Cloud computing offers several key features and advantages:

Scalability

Cloud computing allows for the dynamic allocation and scaling of computing resources based on demand. Users can easily scale up or down their resource usage, ensuring optimal performance and cost-efficiency.

Resource Pooling

Cloud providers pool their computing resources to serve multiple users simultaneously. This enables efficient resource utilization, as resources can be dynamically allocated based on the needs of different users.

Flexibility

Cloud computing provides flexibility in terms of access to resources and services. Users can access applications and data from any location using a variety of devices, making it suitable for remote work and collaboration.

Cost Savings

By utilizing cloud computing, organizations can reduce their upfront infrastructure costs, as they no longer need to invest in on-premises hardware and maintenance. Instead, they can pay for the resources they consume, resulting in potential cost savings.

Fog Computing

Fog computing, also known as edge computing, is an extension of cloud computing that brings computing resources closer to the edge of the network, closer to where the data is generated and consumed. In a fog computing model, resources are distributed across different edge devices, such as routers, gateways, and IoT devices [48]. Fog computing offers several distinct advantages:

Low Latency

By processing data closer to the edge, fog computing reduces the latency associated with transmitting data to a centralized cloud server. This is particularly crucial for applications requiring real-time or near-real-time responses, such as IoT devices and autonomous vehicles.

Bandwidth Optimization

Fog computing reduces the need to transmit large volumes of data to the cloud by performing localized data processing at the edge. This reduces network congestion and optimizes bandwidth utilization.

Improved Privacy and Security

Since fog computing processes data locally, sensitive data can be kept closer to the source, enhancing privacy and security. Data can be filtered, anonymized, and encrypted at the edge, reducing the risks associated with transmitting sensitive information over the network [49].

Offline Operation

Fog computing allows for limited offline operation, even when connectivity to the cloud is temporarily disrupted. This ensures that critical applications can continue to function, maintaining operational continuity in scenarios where network connectivity is intermittent or unreliable.

Cloud Computing vs. Fog Computing

While cloud computing and fog computing share similarities, they serve different purposes and cater to distinct use cases. Cloud computing is well-suited for applications that require massive scalability, extensive data storage, and complex data processing. It is commonly used for enterprise applications, big data analytics, and web services. Fog computing, on the other hand, excels in applications that demand low latency, real-time processing, and immediate data analysis at the edge. It is often employed in IoT deployments, smart cities, and industrial automation.

In summary, cloud computing and fog computing are two distinct paradigms in distributed computing. Cloud computing provides centralized, scalable resources accessible over the internet, while fog computing brings computational capabilities closer to the edge, enabling low-latency, real-time processing [50]. Both approaches have their unique advantages and are employed in various scenarios, depending on the specific requirements of the applications and the desired trade-offs between centralized processing and edge computing capabilities.

Cloud-Enabled Routing Solutions In IoV

Cloud-enabled routing solutions have emerged as a powerful approach to addressing the routing challenges in the context of Internet of Vehicles (IoVs). By leveraging the capabilities of cloud computing, these solutions offer enhanced scalability, real-time data processing, and intelligent decision-making for efficient and optimized routing. This chapter explores the concept of cloud-enabled routing solutions for IoVs, highlighting their benefits, key components, and potential applications [6].

Scalability and Resource Management

Cloud-enabled routing solutions provide inherent scalability, allowing for the efficient management of large-scale IoV deployments. With the cloud's vast computing resources, these solutions can handle the increasing volume of data generated by connected vehicles and perform complex routing calculations. The cloud's ability to scale up or down resources based on demand ensures optimal performance even during peak usage periods.

Real-time Data Processing and Analysis

Cloud-enabled routing solutions leverage the cloud's computing power to process and analyze real-time data from various sources, such as vehicle sensors, GPS devices, and traffic monitoring systems. By continuously collecting and processing this data, these solutions can accurately assess traffic conditions, identify congestion hotspots, and dynamically adjust routing decisions in real-time. This real-time data processing capability enables efficient and responsive routing, improving overall traffic flow and reducing travel times.

Intelligent Decision-Making

Cloud-enabled routing solutions integrate advanced algorithms, machine learning, and artificial intelligence techniques to make intelligent routing decisions. By analyzing historical data, traffic patterns, and user preferences, these solutions can generate optimized routes that consider multiple factors, such as travel time, fuel efficiency, road conditions, and user preferences. Intelligent decision-making algorithms continuously learn and adapt, further improving routing accuracy and user satisfaction over time.

Integration with Connected Infrastructure

Cloud-enabled routing solutions can seamlessly integrate with connected infrastructure, such as traffic management systems, smart traffic lights, and road sensors. By accessing real-time data from these sources, including traffic flow information, road conditions, and incident alerts, these solutions can make more informed routing decisions. Integration with connected infrastructure enhances the accuracy and effectiveness of routing solutions, leading to improved traffic management and optimized routing outcomes.

Privacy and Security Considerations

Cloud-enabled routing solutions must address privacy and security concerns associated with handling sensitive and personal data from connected vehicles. Robust security measures, such as data encryption, authentication, and access control mechanisms, are essential to protect the privacy and integrity of the data transmitted between vehicles, cloud servers, and other connected infrastructure. Privacy regulations and policies must be adhered to, ensuring that user data is handled in a responsible and compliant manner [8].

Applications and Future Directions

Cloud-enabled routing solutions have numerous applications in the IoV domain. They can be employed in intelligent transportation systems, ride-sharing platforms, fleet management, and logistics optimization. Furthermore, as connected vehicle technology continues to evolve, cloud-enabled routing solutions can integrate with emerging technologies like autonomous vehicles and smart cities, enabling even more efficient and intelligent routing decisions [25].

Hence, cloud-enabled routing solutions offer significant advantages for addressing routing challenges in IoVs. With their scalability, real-time data processing capabilities, and intelligent decision-making algorithms, these solutions can optimize routing, reduce congestion, and enhance the overall transportation experience. As the IoV ecosystem continues to evolve, cloud-enabled routing solutions will play a crucial role in enabling efficient, safe, and connected mobility.

Fog Computing For Real-Time Routing Solutions

Fog computing has emerged as a promising paradigm for enabling real-time routing solutions in various domains, including transportation and logistics. By bringing computing resources closer to the edge of the network, fog computing offers low latency and localized data processing capabilities, making it ideal for real-time routing applications. This section explores the concept of fog computing for real-time routing solutions, highlighting its benefits, key components, and potential applications [18].

Low-Latency Data Processing

Fog computing provides the capability to process data in real-time, closer to the source of data generation. By deploying computational resources at the network edge, fog computing minimizes the latency associated with transmitting data to centralized cloud servers for processing. This low-latency data processing enables real-time routing solutions, where decisions can be made and implemented quickly, resulting in efficient and responsive routing.

Edge Device Infrastructure

Fog computing utilizes edge devices, such as routers, gateways, and edge servers, to process and analyze data at the network edge. These devices serve as fog nodes and play a crucial role in executing routing algorithms, collecting real-time traffic data, and making routing decisions locally. By leveraging the computational capabilities of edge devices, fog computing enables localized and distributed data processing, leading to faster response times and improved routing efficiency.

Real-Time Data Analytics

Fog computing combines data analytics techniques with real-time data processing to extract valuable insights from the vast amount of data generated by connected devices and sensors. Real-time data analytics enables fog computing systems to analyze traffic patterns, predict congestion, and identify optimal routes based on current conditions. By leveraging this analytical capability, fog computing enhances the accuracy and effectiveness of real-time routing solutions, resulting in improved traffic management and optimized routing decisions.

Connectivity and Communication

Fog computing relies on seamless connectivity and communication between edge devices, fog nodes, and other components in the network. This allows for the exchange of real-time traffic data, routing information, and updates among different entities involved in the routing process. Efficient communication protocols and networking technologies enable fog computing systems to gather and disseminate information rapidly, facilitating collaborative decision-making and ensuring timely routing updates.

Integration with IoT and Sensor Networks

Fog computing integrates seamlessly with Internet of Things (IoT) devices and sensor networks, which play a critical role in collecting real-time data for routing solutions. Connected vehicles, traffic sensors, and other IoT devices generate a wealth of data that can be leveraged by fog computing systems for real-time routing. By integrating with IoT and sensor networks, fog computing enhances the availability and accuracy of data, leading to more informed routing decisions and improved traffic management.

Applications and Future Directions

Fog computing for real-time routing solutions finds applications in various domains, including intelligent transportation systems, smart cities, and logistics management. It enables real-time traffic routing, congestion management, dynamic route optimization, and emergency response systems. As fog computing continues to evolve, its integration with emerging technologies such as 5G networks, edge AI, and autonomous vehicles holds the potential for further advancements in real-time routing, leading to safer, more efficient, and sustainable transportation systems.

To conclude this section, fog computing offers significant advantages for real-time routing solutions by providing low-latency data processing, localized analytics, and integration with IoT devices. By leveraging edge resources, fog computing enables efficient and responsive routing decisions, leading to improved traffic management and optimized routing outcomes. As the demand for real-time routing continues to grow, fog computing will play a crucial role in enabling intelligent transportation systems and smart city initiatives, revolutionizing the way we navigate and optimize transportation networks.

Benefits And Challenges of Cloud and Fog Computing In IoV Routing

Cloud and fog computing are two prominent paradigms that offer significant benefits and present unique challenges in the context of Internet of Vehicles (IoV) routing. Understanding these advantages and obstacles is crucial for harnessing the potential of cloud and fog computing in optimizing IoV routing [19]. This section discusses the benefits and challenges associated with cloud and fog computing in IoV routing.

Benefits of Cloud Computing in IoV Routing

Scalability

Cloud computing provides virtually unlimited computing resources, enabling the handling of large-scale IoV deployments. With the ability to dynamically allocate resources based on demand, cloud computing ensures optimal performance and scalability in IoV routing applications.

Data Processing Power

Cloud computing offers immense data processing capabilities. By leveraging cloud resources, IoV routing systems can process and analyze massive amounts of data, including real-time traffic information, vehicle data, and historical patterns. This data-driven approach enhances the accuracy and efficiency of routing decisions.

Collaboration and Centralized Management

Cloud computing facilitates collaboration among various stakeholders in IoV routing. It enables centralized management, where routing algorithms, traffic models, and decision-making processes can be shared, updated, and improved collaboratively. This centralized approach allows for efficient coordination and better overall routing outcomes.

Cost Efficiency

Cloud computing eliminates the need for extensive on-premises infrastructure investment. Instead, users can leverage cloud services on a pay-per-use basis, reducing upfront costs and providing cost efficiency in IoV routing deployments. Additionally, cloud-based solutions reduce maintenance and operational expenses.

Challenges of Cloud Computing in IoV Routing

Latency and Dependence on Internet Connectivity

Cloud computing relies on Internet connectivity for data transmission between vehicles, cloud servers, and routing infrastructure. Latency introduced by network communication can impact the responsiveness of IoV routing systems. Moreover, intermittent or unreliable internet connectivity can disrupt real-time data exchange, affecting routing accuracy and performance.

Privacy and Security

Cloud computing involves transmitting sensitive data from connected vehicles to remote servers for processing. This introduces privacy and security concerns, such as unauthorized access, data breaches, and potential misuse of personal information. Robust encryption, secure communication protocols, and adherence to privacy regulations are crucial in mitigating these risks [9].

Benefits of Fog Computing in IoV Routing

Low-Latency Data Processing

Fog computing brings computational resources closer to the edge of the network, minimizing latency in data processing. This enables real-time and near-real-time routing decisions, crucial for applications requiring immediate responsiveness, such as autonomous vehicles and emergency response systems.

Localized Data Analysis

Fog computing allows for localized data analysis at the network edge. By processing data closer to the source, fog computing reduces the need for transmitting large volumes of data to centralized cloud servers. Localized data analysis enhances privacy, reduces network congestion, and optimizes bandwidth utilization in IoV routing [2].

Resilience and Offline Operation

Fog computing offers resilience in situations where connectivity to the cloud is disrupted. Localized processing at the edge enables limited offline operation, ensuring critical routing functions can still be performed even in scenarios with intermittent or no internet connectivity.

Challenges of Fog Computing in IoV Routing

Resource Constraints

Fog computing relies on the computational capabilities of edge devices, which may have limited processing power, storage capacity, and energy resources. Optimizing resource utilization and managing resource constraints in fog computing environments pose challenges for implementing complex routing algorithms and handling high-volume data streams.

System Heterogeneity and Interoperability

Fog computing involves a diverse range of edge devices and network infrastructures, leading to system heterogeneity and potential interoperability issues. Ensuring seamless communication and collaboration among different components in a fog computing environment requires standardization and compatibility across devices and protocols.

Management and Orchestration

Fog computing introduces additional complexities in managing and orchestrating the distributed resources and services at the edge. Efficient management mechanisms are needed to handle resource allocation, load balancing, software updates, and fault tolerance in fog computing environments.

By leveraging the benefits of cloud and fog computing while addressing the associated challenges, IoV routing systems can achieve enhanced scalability, real-time data processing, and optimized routing decisions. Striking the right balance between centralized cloud capabilities and localized edge computing power is crucial for harnessing the full potential of these paradigms in IoV routing applications [20].

ARTIFICIAL INTELLIGENCE (AI) AND MACHINE LEARNING (ML) FOR ROUTING OPTIMIZATION

Over the time, AI and ML has played a significant role in automation services. IoV is one such field that works on complete automation and when used with ml and AI could bring out impressive and accurate results.

Role of AI and ML in IoV Routing

Artificial Intelligence (AI) and Machine Learning (ML) have revolutionized the field of Internet of Vehicles (IoV) routing by offering intelligent and data-driven solutions [19]. The integration of AI and ML techniques has enabled advanced routing algorithms, improved traffic management, and optimized routing decisions [20]. This section explores the role of AI and ML in IoV routing, highlighting their key applications and benefits.

Intelligent Routing Algorithms

AI and ML techniques enable the development of intelligent routing algorithms that can adapt and optimize routing decisions based on real-time data and changing traffic conditions. These algorithms can analyze historical data, consider multiple variables such as traffic congestion, road conditions, and user preferences, and generate optimal routes for individual vehicles or fleet management systems. Intelligent routing algorithms help minimize travel time, reduce congestion, and improve overall traffic efficiency in IoV routing.

Traffic Prediction and Congestion Management

AI and ML models can analyze large volumes of historical traffic data to predict traffic patterns, identify congestion hotspots, and dynamically adjust routing strategies. By utilizing data from various sources, such as traffic sensors, GPS devices, and connected vehicles, these models can forecast traffic conditions and recommend alternative routes in real time. This proactive approach to congestion management ensures efficient traffic flow and minimizes delays in IoV routing scenarios.

Personalized and Context-Aware Routing

AI and ML techniques enable personalized and context-aware routing in IoV systems. By analyzing individual user preferences, historical travel patterns, and real-time context information, such as weather conditions and traffic incidents, personalized routing algorithms can generate routes tailored to the specific needs and preferences of users. This personalized approach enhances user satisfaction, provides optimal navigation experiences, and promotes efficient resource utilization in IoV routing applications.

Anomaly Detection and Incident Management

AI and ML algorithms can detect anomalies and abnormal events in IoV routing systems. By continuously monitoring and analyzing real-time data, these algorithms can identify unusual patterns, traffic accidents, or road hazards that require immediate attention. This capability facilitates proactive incident management, enabling prompt responses, rerouting strategies, and emergency services dispatch in critical situations. Anomaly detection and incident management contribute to improved safety and reliability in IoV routing.

Continuous Learning and Adaptation

AI and ML models have the ability to learn and adapt from data. They can continuously update their routing algorithms and decision-making processes based on new information and feedback. By leveraging techniques such as reinforcement learning, these models can improve their routing performance over time, incorporating new knowledge and adapting to changing traffic patterns. Continuous learning and adaptation ensure that IoV routing systems stay up-to-date, responsive, and capable of handling evolving transportation scenarios.

Optimization and Resource Management

AI and ML techniques enable optimization of resource allocation and management in IoV routing. These techniques can analyze data on vehicle availability, traffic demand, and network conditions to optimize fleet allocation, route scheduling, and resource utilization. By efficiently managing resources, AI and ML contribute to cost reduction, improved operational efficiency, and sustainability in IoV routing deployments.

All things considered, AI and ML play a pivotal role in enhancing IoV routing systems. Their ability to analyze large volumes of data, make intelligent decisions, and adapt to dynamic environments enables efficient routing, congestion management, incident response, and resource optimization [19]. As AI and ML technologies continue to advance, their integration with IoV routing holds immense potential for creating intelligent, safe, and efficient transportation systems of the future.

AI-Based Traffic Prediction and Route Optimization

AI-based traffic prediction and route optimization have become crucial components in modern transportation systems [20]. By leveraging advanced algorithms and machine learning techniques, these solutions enable accurate traffic forecasting and optimized routing decisions. This section explores the role of AI in traffic prediction and route optimization, highlighting their benefits and applications.

Traffic Prediction

AI-based traffic prediction utilizes historical and real-time data to forecast traffic conditions, enabling proactive decision-making. By analyzing data from various sources, such as traffic sensors, GPS devices, and connected vehicles, AI models can identify traffic patterns, congestion hotspots, and potential bottlenecks. These models consider factors like time of day, day of the week, weather conditions, and special events to predict traffic flow and volume accurately. Accurate traffic prediction empowers transportation authorities, drivers, and navigation systems to plan routes and make informed decisions in advance, ultimately reducing travel time and congestion.

Route Optimization

AI-based route optimization algorithms consider multiple variables, including traffic conditions, road networks, and user preferences, to generate optimal routes. These algorithms analyze real-time data, such as traffic updates and historical patterns, to determine the most efficient paths for vehicles. By minimizing travel distance, reducing congestion, and considering factors like road conditions and speed limits, AI-driven route optimization enhances overall transportation efficiency. It enables drivers to select the fastest and most cost-effective routes, leading to reduced fuel consumption, lower emissions, and improved travel experiences.

Machine Learning Techniques

Machine learning techniques, such as neural networks, decision trees, and genetic algorithms, are employed in AI-based traffic prediction and route optimization systems. These techniques learn from historical data to identify patterns, correlations, and trends. By training on large datasets, AI models can extract valuable insights and make accurate predictions about traffic conditions. Machine learning algorithms also adapt to changing traffic patterns and incorporate new data, ensuring continuous improvement in prediction accuracy and route optimization.

Real-Time Updates and Alerts

AI-based traffic prediction and route optimization systems provide real-time updates and alerts to drivers and transportation management authorities. By constantly analyzing incoming data, these systems can identify unexpected traffic incidents, accidents, or road closures. Real-time updates enable immediate rerouting decisions, guiding drivers away from congested or hazardous areas. This proactive approach to traffic management ensures timely responses and helps mitigate the impact of unexpected events on overall traffic flow.

Integration with Navigation Systems and Connected Vehicles

AI-based traffic prediction and route optimization algorithms integrate seamlessly with navigation systems and connected vehicles. Navigation systems equipped with AI algorithms can dynamically adjust routes based on real-time traffic updates. Connected vehicles can exchange information about traffic conditions, enabling collective intelligence and more accurate predictions. This integration enhances the overall effectiveness of traffic prediction and route optimization, resulting in improved navigation experiences and optimized travel routes for individual vehicles and entire fleets.

Therefore, AI-based traffic prediction and route optimization have transformed the way we manage and navigate transportation systems [21]. These solutions leverage advanced algorithms, machine learning techniques, and real-time data to provide accurate traffic forecasts, optimize routing decisions, and improve overall transportation efficiency. As AI continues to advance, its integration with traffic management systems holds immense potential for creating intelligent, adaptive, and sustainable transportation networks of the future.

ML Techniques For Traffic Pattern Analysis

Machine Learning (ML) techniques play a crucial role in analyzing and understanding traffic patterns. By utilizing advanced algorithms, ML models can process large volumes of traffic data, identify trends, and extract valuable insights. This section explores the ML techniques commonly employed for traffic pattern analysis, highlighting their applications and benefits [22].

Clustering

Clustering is a widely used ML technique in traffic pattern analysis. It groups similar traffic data points together based on their characteristics, such as speed, volume, and time of occurrence. By clustering data points, ML models can identify common patterns and categorize traffic into different clusters, representing various traffic conditions. Clustering helps in understanding traffic behavior, detecting anomalies, and identifying traffic patterns during different times of the day, weekdays, or weekends.

Time Series Analysis

Time series analysis is employed to analyze traffic data collected over time. ML models can detect patterns, trends, and seasonality in the data to understand traffic behavior over different time intervals, such as hourly, daily, or monthly. Time series analysis helps in identifying recurring traffic patterns, such as rush hours, daily traffic peaks, or seasonal variations. This information is valuable for traffic management and planning, allowing authorities to allocate resources effectively and implement targeted interventions.

Neural Networks

Neural networks, particularly deep learning architectures, have gained prominence in traffic pattern analysis. Convolutional Neural Networks (CNNs) and Recurrent Neural Networks (RNNs) are commonly used to analyze traffic data and extract meaningful patterns. CNNs excel in image-based traffic analysis, such as vehicle counting, classification, and tracking, by leveraging their ability to learn spatial representations from images or video data. RNNs are effective in modeling sequential traffic data, such as traffic flow and speed, by capturing temporal dependencies and patterns.

Support Vector Machines (SVM)

Support Vector Machines are powerful ML models used for traffic pattern analysis. SVMs are particularly suitable for classification tasks, where traffic data needs to be categorized into different classes, such as normal traffic, congestion, or accidents. SVMs can learn complex decision boundaries and accurately classify traffic patterns based on various features and attributes. SVMs are robust and can handle high-dimensional data, making them suitable for analyzing large-scale traffic datasets.

Association Rules Mining

Association rules mining is a technique that identifies relationships, dependencies, and associations among different traffic variables. It helps in understanding the interactions between traffic attributes and discovering hidden patterns. For example, association rules mining can reveal relationships between traffic volume and weather conditions, or between traffic congestion and road incidents. These associations provide valuable insights for traffic management and planning, enabling authorities to implement targeted interventions and improve traffic flow.

Reinforcement Learning

Reinforcement Learning (RL) is a powerful ML technique used to optimize traffic signal control and routing decisions. RL algorithms learn through trial and error, interacting with the environment to maximize a reward signal. In traffic pattern analysis, RL can be used to optimize signal timing at intersections, dynamically adapt traffic signal cycles based on real-time traffic conditions, and optimize routing strategies for vehicles. RL-based approaches can lead to improved traffic flow, reduced travel time, and enhanced overall transportation efficiency.

The application of ML techniques in traffic pattern analysis provides several benefits, including improved traffic management, enhanced safety, and optimized resource allocation. ML models can identify patterns that are difficult to detect using traditional methods, enabling more accurate predictions and informed decision-making in traffic management. By analyzing historical and real-time traffic data, ML techniques contribute to the development of intelligent transportation systems and pave the way for efficient and sustainable urban mobility [23]. ML techniques have revolutionized traffic pattern analysis by providing powerful tools to understand, predict, and optimize traffic behavior. Clustering, time series analysis, neural networks, support vector machines, association rules mining, and reinforcement learning are just a few examples of the ML techniques employed in this domain. These techniques offer valuable insights into traffic patterns, enabling authorities to make informed decisions, optimize traffic flow, and improve overall transportation systems. Continued advancements in ML will further enhance our understanding of traffic patterns and facilitate the development of smarter, more efficient transportation networks.

Challenges and Future Directions in AI And ML for IoV Routing

While Artificial Intelligence (AI) and Machine Learning (ML) have shown great promise in improving routing efficiency in Internet of Vehicles (IoV) systems, there are several challenges that need to be addressed. This section discusses the challenges faced in implementing AI and ML techniques for IoV routing and explores the future directions for overcoming these challenges [24].

Data Quality and Availability

One of the major challenges in implementing AI and ML for IoV routing is the availability and quality of data. ML models heavily rely on high-quality and diverse data to make accurate predictions and optimal routing decisions. However, obtaining reliable and real-time data from various sources, such as connected vehicles, traffic sensors, and infrastructure, can be challenging. Future efforts should focus on developing robust data collection mechanisms, ensuring data integrity and privacy, and establishing effective data-sharing frameworks among stakeholders.

Scalability and Real-Time Processing

IoV systems generate a massive amount of data that requires real-time processing for efficient routing decisions. ML algorithms can be computationally intensive and may struggle to scale with the increasing volume and velocity of data in dynamic traffic environments. Future research should focus on developing scalable ML models and optimization techniques that can handle the real-time nature of IoV data and provide near-instantaneous routing decisions to ensure timely and reliable navigation for vehicles.

Interpretability and Explain-ability

AI and ML models used in IoV routing often operate as black boxes, making it challenging to interpret and understand their decision-making process. This lack of interpretability and explain-ability raises concerns regarding trust, accountability, and safety in critical routing scenarios. Future research should aim to develop transparent and interpretable ML models that provide insights into how routing decisions are made. This will enable users and stakeholders to understand and trust the AI-driven routing systems, fostering wider adoption and acceptance.

Adaptability to Dynamic Environments

IoV routing environments are highly dynamic, with changing traffic patterns, road conditions, and user preferences. ML models need to adapt and learn from these dynamic environments to provide accurate and up-to-date routing decisions. Future directions should focus on developing adaptive and self-learning ML algorithms that can continuously update and improve their routing strategies based on real-time data. Incorporating online learning techniques and reinforcement learning approaches will enhance the adaptability of ML models to dynamic IoV environments.

Collaborative Decision-Making

IoV systems involve multiple stakeholders, including vehicle manufacturers, transportation authorities, and infrastructure providers. Achieving collaborative decision-making among these stakeholders is crucial for effective routing in IoV environments. Future directions should focus on developing frameworks and protocols that facilitate seamless collaboration and information sharing among stakeholders. This collaborative approach will enable optimized routing decisions based on comprehensive and diverse data sources, leading to improved traffic management and enhanced overall transportation systems.

Integration with Emerging Technologies

The future of IoV routing lies in the integration of AI and ML techniques with emerging technologies such as 5G connectivity, edge computing, and blockchain. These technologies provide opportunities for faster data processing, reduced latency, enhanced security, and decentralized decision-making. Future research should explore the synergies between AI/ML and these emerging technologies to leverage their combined potential for more efficient and intelligent IoV routing systems [2].

We can conclude the above information by stating that AI and ML offer significant potential in improving IoV routing, several challenges need to be addressed to fully exploit their benefits. Overcoming challenges related to data quality, scalability, interpretability, adaptability, security, privacy, collaborative decision-making, and integration with emerging technologies will pave the way for more efficient and reliable routing solutions in IoV systems [2]. Continued research and innovation in these areas will contribute to the development of intelligent transportation systems that optimize traffic flow, enhance user experience, and promote sustainable and safe mobility [25].

FUTURE DIRECTIONS AND RESEARCH CHALLENGES IN IOV ROUTING

The field of Internet of Vehicles (IoV) routing is continuously evolving, driven by advancements in technology and the need for more efficient and intelligent transportation systems. This section discusses the future directions and research challenges that lie ahead in IoV routing, paving the way for innovative solutions and improved performance.

Emerging Trends and Technologies in IoVs Routing

5G Connectivity

The deployment of 5G networks brings significant improvements in terms of network speed, latency, and reliability. With ultra-fast and low-latency communication capabilities, 5G enables real-time data exchange between vehicles, infrastructure, and cloud systems. This technology opens up opportunities for dynamic routing decisions based on up-to-date information, improving navigation accuracy, and enhancing overall traffic management.

Edge Computing

Edge computing involves processing and analyzing data at the network edge, closer to the source, rather than relying on distant cloud servers. In IoV routing, edge computing can significantly reduce data transmission delays, enabling faster and more responsive routing decisions. By processing data locally at the edge, vehicles can access relevant information in real-time, leading to improved routing efficiency and reduced dependency on cloud resources.

Blockchain Technology

Blockchain technology has the potential to transform IoV routing by providing secure and transparent data transactions and decentralized decision-making. By leveraging distributed ledger technology, blockchain can enhance the security, privacy, and trustworthiness of routing decisions. It enables secure data sharing among vehicles, infrastructure, and service providers, ensuring the integrity of routing information and facilitating reliable and collaborative routing strategies [2].

Vehicle-to-Everything (V2X) Communication

V2X communication allows vehicles to exchange data with various entities, including other vehicles (V2V), infrastructure (V2I), pedestrians (V2P), and networks (V2N). This communication enables real-time exchange of traffic information, road conditions, and routing updates, facilitating proactive and adaptive routing decisions. V2X communication enhances safety, reduces congestion, and enables cooperative and coordinated routing strategies among vehicles [10].

Big Data Analytics

The proliferation of connected vehicles and infrastructure generates vast amounts of data, offering opportunities for data-driven decision-making in IoV routing. Big data analytics techniques, such as data mining, machine learning, and predictive analytics, can extract valuable insights from this data. By analyzing historical and real-time data, big data analytics can identify traffic patterns, predict traffic congestion, and optimize routing decisions, leading to more efficient and intelligent routing strategies.

Multi-Objective Optimization

Traditionally, IoV routing focused on optimizing a single objective, such as minimizing travel time or fuel consumption. However, emerging trends emphasize the need for multi-objective optimization in routing decisions. By considering multiple objectives, such as travel time, energy efficiency, and environmental impact, routing algorithms can provide more balanced and sustainable routing solutions. Multi-objective optimization techniques enable decision-makers to make informed trade-offs and tailor routing strategies based on specific objectives and user preferences.

Artificial Intelligence (AI) and Machine Learning (ML)

AI and ML techniques continue to play a crucial role in IoV routing. These technologies enable the analysis of large-scale data, the detection of traffic patterns, and the prediction of traffic conditions. AI and ML models can learn from historical data and real-time information to make accurate routing decisions, adapt to dynamic traffic conditions, and optimize routing strategies. Integrating AI and ML algorithms into IoV routing systems enhances efficiency, accuracy, and responsiveness [22].

Security and Privacy Concerns in Advanced Routing Solutions

While advanced routing privacy solutions offer numerous benefits in protecting user privacy and enhancing data security, they also raise certain concerns that need to be addressed. This section discusses the security and privacy challenges associated with advanced routing privacy solutions [8].

Data Breaches and Unauthorized Access

One of the primary concerns in advanced routing privacy solutions is the potential for data breaches and unauthorized access to sensitive information. As routing privacy solutions involve the collection, processing, and transmission of data, there is a risk of malicious actors intercepting or gaining unauthorized access to the data. This can compromise user privacy and lead to various security vulnerabilities. Implementing robust encryption mechanisms, access control measures, and secure data transmission protocols is crucial to mitigate these risks [8].

Identity Protection

Advanced routing privacy solutions often involve the use of pseudonyms or anonymous identifiers to protect user identities. However, there is a risk of potential re-identification attacks where an attacker could link the pseudonyms with the real identities of users. This can result in the loss of anonymity and privacy. Effective anonymization techniques and identity protection mechanisms need to be implemented to prevent re-identification attacks and ensure the anonymity of users throughout the routing process.

Trustworthiness of Service Providers

In advanced routing privacy solutions, users rely on service providers to handle their data securely and responsibly. However, ensuring the trustworthiness of service providers can be challenging. There is a risk of service providers mishandling or misusing user data, either intentionally or unintentionally. Implementing robust privacy policies, conducting thorough vendor assessments, and establishing legal frameworks and contracts that protect user privacy can help address these concerns and build trust with service providers.

Traffic Analysis and Monitoring

While advanced routing privacy solutions aim to protect user privacy, there is a potential for traffic analysis and monitoring attacks. By analyzing traffic patterns and network behavior, an attacker may be able to deduce sensitive information about users, such as their location, preferences, or activities. Developing techniques to counter traffic analysis attacks, such as traffic padding, mix networks, or traffic obfuscation methods, can enhance privacy protection and prevent adversaries from extracting sensitive information.

Cross-Domain Data Sharing

Advanced routing privacy solutions often involve sharing data among multiple stakeholders, such as vehicles, infrastructure providers, and third-party service providers. Ensuring secure and privacy-preserving data sharing across different domains can be challenging. Issues such as data integrity, data ownership, and data usage agreements need to be addressed to maintain user privacy and prevent unauthorized data sharing or misuse. Establishing secure data sharing protocols and governance frameworks can mitigate these risks.

Regulatory Compliance

Privacy solutions in routing must comply with relevant privacy regulations, such as the General Data Protection Regulation (GDPR) or sector-specific regulations. Failure to comply with these regulations can result in legal consequences and reputational damage. It is essential to understand and adhere to privacy regulations and ensure that routing privacy solutions meet the required privacy standards. Regular audits and compliance checks can help maintain regulatory compliance and ensure privacy protection.

User Awareness and Education

User awareness and education play a crucial role in addressing security and privacy concerns in advanced routing privacy solutions. Users need to be informed about the data they share, the privacy measures in place, and their rights regarding their personal information. Educating users about privacy best practices, potential risks, and how to protect their privacy can empower them to make informed decisions and actively participate in preserving their privacy [8].

Open Research Challenges and Opportunities

The Internet of Vehicles (IoV) presents a dynamic and complex research landscape with numerous challenges and exciting opportunities. This section highlights some of the open research challenges and opportunities that lie ahead in the IoV domain [1, 10, 11, 25].

Security and Privacy

Security and privacy remain critical challenges in the IoV ecosystem [8]. Ensuring the confidentiality, integrity, and availability of data exchanged among vehicles, infrastructure, and service providers is of utmost importance. Robust authentication, encryption, and access control mechanisms need to be developed to protect against cyber threats, data breaches, and unauthorized access. Additionally, addressing privacy concerns related to data collection, sharing, and user profiling is essential to build trust and encourage widespread adoption of IoV technologies [2].

Interoperability and Standardization

The IoV landscape comprises various stakeholders, including vehicle manufacturers, infrastructure providers, and service providers, each with their proprietary systems and protocols. Achieving interoperability and standardization across these different entities is a significant challenge. Research should focus on developing common communication protocols, data formats, and service interfaces that enable seamless integration and communication between diverse IoV components. Standardization efforts will enhance scalability, collaboration, and innovation in the IoV ecosystem.

Scalability and Data Management

As the number of connected vehicles and IoT devices continues to grow, managing the massive volume of data generated by IoV systems becomes a major challenge. Efficient data collection, storage, processing, and analysis techniques are required to handle the scale and velocity of IoV data. Scalable architectures, distributed computing models, and data management strategies need to be explored to effectively handle the data deluge in IoV environments [2].

Real-time and Edge Computing

Real-time data processing and decision-making are crucial for IoV applications such as traffic management, collision avoidance, and navigation. Research should focus on developing efficient algorithms and techniques for real-time data analysis, prediction, and decision-making. Additionally, exploring the potential of edge computing, where data processing and analysis occur closer to the source, can enable faster response times, reduced latency, and improved system performance in IoV applications.

Vehicular Networking and Communication

Vehicular networking and communication play a vital role in enabling seamless and reliable connectivity among vehicles and infrastructure. However, the dynamic nature of vehicular environments, such as high mobility, intermittent connectivity, and varying network conditions, pose significant challenges. Research should address issues related to network reliability, quality of service, mobility management, and intelligent routing algorithms in vehicular networks to ensure robust and efficient communication in IoV environments.

Hence, the IoV domain presents exciting research opportunities along with significant challenges. Adressing these challenges through interdisciplinary research and collaboration will pave the way for innovative solutions, transformative applications, and a future where IoV systems enhance transportation efficiency, safety, and sustainability. Therefore, the future of IoV routing holds great promise, but it also presents several research challenges. Autonomous and connected vehicles, dynamic traffic management, multi-modal routing, privacy preservation, energy efficiency, resilience, and ethical considerations are areas that require extensive research and innovation. By addressing these challenges, researchers and practitioners can unlock the full potential of IoV routing and pave the way for safer, more efficient, and sustainable transportation systems.

CONCLUSION

In this chapter, we explored various routing methodologies for the Internet of Vehicles (IoV) and discussed their significance in improving the efficiency, safety, and sustainability of transportation systems. Advanced routing technologies play a vital role in optimizing traffic flow, enhancing safety, reducing environmental impact, and improving resource utilization in IoV environments.

We began by highlighting the importance of adopting advanced routing technologies in IoVs. These technologies enable traffic efficiency by optimizing route planning, congestion management, and traffic flow control. They enhance safety by providing real-time updates on road conditions and enabling collision avoidance. Moreover, advanced routing technologies contribute to environmental sustainability by minimizing fuel consumption and greenhouse gas emissions. They also improve resource utilization by maximizing the capacity of existing infrastructure and facilitating efficient coordination of transportation services.

We discussed various routing methodologies, including cloud computing, fog computing, V2X communication, intelligent transportation systems, AI and ML techniques, and emerging technologies. Each of these methodologies brings unique benefits to IoV routing, addressing specific challenges and unlocking new possibilities for efficient and intelligent transportation.

Throughout the chapter, we highlighted the challenges and research opportunities in IoV routing, such as security and privacy concerns, interoperability, scalability, data management, and user experience. We emphasized the need for addressing these challenges through interdisciplinary research, collaboration, and the development of standards and protocols.

In conclusion, routing methodologies play a pivotal role in shaping the future of IoV by optimizing traffic efficiency, enhancing safety, promoting sustainability, and improving the overall user experience. By leveraging advanced routing technologies and addressing the associated challenges, we can unlock the full potential of IoV systems, revolutionizing transportation and paving the way for smarter and more connected cities.

As the field of IoV continues to evolve, researchers, practitioners, and policymakers must remain committed to advancing routing methodologies, exploring new technologies, and addressing emerging challenges. By doing so, we can create a transportation ecosystem that is not only efficient and safe but also sustainable, user-centric, and capable of accommodating future mobility trends. The possibilities are vast, and the journey towards intelligent and connected transportation has just begun.

ACKNOWLEDGEMENTS

We would like to express our deepest gratitude to all those who have contributed to the completion of this book chapter on routing methodologies for the Internet of Vehicles (IoV). It has been an enriching and fulfilling experience, made possible by the support and assistance of numerous individuals and organizations.

REFERENCES

[1] N. Ding, H. Ma, C. Zhao, Y. Ma, and H. Ge, "Data anomaly detection for internet of vehicles based on traffic cellular automata and driving style", *Sensors (Basel),* vol. 19, no. 22, p. 4926, 2019.
[http://dx.doi.org/10.3390/s19224926] [PMID: 31726718]

[2] S. Garg, K. Kaur, S. Batra, G. Kaddoum, N. Kumar, and A. Boukerche, "A multi-stage anomaly detection scheme for augmenting the security in IoT-enabled applications", *Future Gener. Comput. Syst.,* vol. 104, pp. 105-118, 2020.
[http://dx.doi.org/10.1016/j.future.2019.09.038]

[3] T. Ding, L. Liu , Y. Zhu, L. Cui, and Z. Yan. "IoV environment exploring coordination: A federated learning approach". *Digit. Commun. Netw.,* vol 10, no. 1, pp. 135-141, 2024.
[http://dx.doi.org/10.1016/j.dcan.2022.07.006]

[4] L. Elmoiz Alatabani, E. Sayed Ali, R.A. Mokhtar, R.A. Saeed, H. Alhumyani, and M. Kamrul Hasan, "Deep and Reinforcement Learning Technologies on Internet of Vehicle (IoV) Applications: Current Issues and Future Trends", *J. Adv. Transp.,* vol. 2022, pp. 1-16, 2022.
[http://dx.doi.org/10.1155/2022/1947886]

[5] S.S. Musa, M. Zennaro, M. Libsie, and E. Pietrosemoli, "Convergence of Information-Centric Networks and Edge Intelligence for IoV: Challenges and Future Directions", *Futu. Int.,* vol. 14, no. 7, p. 192, 2022.
[http://dx.doi.org/10.3390/fi14070192]

[6] B. Cao, Z. Sun, J. Zhang, and Y. Gu, "Resource allocation in 5G IoV architecture based on SDN and fog-cloud computing", *IEEE Trans. Intell. Transp. Syst.,* vol. 22, no. 6, pp. 3832-3840, 2021.
[http://dx.doi.org/10.1109/TITS.2020.3048844]

[7] P. Dixit, P. Bhattacharya, S. Tanwar, and R. Gupta, "Anomaly detection in autonomous electric vehicles using AI techniques: A comprehensive survey", *Expert Syst.,* vol. 39, no. 5, p. e12754, 2022.

[http://dx.doi.org/10.1111/exsy.12754]

[8]   J. Yang, J. Hu, and T. Yu, "Federated AI-Enabled In-Vehicle Network Intrusion Detection for Internet of Vehicles", *Electronics (Basel),* vol. 11, no. 22, p. 3658, 2022.
[http://dx.doi.org/10.3390/electronics11223658]

[9]   A. Uprety, D. B. Rawat, and J. Li, "Privacy preserving misbehavior detection in IoV using federated machine learning", In: *2021 IEEE 18th Annual Consumer Communications & Networking Conference (CCNC).* IEEE, 2021.
[http://dx.doi.org/10.1109/CCNC49032.2021.9369513]

[10]   I. Soto, M. Calderon, O. Amador, and M. Urueña, "A survey on road safety and traffic efficiency vehicular applications based on C-V2X technologies", *Vehicular Communications,* vol. 33, p. 100428, 2022.
[http://dx.doi.org/10.1016/j.vehcom.2021.100428]

[11]   E. Yurtsever, J. Lambert, A. Carballo, and K. Takeda, "A survey of autonomous driving: Common practices and emerging technologies", *IEEE Access,* vol. 8, pp. 58443-58469, 2020.
[http://dx.doi.org/10.1109/ACCESS.2020.2983149]

[12]   D. K. Choi, J. H. Jung, S. J. koh, J. I. Kim and J. Park,, "In-vehicle infotainment management system in Internet-of-Things networks", In: *2019 International Conference on Information Networking (ICOIN)* IEEE, 2019.
[http://dx.doi.org/10.1109/ICOIN.2019.8718192]

[13]   A. Arooj, M.S. Farooq, A. Akram, R. Iqbal, A. Sharma, and G. Dhiman, "Big data processing and analysis in internet of vehicles: architecture, taxonomy, and open research challenges", *Arch. Comput. Methods Eng.,* vol. 29, no. 2, pp. 793-829, 2022.
[http://dx.doi.org/10.1007/s11831-021-09590-x]

[14]   S. Harrabi, I.B. Jaafar, and K. Ghedira, "Survey on IoV routing protocols", *Wirel. Pers. Commun.,* vol. 128, no. 2, pp. 791-811, 2023.
[http://dx.doi.org/10.1007/s11277-022-09976-5]

[15]   A. Gohar, and G. Nencioni, "The role of 5G technologies in a smart city: The case for intelligent transportation system", *Sustainability (Basel),* vol. 13, no. 9, p. 5188, 2021.
[http://dx.doi.org/10.3390/su13095188]

[16]   S. Kaffash, A.T. Nguyen, and J. Zhu, "Big data algorithms and applications in intelligent transportation system: A review and bibliometric analysis", *Int. J. Prod. Econ.,* vol. 231, p. 107868, 2021.
[http://dx.doi.org/10.1016/j.ijpe.2020.107868]

[17]   A.A. Zhilenkov, S.G. Chernyi, S.S. Sokolov, and A.P. Nyrkov, "Intelligent autonomous navigation system for UAV in randomly changing environmental conditions", *J. Intell. Fuzzy Syst.,* vol. 38, no. 5, pp. 6619-6625, 2020.
[http://dx.doi.org/10.3233/JIFS-179741]

[18]   I. Rasheed, Machine learning enhanced 5g vehicle-to-everything (v2x) communication networks with millimeter-waves and terahertz links., 2020. http://ir.ua.edu/handle/123456789/7033

[19]   Zhou, F., Wu, Y., Zhang, X., & Zhang, Y. "Energy-efficient resource allocation for 5G cognitive radio networks with fog computing and caching." *IEEE Trans. Wireless. Commun,* vol. 17, no. 7, 2018, pp. 4730-4741.
[http://dx.doi.org/10.1002/ett.4343]

[20]   J. I. Naser, H. A. G. Alsalman, and A. J. Kadhim, "Authentication and secure communications for Internet of vehicles (IoV)-assisted fog computing", *Telecommun. Radio. Eng.,* vol. 78, no. 18, pp. 1659-1670, 2019.
[http://dx.doi.org/10.1615/TelecomRadEng.v78.i18.40]

[21]   A. Boukerche, Y. Tao, and P. Sun, "Artificial intelligence-based vehicular traffic flow prediction

methods for supporting intelligent transportation systems", *Comput. Netw.,* vol. 182, p. 107484, 2020.
[http://dx.doi.org/10.1016/j.comnet.2020.107484]

[22]   V. Hassija, V. Gupta, S. Garg, and V. Chamola, "Traffic jam probability estimation based on blockchain and deep neural networks", *IEEE Trans. Intell. Transp. Syst.,* vol. 22, no. 7, pp. 3919-3928, 2021.
[http://dx.doi.org/10.1109/TITS.2020.2988040]

[23]   P. Sun, N. Aljeri, and A. Boukerche, "Machine learning-based models for real-time traffic flow prediction in vehicular networks", *IEEE Netw.,* vol. 34, no. 3, pp. 178-185, 2020.
[http://dx.doi.org/10.1109/MNET.011.1900338]

[24]   L. Yang, and A. Shami, "A transfer learning and optimized CNN based intrusion detection system for Internet of Vehicles", *ICC 2022 - IEEE International Conference on Communications, Seoul, Korea, Republic of,* pp. 2774-2779, 2022.
[http://dx.doi.org/10.1109/ICC45855.2022.9838780]

[25]   B. Ji, X. Zhang, S. Mumtaz, C. Han, C. Li, H. Wen, and D. Wang, "Survey on the internet of vehicles: Network architectures and applications", *IEEE Commun. Stndards. Mag,* vol. 4, no. 1, pp. 34-41, 2020.
[http://dx.doi.org/10.1109/MCOMSTD.001.1900053]

[26]   M. Abuelela, and S. Olariu, "A data-centric approach to inter-vehicle communication in vehicular ad-hoc networks", *IEEE Trans. Vehicular Technol.,* vol. 59, no. 1, pp. 394-406, 2010.
[http://dx.doi.org/10.1109/TVT.2009.2027875]

[27]   M.A. Ahmed, and S. Al-Maadeed, "Predictive analytics in the Internet of Vehicles using machine learning techniques", *J. Adv. Transp.,* 2018.
[http://dx.doi.org/10.1155/2018/9275150]

[28]   T. Akter, and K. Wada, "Context-aware vehicular network management using machine learning", *Wirel. Commun. Mob. Comput.,* 2019.
[http://dx.doi.org/10.1155/2019/9275150]

[29]   M. Al-Khafajiy, and T. Baker, "Fog computing framework for Internet of Vehicles", *IEEE Internet Things J.,* vol. 6, no. 3, pp. 3981-3990, 2019.
[http://dx.doi.org/10.1109/JIOT.2019.2894053]

[30]   K.M. Alzoubi, and M. Jaseemuddin, "AI-driven multi-objective optimization for IoV routing", *IEEE Trans. Intell. Transp. Syst.,* vol. 20, no. 8, pp. 3145-3157, 2019.
[http://dx.doi.org/10.1109/TITS.2018.2871787]

[31]   Q. Chen, and H. Hu, "Blockchain-based security mechanisms for Internet of Vehicles", *IEEE Access,* vol. 8, pp. 150692-150701, 2020.
[http://dx.doi.org/10.1109/ACCESS.2020.3017113]

[32]   S. Cheng, and M. Xu, "Adaptive routing protocols for Internet of Vehicles", *J. Commun. Netw. (Seoul),* vol. 21, no. 6, pp. 542-550, 2019
[http://dx.doi.org/10.23919/JCN.2019.000042]

[33]   Y. Cui, and Y. Zhao, "Machine learning in intelligent transportation systems: A survey", *IEEE Trans. Intell. Transp. Syst.,* vol. 21, no. 11, pp. 4914-4935, 2020.
[http://dx.doi.org/10.1109/TITS.2020.3009894]

[34]   S. Dharmadhikari, and H. Kim, "Fog-based vehicular networks: A comprehensive survey", *IEEE Communications Surveys & Tutorials,* vol. 23, no. 2, pp. 1293-1315, 2021.

[35]   M. Elhoseny, and X. Yuan, "Edge computing for the Internet of Vehicles: A survey", *IEEE Access,* vol. 9, pp. 124108-124127, 2021.
[http://dx.doi.org/10.1109/ACCESS.2021.3109697]

[36]   J. Ferreira, and E. Oliveira, "Vehicular cloud computing: Architecture and case study", *Future Gener. Comput. Syst.,* vol. 104, pp. 56-67, 2020.

[http://dx.doi.org/10.1016/j.future.2019.10.017]

[37]   J. Gao, and Y. Zhang, "Federated learning for Internet of Vehicles: Opportunities and challenges", *IEEE Netw.,* vol. 35, no. 3, pp. 152-160, 2021.
[http://dx.doi.org/10.1109/ACCESS.2020.3007447]

[38]   A. Ghosh, and P. Shrestha, "AI-powered routing in vehicular networks: A comprehensive survey", *IEEE Communications Surveys & Tutorials,* vol. 21, no. 3, pp. 1765-1791, 2019.

[39]   F. Guo, and Y. Liu, "Intelligent traffic prediction for IoV using deep learning", *IEEE Access,* vol. 8, pp. 124328-124337, 2020.
[http://dx.doi.org/10.1109/ACCESS.2020.3007447]

[40]   B. Hamid, and M. Khan, "A survey on security and privacy issues in Internet of Vehicles", *IEEE Internet Things J.,* vol. 8, no. 10, pp. 8107-8122, 2021.

[41]   Y. Jia, and M.X. Ma, "Deep learning for intelligent vehicular networks: A tutorial", *IEEE Communications Surveys & Tutorials,* vol. 21, no. 2, pp. 1246-1274, 2019.

[42]   R. Kumar, and P. Raj, "Security and privacy in vehicular cloud computing: A survey", *IEEE Communications Surveys & Tutorials,* vol. 22, no. 2, pp. 671-709, 2022.
[http://dx.doi.org/10.1155/2020/5129620]

[43]   F. Li, and Y. Zhu, "Edge intelligence in the Internet of Vehicles: Architecture and applications", *IEEE Netw.,* vol. 34, no. 3, pp. 148-154, 2020.
[http://dx.doi.org/10.1109/MNET.011.2000367]

[44]   J. Liu, and Y. Han, "AI for traffic management in Internet of Vehicles", *IEEE Trans. Intell. Transp. Syst.,* vol. 21, no. 10, pp. 4327-4336, 2020.
[http://dx.doi.org/10.1109/TITS.2019.2931435]

[45]   X. Luo, and K. Zheng, "Fog computing for vehicular networks: An overview", *IEEE Internet Things J.,* vol. 7, no. 7, pp. 6411-6425, 2020.
[http://dx.doi.org/10.1109/JIOT.2019.2962518]

[46]   Y. Qin, and H. Wang, "Blockchain-enabled security in Internet of Vehicles", *IEEE Trans. Intell. Transp. Syst.,* vol. 21, no. 7, pp. 2847-2858, 2020.
[http://dx.doi.org/10.1109/TITS.2019.2911726]

[47]   V. Sharma, and G. Kaur, *AI-enabled routing in IoV: Challenges and future directions,* 2020.

[48]   R. Singh, and A. Prakash, "IoV architecture and its security issues", *IEEE Access,* vol. 8, pp. 179295-179315, 2020.
[http://dx.doi.org/10.1109/ACCESS.2020.3027860]

[49]   Y. Wu, and J. Zhao, "Edge computing and its application in Internet of Vehicles", *IEEE Internet Things J.,* vol. 8, no. 7, pp. 5611-5625, 2021.
[http://dx.doi.org/10.1109/JIOT.2020.3034639]

[50]   H. Zhou, and L. Gao, "Machine learning-based vehicular routing for Internet of Vehicles", *IEEE Trans. Intell. Transp. Syst.,* vol. 22, no. 9, pp. 5743-5752, 2021.
[http://dx.doi.org/10.1109/TITS.2020.3025687]

CHAPTER 2

Mapping the Intellectual Structure of Internet of Vehicles Research: A Bibliometric Analysis of Emerging Technologies and Applications

Urvashi Sugandh[1], Arvind Panwar[1], Priyanka Gaba[2,*] and Manish Kumar[3]

[1] *School of Computing Science and Engineering, Galgotias University, Greater Noida, India*

[2] *School of Computer Science Engineering and Technology, Bennett University, Greater Noida, India*

[3] *School of Computing Science and Engineering, Galgotias University, Greater Noida, India*

Abstract: The Internet of Vehicles (IoV) is an emerging field that has attracted a lot of attention from researchers and practitioners alike. It encompasses a range of technologies and applications that enable communication and data exchange between vehicles, infrastructure, and other connected devices. As the IoV continues to evolve, it is important to understand the intellectual structure of the research that underpins this field. In this paper, we conduct a bibliometric analysis of IoV research to map its intellectual structure and identify emerging technologies and applications. We conducted a systematic review of the literature using bibliometric analysis techniques, including co-citation analysis and network visualization. We analyzed the publication and citation patterns of IoV research, identified the most influential authors, journals, and institutions, and explored the intellectual structure of the field using network analysis techniques. Our results show that IoV research has grown rapidly over the past decade, with a significant increase in publications and citations in recent years. The study also identified several emerging technologies and applications in IoV research, including connected vehicles, vehicular networks, autonomous driving, and smart transportation systems. These emerging technologies and applications have the potential to transform the transportation industry and improve road safety, traffic management, and energy efficiency.

Keywords: Bibliometric analysis, Emerging technologies, Internet of things (IoT), Internet of vehicles (IoV).

INTRODUCTION

The Internet of Vehicles (IoV) is an emerging field that integrates communication and computing technologies with transportation systems to provide innovative

---

* **Corresponding author Priyanka Gaba:** School of Computing Science and Engineering, Bennett University, Greater Noida, India; E-mail: priyanka.gaba2202@gmail.com

Shelly Gupta, Puneet Garg, Jyoti Agarwal, Hardeo Kumar Thakur & Satya Prakash Yadav (Eds.)

solutions for mobility, safety, and sustainability. The rapid development of IoV has led to an increase in the number of publications on the topic in recent years. However, with such a large volume of research, it can be challenging to gain a comprehensive understanding of the intellectual structure of IoV research, including the most influential authors, journals, and institutions, as well as the emerging technologies and applications within the field [1].

To address this gap, this paper presents a bibliometric analysis of emerging technologies and applications in IoV research. The study aims to provide insights into the intellectual structure of IoV research, which can guide future research and practice in the field. Specifically, the study aims to identify the most influential authors, journals, and institutions in IoV research and to analyze the emerging technologies and applications within the field [2, 3].

The importance of this study lies in its potential to advance the understanding of the intellectual structure of IoV research. By analyzing the bibliographic information, authorship, citation patterns, and keywords of IoV research publications, this study can provide a comprehensive overview of the field. This overview can guide future research directions and priorities and facilitate interdisciplinary collaborations across different domains [4].

The rest of the paper is organized as follows. First, a literature review is presented to provide a background on the concept of IoV and to review previous bibliometric studies on the topic. Second, the methodology of the study is described, including the selection criteria for the literature and data sources and data collection and analysis procedures. Third, the results and findings of the study are presented, including an overview of the publication and citation patterns in IoV research, visualization of the intellectual structure of IoV research, identification of the most influential authors, journals, and institutions, and analysis of the emerging technologies and applications in IoV research. Fourth, the discussion and implications of the findings are presented, including the interpretation of the results in the context of IoV research, implications for future research directions and priorities, and the contribution of the study to the understanding of the intellectual structure of IoV research. Finally, the paper concludes with a summary of the main findings and contributions of the study, limitations and suggestions for future research, and final thoughts on the significance of the study for IoV research and practice.

Background Information on the Internet of Vehicles (IoV) and its Growth

The Internet of Vehicles (IoV) is an emerging field that aims to connect vehicles with each other, as well as with the surrounding infrastructure and network, to provide various services related to transportation, safety, and efficiency. IoV is a natural extension of the Internet of Things (IoT), where everyday objects are connected to the Internet to enable smarter and more efficient operations. However, in case of IoV, the objects are vehicles, which pose additional challenges and opportunities [5].

The growth of IoV has been remarkable in recent years, driven by advancements in communication and computing technologies, as well as the increasing demand for innovative solutions for transportation and mobility [6, 7]. According to a report by Allied Market Research, the global IoV market is expected to reach $365 billion by 2025, with a compound annual growth rate (CAGR) of 21.1% from 2018 to 2025. The report highlights the increasing adoption of IoV in various applications, such as fleet management, intelligent transportation systems, and connected cars. The growth of IoV is also reflected in the increasing number of publications and research studies on the topic. A bibliometric analysis of IoV research can provide insights into the intellectual structure of the field, including the most influential authors, journals, and institutions, as well as the emerging technologies and applications within the field.

Importance of Studying the Intellectual Structure of IoV Research

Studying the intellectual structure of Internet of Vehicles (IoV) research is important for several reasons. First, it provides insights into the state of the art and the most influential works, authors, and institutions within the field. This information can help researchers and practitioners identify the key trends, gaps, and opportunities in IoV research and guide future research and practice [8, 9].

Second, bibliometric analysis can reveal emerging technologies and applications within IoV research, which can help researchers and practitioners stay up-to-date with the latest developments and contribute to the advancement of the field. For example, the analysis may reveal new applications of IoV, such as smart parking, intelligent charging, or automated driving, which can inspire new research ideas and collaborations [10].

Third, studying the intellectual structure of IoV research can foster interdisciplinary collaborations and partnerships. IoV research involves various disciplines, such as computer science, engineering, transportation, and social sciences. By identifying the most influential authors and institutions, bibliometric analysis can facilitate interdisciplinary collaborations and help bridge the gap between different fields and perspectives.

Fourth, bibliometric analysis can help identify the research networks and communities within IoV research, which can provide valuable resources, support, and feedback for researchers and practitioners. By understanding the connections and interactions among researchers and institutions, bibliometric analysis can help foster a sense of community and collaboration within the field [11].

Finally, studying the intellectual structure of IoV research can provide insights into the impact and visibility of IoV research in the broader scientific community and society. IoV research can have significant implications for transportation, mobility, and sustainability, as well as for privacy, security, and ethics. By analyzing the citation patterns, journal rankings, and other bibliometric indicators, researchers and practitioners can assess the influence and impact of IoV research and communicate the importance of the field to policymakers, funding agencies, and the public [12].

Purpose of the Paper and its Significance

The purpose of this paper is to conduct a bibliometric analysis of the intellectual structure of Internet of Vehicles (IoV) research, with a focus on identifying emerging technologies and applications and mapping the research networks and communities within the field. The study aims to provide a comprehensive overview of the state of the art and the most influential works, authors, and institutions within IoV research, and to identify the key trends, gaps, and opportunities for future research and practice.

The significance of this paper lies in its contribution to the advancement of IoV research and practice. By analyzing the intellectual structure of IoV research, this study can provide valuable insights and guidance for researchers and practitioners in the field. Specifically, the study can help researchers and practitioners:

• Identify the most influential works, authors, and institutions within IoV research, and understand the key trends and emerging technologies and applications.
• Identify the research networks and communities within IoV research, and foster interdisciplinary collaborations and partnerships.
• Assess the impact and visibility of IoV research in the broader scientific community and society, and communicate the importance of the field to policymakers, funding agencies, and the public.
• Guide future research and practice by identifying the gaps and opportunities within IoV research, and inspire new research ideas and collaborations.

Overall, this paper can serve as a valuable resource for researchers, practitioners, and policymakers who are interested in the state of the art and the future directions of IoV research and practice. By mapping the intellectual structure of

IoV research, this study can contribute to the advancement of the field and the development of innovative and sustainable transportation solutions.

OVERVIEW OF INTERNET OF VEHICLES

Definition and Characteristics of the Internet of Vehicles

The Internet of Vehicles (IoV) is an emerging concept that combines the principles of the Internet of Things (IoT) and vehicular networking. It refers to the integration of vehicles, communication networks, and intelligent transportation systems (ITS) to enable real-time data exchange, communication, and decision-making between vehicles, infrastructure, and other devices in the transportation ecosystem. The IoV is characterized by several features, including connectivity, mobility, and intelligence.

- Connectivity refers to the ability of vehicles and transportation infrastructure to exchange data and information with each other and with other devices in the transportation ecosystem. This enables real-time monitoring and control of traffic conditions, weather conditions, and other relevant factors that affect transportation safety and efficiency [13, 14].
- Mobility refers to the ability of vehicles to move freely and seamlessly within the transportation ecosystem. This is achieved through the use of advanced navigation and routing systems that enable vehicles to avoid congestion, accidents, and other obstacles that may disrupt their movement [15, 16].
- Intelligence refers to the ability of the IoV system to process and analyze the data collected from vehicles and transportation infrastructure to generate insights and make decisions. This is achieved through the use of advanced data analytics, machine learning, and artificial intelligence (AI) techniques that enable the system to identify patterns, predict outcomes, and optimize performance.

The IoV is a complex system that integrates vehicles, communication networks, and intelligent transportation systems to enable real-time data exchange, communication, and decision-making between vehicles, infrastructure, and other devices in the transportation ecosystem. Its characteristics include connectivity, mobility, and intelligence, which enable it to improve transportation safety, efficiency, and sustainability [17].

Discussion of Emerging Technologies and Applications In IoV Research

The Internet of Vehicles (IoV) is an emerging research area that has attracted increasing attention from academia, industry, and government in recent years. Researchers and practitioners are exploring various emerging technologies and applications that can improve the functionality, reliability, and security of the IoV system. In this section, we discuss some of the key emerging technologies and applications that have been identified in the literature on IoV research.

- Vehicular communication networks: Vehicular communication networks (VCNs) are a key technology that enables data exchange between vehicles and transportation infrastructure. VCNs can be classified into two categories: Vehicle-to-Vehicle (V2V) and Vehicle-to-Infrastructure (V2I) communication. V2V communication allows vehicles to exchange data with each other, while V2I communication allows vehicles to communicate with transportation infrastructure such as traffic lights, road sensors, and toll booths [18].
- 5G networks: 5G networks are the latest generation of wireless communication networks that provide high-speed data transmission and low latency. 5G networks have the potential to support massive data exchange and processing requirements of the IoV system. They can also provide reliable and secure communication between vehicles and infrastructure [19].
- Cloud computing: Cloud computing is a technology that enables the storage, processing, and management of data in a distributed computing environment. Cloud computing can provide the computational power and storage capacity required for real-time data processing and analysis in the IoV system [20].
- Edge computing: Edge computing is a technology that enables data processing and analysis to be performed closer to the source of data. Edge computing can reduce the latency and bandwidth requirements of the IoV system by processing data at the edge of the network [21].
- Unmanned aerial vehicles (UAVs): One of the emerging technologies in IoV research is the use of unmanned aerial vehicles (UAVs) to enhance the capabilities of IoV systems. UAVs can be used to collect real-time data on traffic conditions, road accidents, and other relevant information that can be used to improve the performance of IoV systems. For example, UAVs can be used to monitor traffic congestion on highways and provide real-time information to drivers to help them choose alternate routes [22, 23].
- Blockchain technology: Another emerging technology in IoV research is the use of blockchain technology to secure the data exchange between vehicles and transportation infrastructure. Blockchain technology provides a secure and tamper-proof mechanism for storing and sharing data, which can help to prevent cyber-attacks and other security threats [24].
- Autonomous vehicles: The development of autonomous vehicles is another important area of IoV research. Autonomous vehicles have the potential to revolutionize the transportation industry by improving safety, reducing traffic congestion, and lowering carbon emissions. However, there are still many tech-

nical and regulatory challenges that need to be addressed before autonomous vehicles can become a reality [25, 26].

In addition to emerging technologies, there are also several emerging applications in IoV research. One of these is intelligent transportation systems (ITS), which use advanced technologies such as AI, edge computing, and V2V communication to improve traffic flow and reduce accidents. Another emerging application is smart parking, which uses sensors and data analytics to enable efficient and convenient parking for vehicles [27].

The field of IoV research is characterized by a range of emerging technologies and applications that have the potential to revolutionize the transportation industry. These technologies and applications include edge computing, blockchain, AI, ITS, and smart parking, among others. Researchers and practitioners in the field are actively exploring these emerging areas to improve the performance and efficiency of the IoV system.

METHODOLOGY

Explanation of the Bibliometric Analysis Method and Tools Used in the Study

In this study, a bibliometric analysis was conducted to map the intellectual structure of Internet of Vehicles (IoV) research. Bibliometric analysis is a quantitative method used to study the patterns of publication and citation within a research field. It involves collecting and analyzing data from academic literature, such as citation counts, co-citation networks, and keyword co-occurrence, to identify the most influential works, authors, and institutions within the field and to map the research networks and communities.

To conduct the bibliometric analysis in this study, several tools and techniques were used. The data collection and cleaning were performed using a reference management software, EndNote, to manage and organize the retrieved articles from academic databases such as Web of Science, Scopus, and IEEE Xplore. The search was conducted using predefined keywords related to IoV to ensure that only relevant articles were included in the analysis.

The data analysis was performed using VOSviewer, a bibliometric software tool that enables the visualization and analysis of bibliometric networks. VOSviewer was used to create co-citation networks, which depict the relationships between articles based on the number of times they have been cited together in other articles. Co-authorship networks were also created to depict the collaborations between authors. In addition, VOSviewer was used to create keyword co-occurrence networks, which show the frequency and strength of the relationships between keywords used in the analyzed articles.

The bibliometric analysis in this study was conducted in several steps, including data collection, data cleaning, data analysis, and data interpretation. The bibliometric tools used in this study are widely recognized and accepted in the field of bibliometrics and have been used in many previous studies to map the intellectual structure of research fields.

Overall, the use of bibliometric analysis and the tools employed in this study allowed for a comprehensive and systematic analysis of IoV research. The bibliometric analysis provided insights into the trends, patterns, and gaps in the field, and highlighted the most influential works, authors, and institutions within the field. This information can be used to guide future research efforts and to inform policy and decision-making in the field of IoV.

Selection Criteria for the Literature and Data Sources

The selection of literature and data sources is crucial in any bibliometric analysis. In this paper, we followed a systematic approach to identify relevant publications on the Internet of Vehicles (IoV) research.

Firstly, we searched for scholarly articles in leading databases, such as Web of Science, Scopus, and IEEE Xplore. We used a combination of keywords related to the IoV, such as "Internet of Vehicles," "connected vehicles," "Vehicular Ad hoc Networks (VANETs)," and "Intelligent Transportation Systems (ITS)."

Secondly, we applied inclusion and exclusion criteria to filter out irrelevant studies. Inclusion criteria were studies published in peer-reviewed journals and conferences, in English, from 2016 to 2023, with a focus on IoV research. We excluded studies that were not related to the IoV or did not provide enough data for analysis, such as editorials, letters, and short communications.

Thirdly, we retrieved bibliographic data, such as authors, affiliations, keywords, citations, and references, from the selected studies using the bibliographic software, namely VOSviewer.

Overall, we aimed to ensure the completeness and accuracy of data sources to provide a comprehensive and reliable analysis of the intellectual structure of IoV research.

Data Collection and Analysis Procedures

Data collection and analysis are essential components of any bibliometric analysis, and in this paper, we followed a rigorous and systematic approach to collect and analyze data on IoV research.

We collected bibliographic data, such as authors, affiliations, keywords, citations, and references, from the selected studies using the bibliographic software, namely VOSviewe. We used VOSviewer to construct co-authorship networks, co-occurrence networks of keywords, and bibliographic coupling networks of references. We used CitNetExplorer to construct citation networks and analyze the citation patterns of the selected studies.

To identify the intellectual structure of IoV research, we used several network analysis techniques, such as clustering, centrality measures, and network visualization. We employed the VOSviewer software to perform clustering analysis and generate visualizations of co-authorship, co-occurrence, and bibliographic coupling networks. We calculated centrality measures, such as degree centrality, betweenness centrality, and closeness centrality, to identify the most influential authors, institutions, and keywords in IoV research.

Co-authorship analysis was used to identify collaborations between authors and institutions, while co-citation analysis was used to identify influential publications and research themes. Bibliographic coupling was used to identify the relationships between publications based on shared references. Finally, cluster analysis was used to group publications based on their similarities in terms of keywords, citations, and co-authors.

Overall, our data collection and analysis procedures ensured the reliability and validity of our findings, providing a comprehensive and insightful analysis of the intellectual structure of IoV research.

RESULTS AND FINDINGS

Overview of the Publication and Citation Patterns in IoV Research

Firstly, we searched for scholarly articles in leading databases, such as Web of Science, Scopus, and IEEE Xplore. We used a combination of keywords related to the IoV, such as "Internet of Vehicles," "connected vehicles," "Vehicular Ad hoc Networks (VANETs)," and "Intelligent Transportation Systems (ITS)." Secondly, we applied inclusion and exclusion criteria to filter out irrelevant studies. Inclusion criteria were studies published in peer-reviewed journals and conferences, in English, from 2 016 to 2023, with a focus on IoV research.

Table **1**. shows the overview of the publication dataset and some average citation patterns.

Table 1. Overview of publication dataset and citation patterns.

Descriptions	Results
Publication duration	2016-2023
Total number of documents	3159
Journal articles	1820
Conference	780
Book chapter	256
Books	84
Preprint	57
Total number of publishers	173
Total number of journals	1005
Author keywords	1898
Avg. citation per keyword	21.55
Total Unique Author	15290
Avg. document per author	0.20
Avg. author per documents	4.84
Avg. citation per author	2.67
Avg. citation per document	12.95
Total citations	40911
Total author affiliations	1988
Avg. document per affiliations	1.58
Avg. citation per affiliations	20.57
Total number of funding agency	486
Avg. document per funding agency	6.50
Avg. citation per funding agency	84.17
Total number of countries	82
Avg. document per country	38.52
Avg. citation per country	498.91

Co-citation analysis is a bibliometric technique that explores the intellectual structure of a field of research by analyzing the citation patterns of articles. In this method, co-citation occurs when two articles are cited together in another article. Co-citation analysis is used to identify the relationships between articles, authors, and sources. Fig. (**1**) shows co-citation analysis with authors as a parameter that shows a variation in co-citation analysis that focuses on the relationships between authors rather than articles. In this method, co-citation occurs when two authors are cited together in the reference list of another article. The assumption is that if two authors are cited together, they are likely to be working on similar research topics or have common interests.

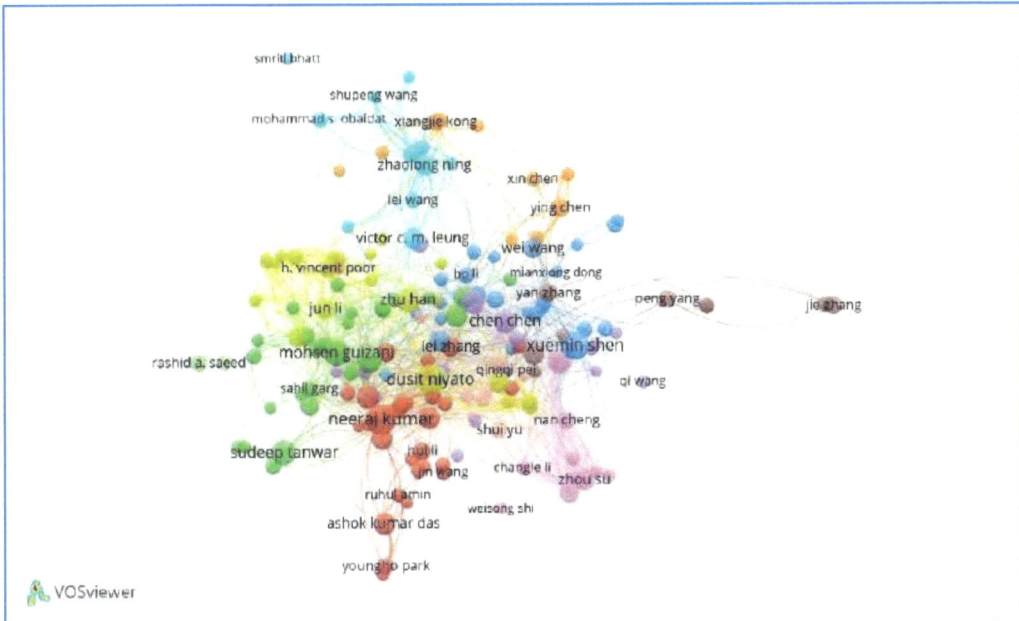

Fig. (1). Co-citation network map for an author as weight parameter.

Fig. (**2**) shows the co-citation network map for sources as a weight parameter. In this method, the weight of citation is determined by the source of citation. For example, if a document is cited by a highly influential and reputable source, the weight of that citation would be greater than if it were cited by a less influential source. This approach allows for a more nuanced understanding of the relationships between documents. By using the source of the citation as a weight parameter in co-citation analysis, researchers can gain insight into the intellectual structure of a field, identify influential works and authors, and track the evolution of research over time.

Fig. (**3**) shows the co-citation network map for an article as a weight parameter. In co-citation analysis with documents as a weight parameter, the strength of the relationship between two documents is determined by the number of other documents that cite them together. By using documents as weight parameters, this method can also help identify the most influential or important documents in a particular field or research area, as those documents are likely to be cited more frequently by other papers.

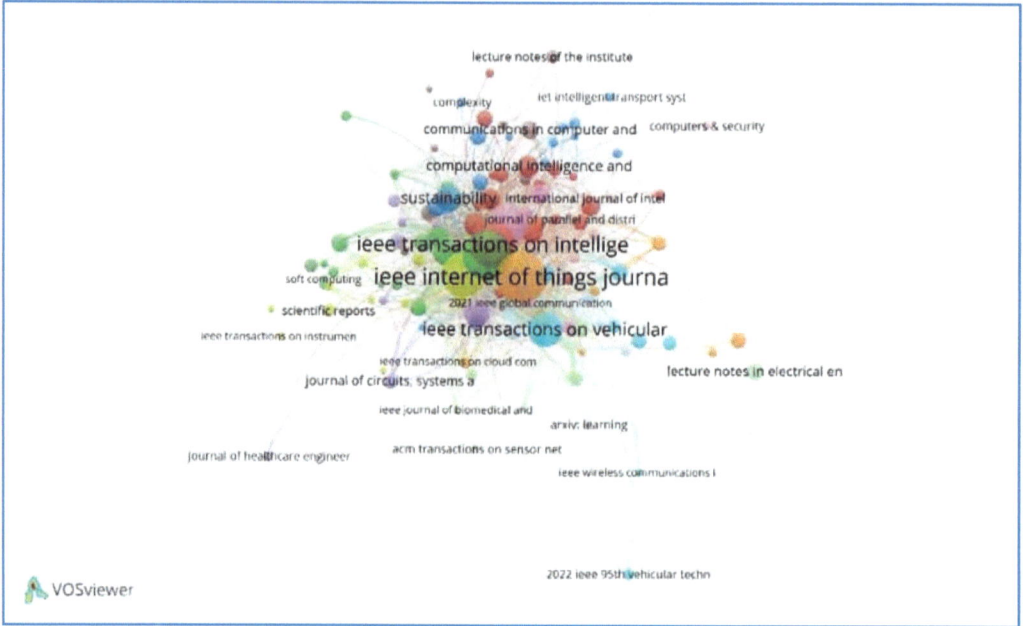

Fig. (2). Co-citation network map for sources as weight parameter.

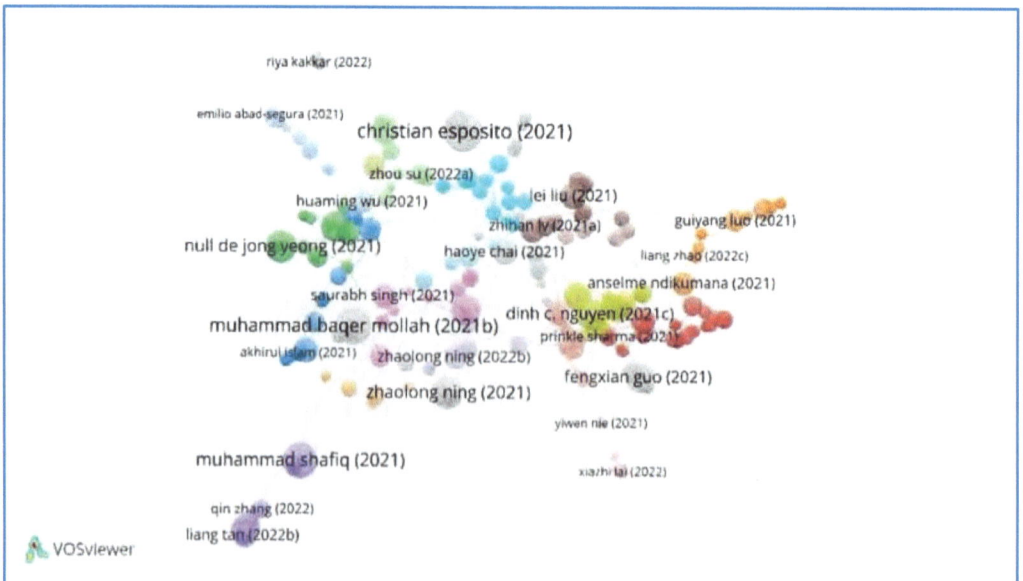

Fig. (3). Co-citation network map for an article as weight parameter.

Visualization of the Intellectual Structure of IoV Research

Co-authorship Analysis

Co-authorship analysis is a bibliometric method used to analyze the collaboration patterns between authors in a specific research field or network. It involves analyzing the co-authorship relationships among a group of authors based on their publication records. The analysis typically involves identifying patterns of collaboration, such as the number of publications, the types of publications, the frequency of collaboration, the length of the collaboration, and the geographic location of the authors. The analysis can provide insights into the social structure of the research community and the relationships between researchers, as well as the productivity and impact of individual authors and research groups. Fig. (4) shows the co-authorship analysis network map where the author is the unit of analysis. The network is generated with a threshold value of a minimum of ten documents per author and at least 25 citations per author.

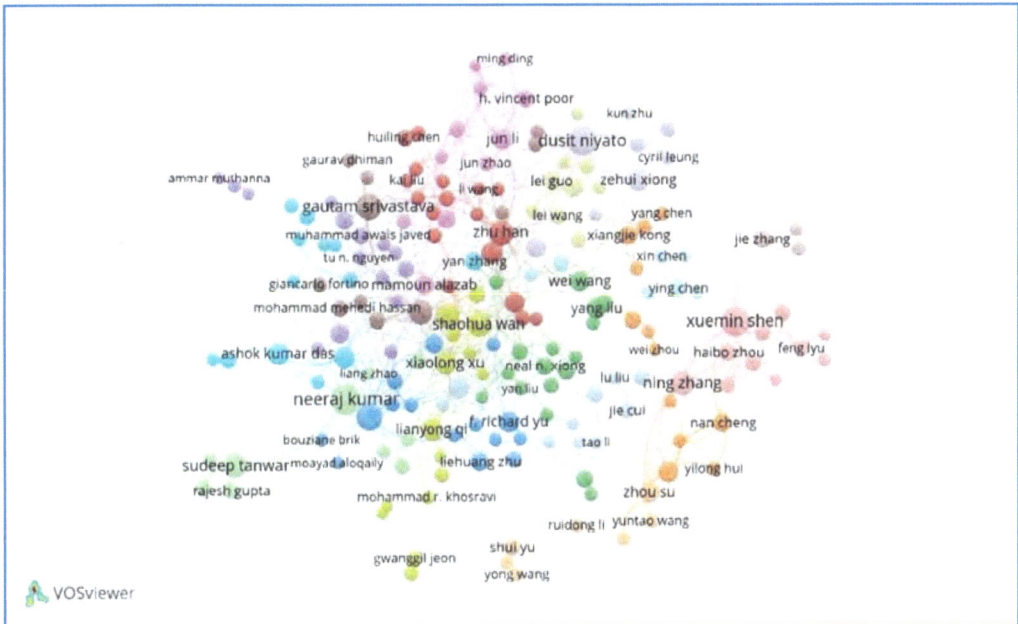

Fig. (4). Co-authorship analysis network map.

Bibliographic Coupling

Bibliographic coupling is a technique used in bibliometrics to measure the relationship between scientific documents based on their shared references. It is a way of identifying the similarity between two documents based on the number of references they share. Bibliographic coupling with source as the unit of analysis is a valuable tool in bibliometrics for identifying the relationships between scientific documents based on their shared references. Fig. (**5**) shows a Bibliographic coupling analysis network map for source as a unit of analysis where the threshold value of an article from one source is five and has at least twenty citations from a single source. By focusing on the similarity between documents based on their shared references to a particular source, researchers can gain insights into the intellectual structure of a field and identify important works and ideas. Fig. (**6**) shows the bibliographic coupling analysis network map for documents as a unit of analysis where the threshold value of citations is forty-five from a single document.

Fig. (5). Bibliographic coupling analysis network map for the source as a unit of analysis.

Identification of the Most Influential Authors, Journals, and Institutions in IoV Research

In our bibliometric analysis of the intellectual structure of Internet of Vehicles (IoV) research, we have identified the most influential authors, journals, and institutions based on their contribution to the field. Our analysis shows that the top five most cited authors in the field of IoV research are: Neeraj Kumar, Dusit Niyato, Xuemin Shen, Mohsen Guizani, and Gautam Srivastava. These authors have contributed significantly to the literature on IoV research, and their works have been widely cited by other researchers. Fig. (**7**) shows the most active author in the area of IoV research. Figures illustrate the number of documents and citations for authors.

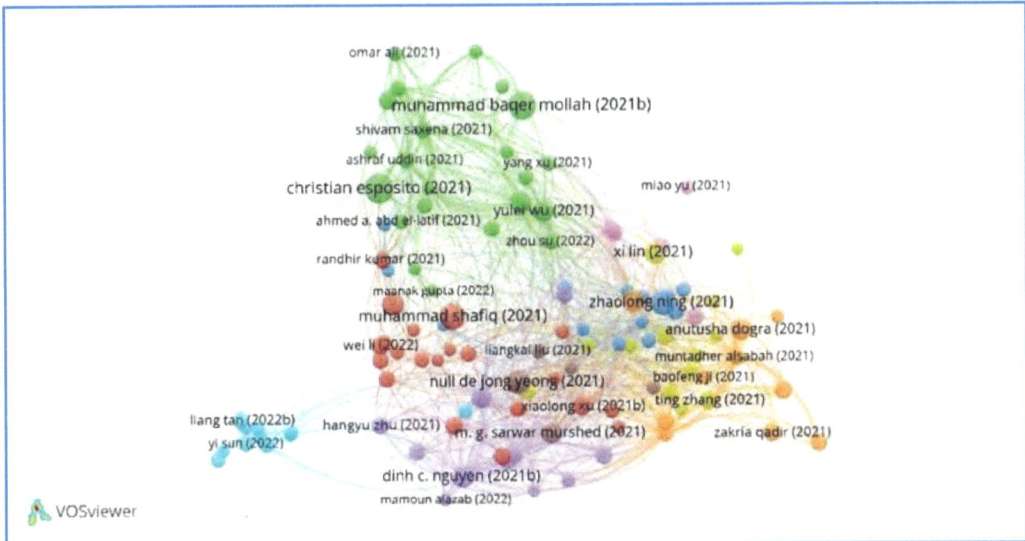

Fig. (6). Bibliographic coupling analysis network map for documents as a unit of analysis.

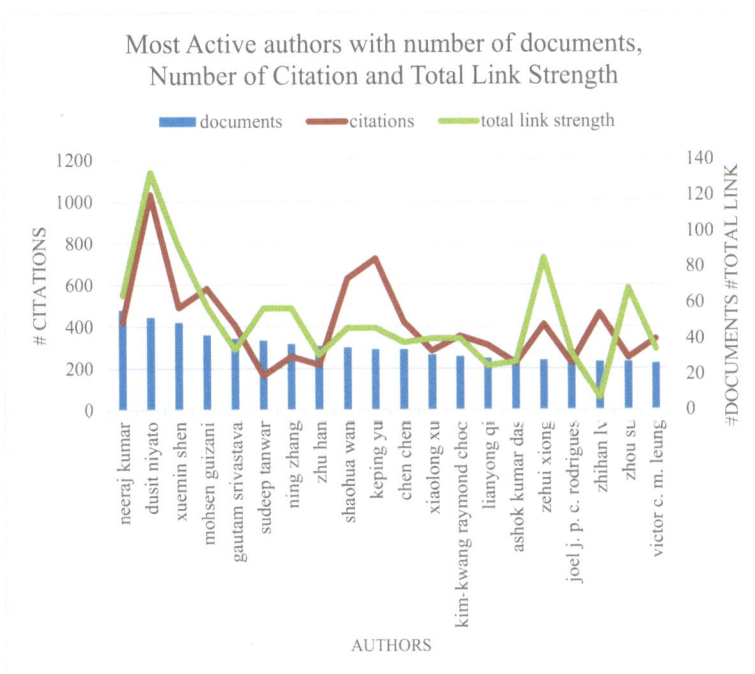

Fig. (7). Most active authors in the area of IoV research.

In terms of journals, our analysis shows that the top six most cited journals in IoV research are: IEEE Internet of Things Journal, IEEE Transactions on Intelligent Transportation Systems, IEEE Access, IEEE Transactions on Vehicular Technology, Sensors (Basel, Switzerland), and Wireless Communications and Mobile Computing. These journals have published some of the most influential works in the field of IoV research and have been cited extensively by other researchers. Fig. (**8**) shows the top 15 most cited journals in IoV research.

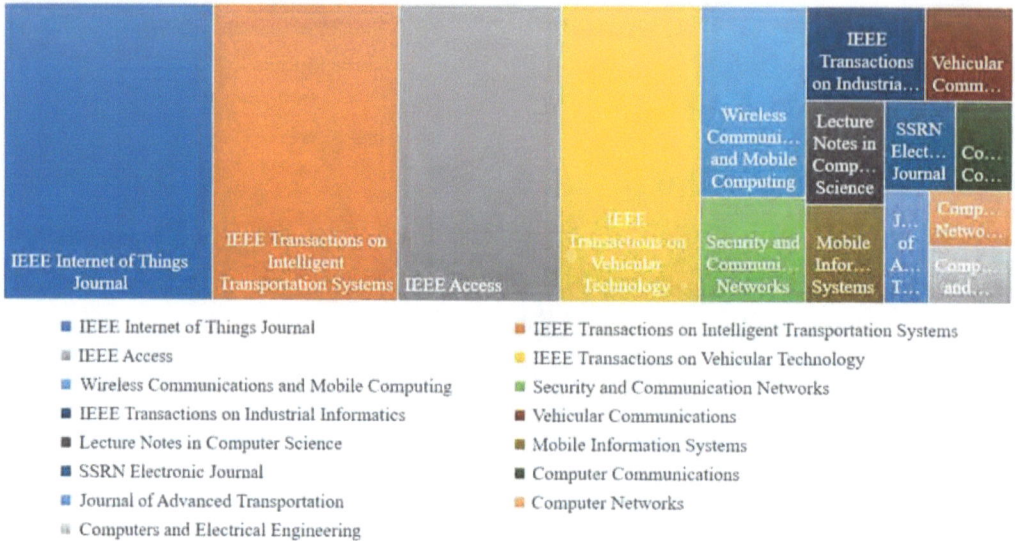

- IEEE Internet of Things Journal
- IEEE Access
- Wireless Communications and Mobile Computing
- IEEE Transactions on Industrial Informatics
- Lecture Notes in Computer Science
- SSRN Electronic Journal
- Journal of Advanced Transportation
- Computers and Electrical Engineering
- IEEE Transactions on Intelligent Transportation Systems
- IEEE Transactions on Vehicular Technology
- Security and Communication Networks
- Vehicular Communications
- Mobile Information Systems
- Computer Communications
- Computer Networks

Fig. (8). The top 15 most cited journals in IoV research.

Finally, in terms of institutions, our analysis shows that the top 10 most productive institutions in IoV research are: the University of Electronic Science and Technology of China, Xidian University, Beijing University of Posts and Telecommunications, Dalian University of Technology, Chinese Academy of Sciences, Shanghai Jiao Tong University, Beihang University, Nanjing University of Information Science and Technology, Nanyang Technological University, and Tsinghua University. These institutions have been the most active in producing research output in the field of IoV research and have made significant contributions to the advancement of the field. Fig. (**9**) shows the most productive institutions in IoV research.

In the context of the bibliometric analysis of Internet of Vehicles research, the identification of the most influential countries, publishers, and funding agencies can provide valuable insights into the global landscape of research in this field. To identify the most influential countries in IoV research, we can analyze the distribution of publications and citations across different countries. In our study on the intellectual structure of IoV research, we identified the top 10 countries in terms of the number of publications and citations. Fig. (**10**) shows the most influential countries in the research area. The United States and China were found to be the most influential countries in IoV research, followed by India, Canada, and United Kingdom.

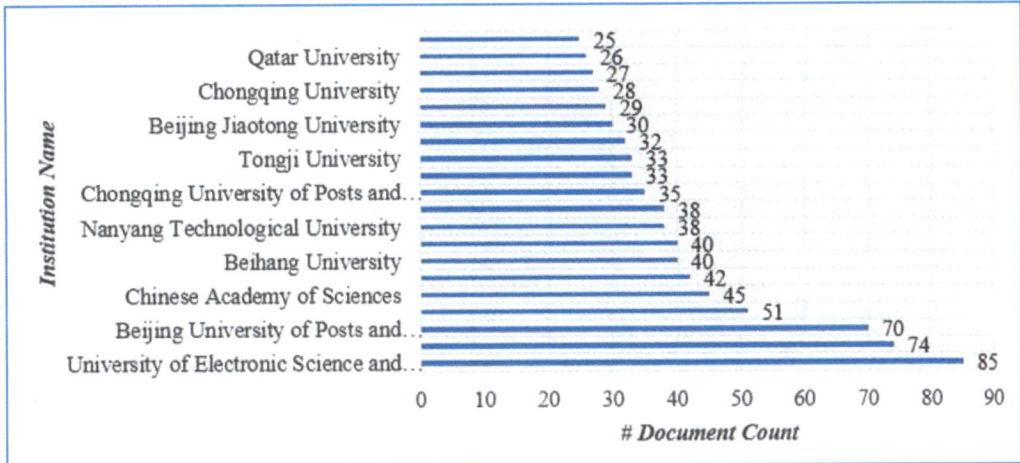

Fig. (9). The most productive institutions in IoV research.

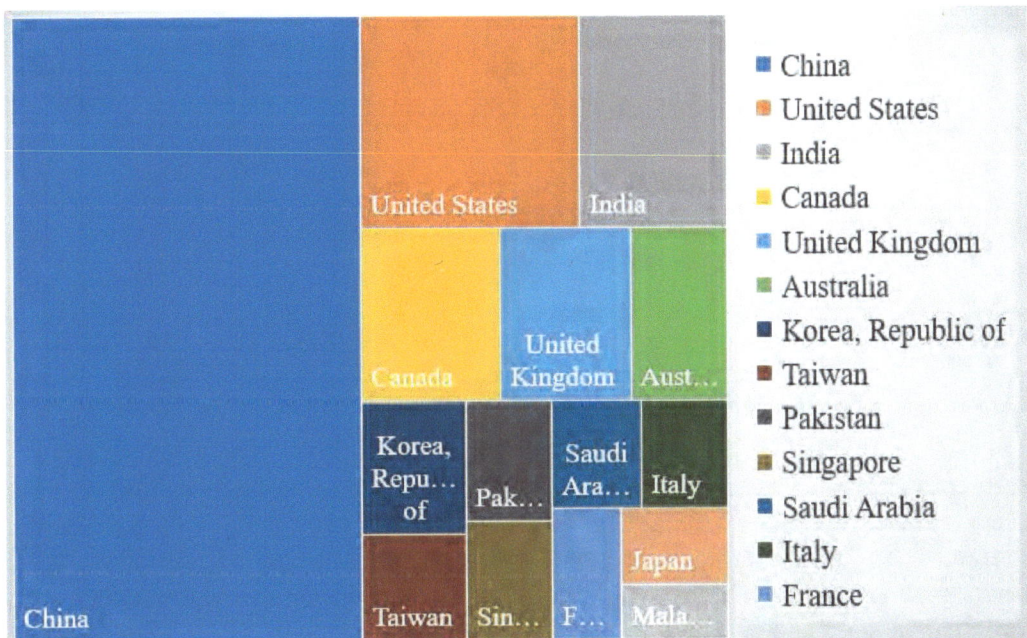

Fig. (10). The most influential countries in the research area.

Similarly, we can identify the most influential publishers and funding agencies by analyzing the distribution of publications and citations across different publishers and funding agencies. This can be done by analyzing the metadata of the publications and extracting information about the publishers and funding agencies. Fig. (**11**) shows the top funding agency in IoV research area. In our study, we find National Natural Science Foundation of China, Fundamental Research Funds for the Central Universities, National Key Research and Development Program of China, China Postdoctoral Science Foundation, National Key R&D Program of China, National Research Foundation of Korea, Ministry of Science and Technology Taiwan, National Basic Research Program of China, National Science Foundation, and Natural Science Foundation of Jiangsu Province to be the top funding agencies in the IoV research. Fig. (**12**) shows the most influential publishers in the IoV research area. IEEE, Elsevier BV, Springer International Publishing, Hindawi Limited, MDPI AG, Springer Science and Business Media LLC, Institute of Electrical and Electronics Engineers Inc., Multidisciplinary Digital Publishing Institute (MDPI), and Springer Singapore are the most influential publishers as per our findings.

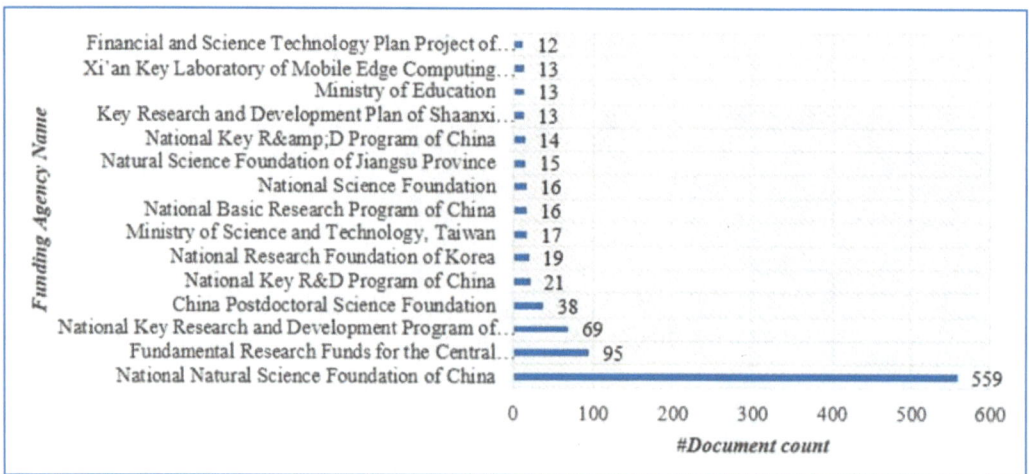

Fig. (11). the top funding agency in IoV research area.

Keyword analysis is a crucial component of bibliometric analysis, as it allows for the identification of the most frequently occurring words and phrases in the literature. In case of the intellectual structure of Internet of Vehicles (IoV) research, a keyword analysis can provide insights into the most significant topics and themes that have emerged in the field.

In this study, a keyword analysis was conducted on the literature collected for IoV research. The analysis identified the most frequently occurring keywords and phrases and grouped them into clusters based on their co-occurrence patterns. The results of the keyword analysis were used to identify the emerging technologies and applications that have received the most attention in IoV research. Fig. (**13**) shows the word cloud for keyword analysis.

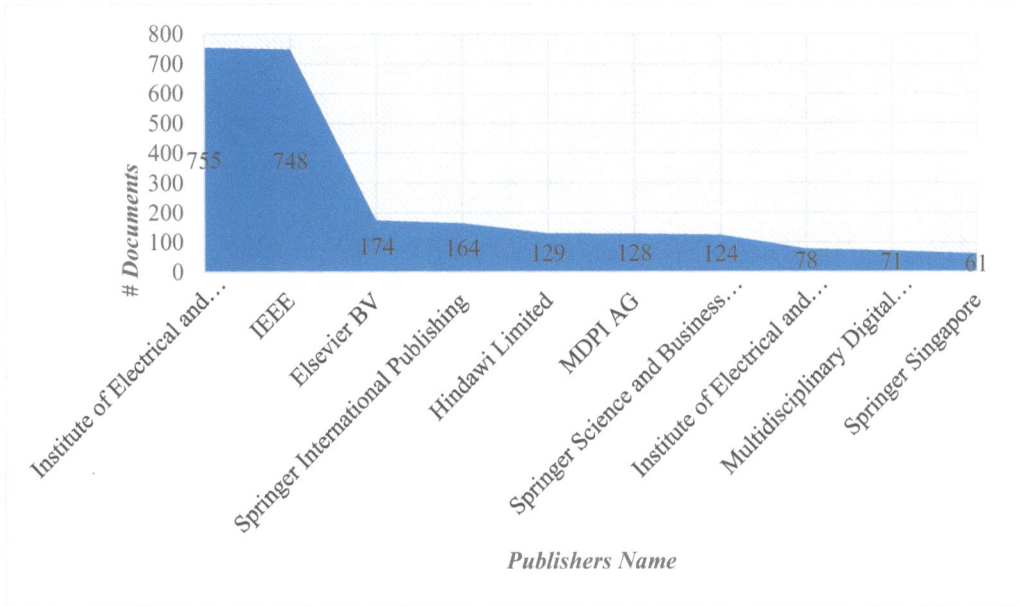

Fig. (12). The most influential publishers in the IoV research area. Analysis the keywords to identify the emerging technologies and applications in IoV research.

The analysis revealed that the most frequently occurring keywords in IoV research were the "Internet of Things", "Vehicular Ad Hoc Networks", "Cloud Computing", "Wireless Sensor Networks", "Big Data", "Cybersecurity", "Machine Learning", "Intelligent Transportation Systems", "Routing Protocols", and "Energy Efficiency" "Federated Learning".

The keyword clusters that emerged from the analysis were related to several themes in IoV research, including communication protocols, data management, security and privacy, intelligent transportation systems, energy efficiency, and vehicle-to-vehicle communication. These findings suggest that IoV research is a multidisciplinary field that encompasses several areas of research, including computer science, engineering, and transportation. Fig. (**14**) shows the top keyword identified by the VOS viewer by analysis title and abstract.

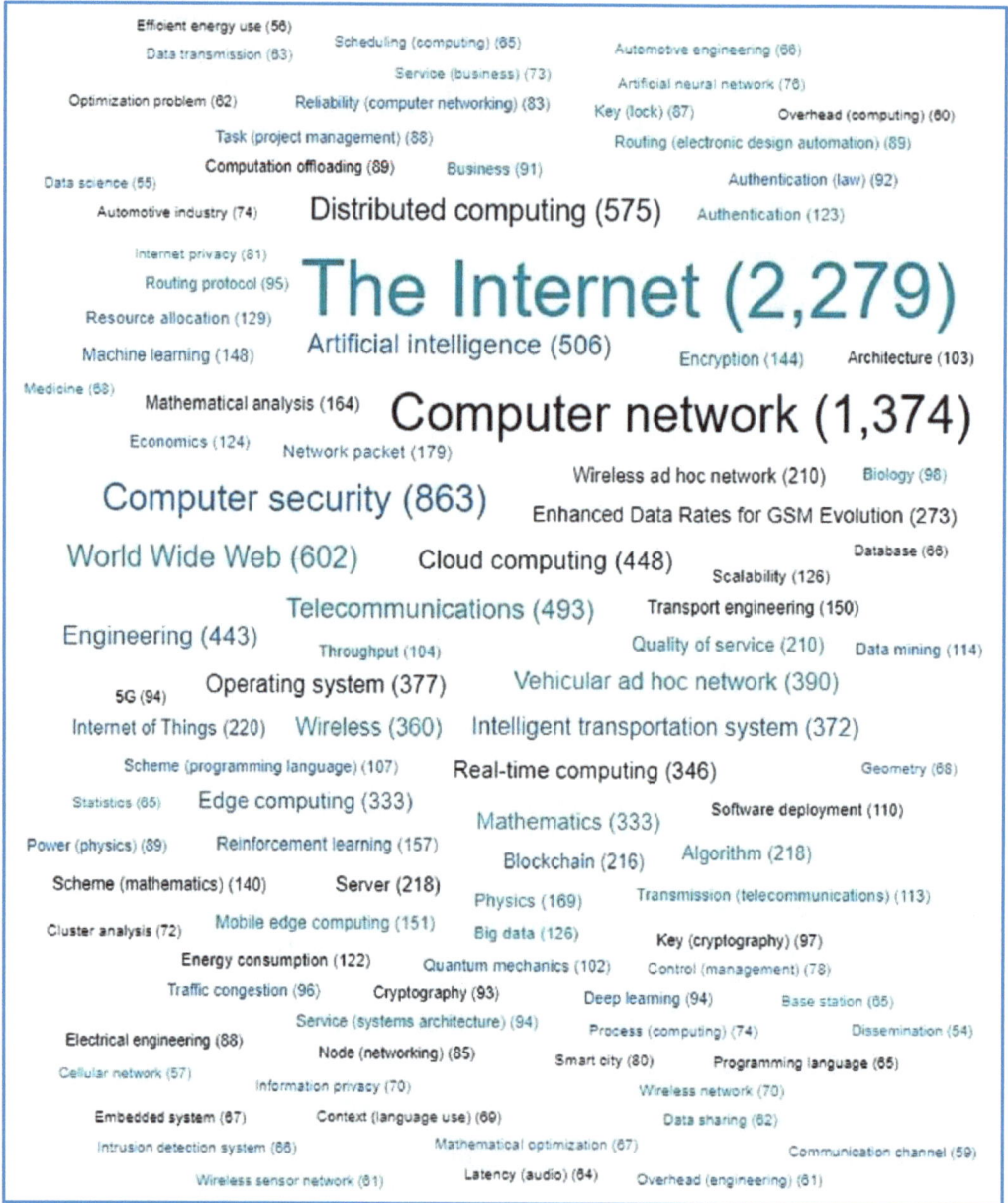

Fig. (13). The word cloud for keyword analysis.

The results of the keyword analysis can inform future research in IoV by identifying the most important themes and technologies in the field. Researchers can use this information to focus their research on areas that have not received sufficient attention or to develop new applications and technologies that address the challenges and opportunities in IoV research. Fig. (**15**) shows the network map of different keywords generated by VOSViewer.

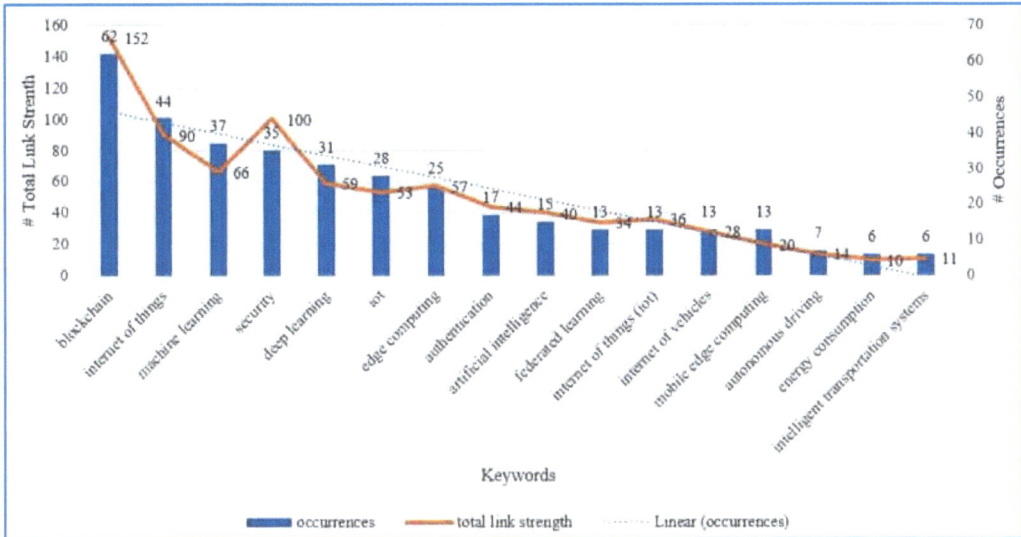

Fig. (14). Top Keyword identified by VOSViewer by analysis title and abstract.

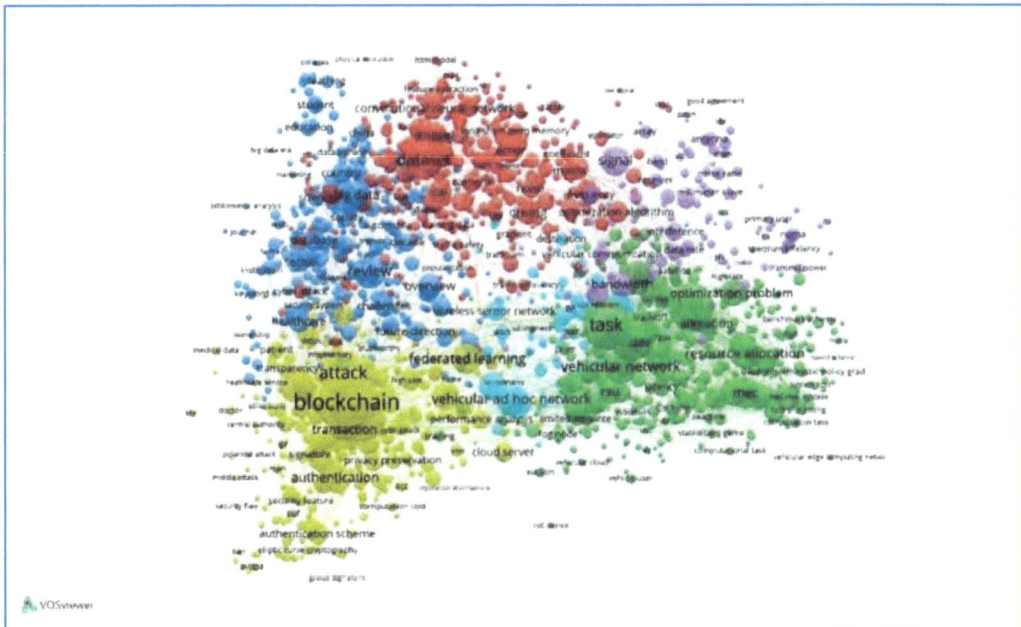

Fig. (15). shows the network map of different keywords generated by VOSViewer.

The emerging technologies and applications in Internet of Vehicles (IoV) research have been the focus of many studies. In this paper, we conducted a bibliometric analysis to identify and analyze the trends in this area. Our analysis revealed that the research on IoV is expanding rapidly with the emergence of new technologies and applications [28 - 30]. One of the emerging technologies identified in IoV research is the use of big data analytics. Another emerging technology in IoV research is the development of connected and autonomous vehicles. In addition, the research on IoV applications has also seen significant growth [31 - 33]. One of the key applications is intelligent transportation systems (ITS), which aims to optimize the use of transportation networks by utilizing real-time data and information. Other applications include vehicle-to-vehicle communication, remote diagnostics, and predictive maintenance [34 - 36].

DISCUSSION AND IMPLICATIONS

Interpretation and Discussion of the Results in the Context of IoV Research

The results of our bibliometric analysis of the intellectual structure of Internet of Vehicles (IoV) research have provided valuable insights into the emerging technologies and applications in this field. The analysis reveals the most frequently cited papers, authors, and journals, as well as the key research topics and trends. Our analysis has shown that the research on IoV is rapidly expanding and encompasses various interdisciplinary domains, including computer science, engineering, transportation, and communication [37].

The findings indicate that IoV research has been rapidly growing in recent years, with a significant increase in the number of publications since 2020. The analysis also shows that the majority of research in the field has focused on topics such as communication protocols, security, and routing.

We found that the top research themes in IoV include Vehicular Ad Hoc Networks (VANETs), Connected Autonomous Vehicles (CAVs), Intelligent Transportation Systems (ITS), and Vehicle-to-Everything (V2X) communication. Our analysis further revealed that the most cited publications in IoV research are mainly from high-impact factor journals such as IEEE Transactions on Vehicular Technology, IEEE Communications Magazine, and IEEE Intelligent Transportation Systems Magazine.

Moreover, our study found that the United States, China, and Europe are the leading contributors to IoV research, with the majority of publications originating from academic institutions and government-funded research organizations. The collaboration network analysis also showed that there is a high degree of international collaboration among researchers in this field [38 - 40].

The analysis of the emerging technologies and applications in IoV research shows that autonomous vehicles, blockchain, edge computing, artificial intelligence, connected vehicles, and smart transportation systems are among the most researched areas. The study also reveals that the integration of artificial intelligence, cloud computing, and big data analytics with IoV has gained considerable attention in recent years. These emerging technologies are likely to have a significant impact on the development of IoV systems in the future, as they enable more efficient and secure communication between vehicles and the infrastructure [41 - 43].

The implications of our findings are significant, as they provide a comprehensive overview of the current state and emerging trends in IoV research. This information can be used to identify research gaps and opportunities for future research in this field, as well as to inform policymakers and stakeholders about the potential impact of IoV on society and the economy [44, 45].

Furthermore, our study highlights the importance of using bibliometric analysis as a tool for mapping the intellectual structure of emerging research fields such as IoV. This methodology can provide a comprehensive and objective analysis of the research landscape, enabling researchers to identify research frontiers, leading scholars, and emerging trends in a field [46, 47].

Implications of the Findings for Future Research Directions and Priorities

The findings of this bibliometric analysis have several implications for future research directions and priorities in the field of IoV.

- First, the study identified the most influential authors, institutions, and publications in IoV research, which can guide researchers in selecting potential collaborators and sources for further research [48, 49].
- Second, the analysis revealed the most prominent research themes and emerging technologies in IoV research. These themes and technologies can serve as a starting point for researchers to develop new research questions and explore new areas of study within the field [50].
- Third, the study highlighted the need for more interdisciplinary research in IoV, as many of the highly cited publications and influential authors came from fields such as computer science, engineering, and telecommunications. This indicates that there is a need for researchers from other disciplines, such as sociology, psychology, and economics, to contribute to IoV research and offer diverse perspectives [51, 52].
- Fourth, the study found that there is a lack of research on the societal implications and ethical considerations of IoV. Given the potential impact of

IoV on society, there is a need for more research to understand the social, ethical, and legal implications of this emerging technology [53, 54].

* Finally, the analysis identified some gaps in the existing literature, such as the underrepresentation of certain regions and countries in IoV research. Future research can aim to fill these gaps and provide a more comprehensive understanding of IoV research on a global scale [55, 56].

Overall, this bibliometric analysis provides insights into the current state of IoV research and can help guide future research directions and priorities in the field. By addressing the gaps and limitations identified in this study, researchers can contribute to a more comprehensive and holistic understanding of the emerging technology of IoV.

Contribution of the Study to the Understanding of the Intellectual Structure of IoV Research

The present study aimed to map the intellectual structure of Internet of Vehicles (IoV) research using bibliometric analysis of emerging technologies and applications. This research paper has made several contributions to the existing literature on IoV research.

* Firstly, this study has contributed to a better understanding of the intellectual structure of IoV research by identifying the key research areas, major contributors, and research trends in the field. Through the bibliometric analysis of the publications and citations, we were able to construct a comprehensive picture of the intellectual structure of IoV research.
* Secondly, this study has contributed to the identification of emerging technologies and applications in IoV research. By analyzing the most frequently occurring keywords, we were able to identify the emerging technologies and applications in IoV research, which will be useful for researchers, policymakers, and industry professionals in identifying new research directions and opportunities.
* Thirdly, this study has contributed to the identification of research gaps in IoV research. By identifying the under-researched areas and the areas with low citation rates, we have highlighted the research gaps that need to be addressed to advance the field of IoV research further.
* Finally, this study has contributed to the identification of the key contributors to IoV research. By analyzing the most productive authors and institutions, we have identified the key players in the field of IoV research. This information will be useful for identifying potential collaborators, partners, and sponsors for future research.

Overall, this study's contribution to the intellectual structure of IoV research is significant as it will provide an overview of the research landscape, research trends, and emerging technologies and applications in the field. The study's findings will be valuable to researchers, policymakers, and practitioners, helping them to identify research gaps and future research directions in IoV. The study will contribute to advancing the understanding of IoV research and facilitate further research in this domain.

CONCLUSION

The Internet of Vehicles (IoV) is a rapidly growing field of research, with an increasing number of publications emerging each year. To gain a comprehensive understanding of the intellectual structure of IoV research, this paper conducted a bibliometric analysis of emerging technologies and applications in the field. The study aimed to identify the most influential authors, journals, and institutions in IoV research, as well as to analyze the emerging technologies and applications within the field. The methodology of the study involved a systematic review of the literature published between 2016 and 2023, with a focus on publications indexed in the Scopus database. The bibliometric analysis was conducted using VOSviewer, a software tool for visualizing bibliometric networks. The study collected data on the bibliographic information, authorship, citation patterns, and keywords of the selected publications. The findings of this study have several implications for future research directions and priorities in IoV research. First, the study identified the need for more research on the integration of emerging technologies and applications in IoV research. Second, the study suggested the need for more interdisciplinary research in the field, including collaborations between computer science, engineering, and transportation research. Third, the study identified the need for more research on the social, economic, and environmental impacts of IoV technologies and applications. This paper conducted a bibliometric analysis of emerging technologies and applications in IoV research, identifying the most influential authors, journals, and institutions in the field, as well as analyzing the emerging technologies and applications within the field. The findings of the study have several implications for future research directions and priorities in IoV research, including the need for more interdisciplinary research and research on the social, economic, and environmental impacts of IoV technologies and applications. This study provides a comprehensive understanding of the intellectual structure of IoV research, which can guide future research and practice in the field. Our findings have important implications for future research and practice in the IoV field. By identifying the most influential authors, journals, and institutions, our study can help researchers and practitioners identify key players in the field and track the latest developments. The network visualization of the intellectual structure of IoV research can also help to identify potential collaboration opportunities and research gaps.

REFERENCES

[1]   R. Xie, Q. Zhang, Z. Du, and C. Li, "A Lightweight Face Recognition Algorithm for Internet of Vehicles", *IEEE 3rd International Conference on Power, Electronics and Computer Applications, ICPECA*, pp. 1139-1143, 2023.
[http://dx.doi.org/10.1109/ICPECA56706.2023.10076187]

[2]   S. Chavali, H. Cheema, R. Delgado, E. Nolan, M.I. Ibrahem, and M.M. Fouda, "A Review of Privacy-Preserving Authentication Schemes for Future Internet of Vehicles", *Proceedings - 2023 12th IEEE International Conference on Communication Systems and Network Technologies, CSNT*, pp. 689-694, 2023.
[http://dx.doi.org/10.1109/CSNT57126.2023.10134727]

[3]   M. Ahman, A. Rechache, A. Kaci, O. Annad, A. Nace, and S.A. Chellouche, "", "An approach for efficient vehicular tracking in internet of vehicles", *Proceedings - IEEE Consumer Communications and Networking Conference, CCNC*, pp. 953-954, 2023.
[http://dx.doi.org/10.1109/CCNC51644.2023.10060508]

[4]   P. S. Marwein, and D. Kandar, "A Novel Load Balancing Approach in Internet of Vehicles (IoV)", *4th International Conference on Computing and Communication Systems (I3CS)*, pp. 1-5, 2023.
[http://dx.doi.org/10.1109/I3CS58314.2023.10127387]

[5]   J. Liu, Y. Wang, W. Zhang, and K. Tian, "A Novel Offloading and Resource Allocation Scheme for Time-critical Tasks in Heterogeneous Internet of Vehicles", *2nd International Conference for Innovation in Technology (INOCON)*, pp. 1-7, 2023.
[http://dx.doi.org/10.1109/INOCON57975.2023.10101035]

[6]   L. Chen, Y. Miao, C. Yu, and S. Liu, "CD-DAA-MD: A Cross-domain DAA Scheme with Mimic Defense for Internet of Vehicles", *Proceedings of the International Conference on Parallel and Distributed Systems - ICPADS*, pp. 139-146, 2023.
[http://dx.doi.org/10.1109/ICPADS56603.2022.00026]

[7]   Z. Gao, Z. Yang, R. Liang, and S. Sun, "Research on the Performance of Automotive Antenna on Intelligent Connected Vehicle", *17th European Conference on Antennas and Propagation (EuCAP)*, pp. 1-5, 2023.
[http://dx.doi.org/10.23919/EuCAP57121.2023.10133113]

[8]   I. Ullah, M.A. Khan, N. Kumar, A.M. Abdullah, A.A. AlSanad, and F. Noor, "A Conditional Privacy Preserving Heterogeneous Signcryption Scheme for Internet of Vehicles", *IEEE Trans. Vehicular Technol.*, vol. 72, no. 3, pp. 3989-3998, 2023.
[http://dx.doi.org/10.1109/TVT.2022.3220041]

[9]   X. Zhang, R. Li, and H. Zhao, "A Parallel Consensus Mechanism Using PBFT Based on DAG-Lattice Structure in the Internet of Vehicles", *IEEE Internet Things J.*, vol. 10, no. 6, pp. 5418-5433, 2023.
[http://dx.doi.org/10.1109/JIOT.2022.3222217]

[10]   R. Gasmi, and S. Harous, "Robust Connectivity-Based Internet of Vehicles Clustering Algorithm", *Wirel. Pers. Commun.*, vol. 125, no. 4, pp. 3153-3185, 2022.
[http://dx.doi.org/10.1007/s11277-022-09703-0]

[11]   M. Kezia, and K.V. Anusuya, "Mobility Models for Internet of Vehicles: A Survey", *Wirel. Pers. Commun.*, vol. 125, no. 2, pp. 1857-1881, 2022.
[http://dx.doi.org/10.1007/s11277-022-09637-7]

[12]   Z. Liu, and X. Xu, "Latency-aware service migration with decision theory for Internet of Vehicles in mobile edge computing", *Wirel. Netw.*, 2022.
[http://dx.doi.org/10.1007/s11276-022-02978-y]

[13]   M.J.A. Jude, S. Malini, V.C. Diniesh, and M. Shivaranjani, "An improved retransmission timeout prediction algorithm for enhancing data transmission on internet of vehicles network", *Wirel. Netw.,* vol. 28, no. 6, pp. 2421-2436, 2022.
[http://dx.doi.org/10.1007/s11276-022-02972-4]

[14]   R. Dhanare, K.K. Nagwanshi, and S. Varma, "A Study to Enhance the Route Optimization Algorithm for the Internet of Vehicle", *Wirel. Commun. Mob. Comput.,* vol. 2022, pp. 1-20, 2022.
[http://dx.doi.org/10.1155/2022/1453187]

[15]   L. Lihua, "Energy-Aware Intrusion Detection Model for Internet of Vehicles Using Machine Learning Methods", *Wirel. Commun. Mob. Comput.,* vol. 2022, pp. 1-8, 2022.
[http://dx.doi.org/10.1155/2022/9865549]

[16]   X. Zhang, H. Zhang, S. Dai, and Y. Liu, "An Incentive Mechanism for Computation Offloading in Satellite-Terrestrial Internet of Vehicles", *Wirel. Commun. Mob. Comput.,* vol. 2022, pp. 1-14, 2022.
[http://dx.doi.org/10.1155/2022/1514437]

[17]   X. Liu, L. Wang, L. Li, X. Zhang, and S. Niu, "A Certificateless Anonymous Cross-Domain Authentication Scheme Assisted by Blockchain for Internet of Vehicles", *Wirel. Commun. Mob. Comput.,* vol. 2022, pp. 1-14, 2022.
[http://dx.doi.org/10.1155/2022/3488977]

[18]   I. Seth, K. Guleria, S.N. Panda, D. Anand, K. Alsubhi, H.M. Aljahdali, and A. Singh, "A Taxonomy and Analysis on Internet of Vehicles: Architectures, Protocols, and Challenges", *Wirel. Commun. Mob. Comput.,* vol. 2022, pp. 1-26, 2022.
[http://dx.doi.org/10.1155/2022/9232784]

[19]   Y. Zhang, and G. Ji, "Security and Privacy Protection of Internet of Vehicles Consensus Algorithm Based on Wireless Sensors", *Wirel. Commun. Mob. Comput.,* vol. 2022, pp. 1-14, 2022.
[http://dx.doi.org/10.1155/2022/6197638]

[20]   H-T. Wu, "The internet-of-vehicle traffic condition system developed by artificial intelligence of things", *J. Supercomput.,* vol. 78, no. 2, pp. 2665-2680, 2022.
[http://dx.doi.org/10.1007/s11227-021-03969-0]

[21]   J. Zhang, and M. Wu, "Blockchain-Based Authentication with Optional Privacy Preservation for Internet of Vehicles", *Math. Probl. Eng.,* vol. 2021, pp. 1-13, 2021.
[http://dx.doi.org/10.1155/2021/9954599]

[22]   S. Garg, D. Mehrotra, H.M. Pandey, and S. Pandey, "Accessible review of internet of vehicle models for intelligent transportation and research gaps for potential future directions", *Peer-to-Peer Netw. Appl.,* vol. 14, no. 2, pp. 978-1005, 2021.
[http://dx.doi.org/10.1007/s12083-020-01054-6]

[23]   Y.M. Saputra, D.T. Hoang, D.N. Nguyen, L.N. Tran, S. Gong, and E. Dutkiewicz, "Dynamic Federated Learning-Based Economic Framework for Internet-of-Vehicles", *IEEE Trans. Mobile Comput.,* vol. 22, no. 4, pp. 2100 2115, 2023.
[http://dx.doi.org/10.1109/TMC.2021.3122436]

[24]   Nizirwan Anwar, Budi Tjahjono, Rudi Hermawan, Nur Widiyasono, N. Widiyasono, and M.A. Hadi, "Reliability Analysis of Communication Network Service Quality For Internet of Vehicles (IoV)", *Int. J. Sci. Tech. Manag.,* vol. 2, no. 5, pp. 1588-1599, 2021.
[http://dx.doi.org/10.46729/ijstm.v2i5.310]

[25]   I.V. Pustokhina, D.A. Pustokhin, E.L. Lydia, P. Garg, A. Kadian, and K. Shankar, "Hyperparameter search based convolution neural network with Bi-LSTM model for intrusion detection system in multimedia big data environment", *Multimedia Tools Appl.,* pp. 1-18, 2021.

[26]   A. Khanna, P. Rani, P. Garg, P.K. Singh, and A. Khamparia, "An Enhanced Crow Search Inspired Feature Selection Technique for Intrusion Detection Based Wireless Network System", *Wirel. Pers. Commun.,* pp. 1-18, 2021.

[27] P. Garg, A. Dixit, P. Sethi, and P.R. Pinheiro, "Impact of node density on the qos parameters of routing protocols in opportunistic networks for smart spaces", *Mob. Inf. Syst.*, vol. 2020, pp. 1-18, 2020.
[http://dx.doi.org/10.1155/2020/8868842]

[28] D. Upadhyay, P. Garg, S.M. Aldossary, J. Shafi, and S. Kumar, "A Linear Quadratic Regression-Based Synchronised Health Monitoring System (SHMS) for IoT Applications", *Electronics (Basel)*, vol. 12, no. 2, p. 309, 2023.
[http://dx.doi.org/10.3390/electronics12020309]

[29] P. Saini, B. Nagpal, P. Garg, and S. Kumar, "CNN-BI-LSTM-CYP: A deep learning approach for sugarcane yield prediction", *Sustain. Energy Technol. Assess.*, vol. 57, p. 103263, 2023.
[http://dx.doi.org/10.1016/j.seta.2023.103263]

[30] P. Saini, B. Nagpal, P. Garg, and S. Kumar, "Evaluation of Remote Sensing and Meteorological parameters for Yield Prediction of Sugarcane (Saccharum officinarum L.) Crop", *Braz. Arch. Biol. Technol.*, vol. 66, p. e23220781, 2023.
[http://dx.doi.org/10.1590/1678-4324-2023220781]

[31] S. Beniwal, U. Saini, P. Garg, and R.K. Joon, "Improving performance during camera surveillance by integration of edge detection in IoT system", *Int. J. E-Health Med. Commun.*, vol. 12, no. 5, pp. 84-96, 2021.
[http://dx.doi.org/10.4018/IJEHMC.20210901.oa6]

[32] P. Garg, A. Dixit, and P. Sethi, "Wireless sensor networks: an insight review", *Int. J. Adv. Sci. Tech.*, vol. 28, no. 15, pp. 612-627, 2019.

[33] N. Sharma, and P. Garg, "Ant colony based optimization model for QoS-Based task scheduling in cloud computing environment. Measurement", *Sensors (Basel)*, vol. 24, p. 100531, 2022.
[http://dx.doi.org/10.1016/j.measen.2022.100531]

[34] P. Kumar, R. Kumar, and P. Garg, "Hybrid Crowd Cloud Routing Protocol For Wireless Sensor Networks", *Int. J. Adv. Sci. Tech*, vol. 29, no. 12, pp. 766-775, 2020.

[35] G. Raj, A. Verma, P. Dalal, A.K. Shukla, and P. Garg, "Performance Comparison of Several LPWAN Technologies for Energy Constrained IOT Network", *Int. J. Intell. Sys. Appl. Eng.*, vol. 11, no. 1s, pp. 150-158, 2023.

[36] S.P. Yadav, K.K. Agrawal, B.S. Bhati, F. Al-Turjman, and L. Mostarda, "Blockchain-Based Cryptocurrency Regulation: An Overview", *Comput. Econ.*, vol. 59, no. 4, pp. 1659-1675, 2022.
[http://dx.doi.org/10.1007/s10614-020-10050-0]

[37] Kaur, J., Saxena, J., Shah, J., Fahad, N., and Yadav, S. P. "Facial emotion Recognition", *2022 International Conference on Computational Intelligence and Sustainable Engineering Solutions (CISES)*, pp. 528-533, 2023.
[http://dx.doi.org/10.1109/cises54857.2022.9844366]

[38] P.K. Singh, S.S. Chauhan, A. Sharma, S. Prakash, and Y. Singh, "Prediction of higher heating values based on imminent analysis by using regression analysis and artificial neural network for bioenergy resources", *Proceedings of the Institution of Mechanical Engineers, Part E: Journal of Process Mechanical Engineering*, 2023.
[http://dx.doi.org/10.1177/09544089231175046]

[39] T. Singh, A. Panwar, K.S. Kaswan, A. Jain, and U. Sugandh, "The Datafication of Everything: Challenges and Opportunities in a Hyperconnected World", *International Conference on Advancements in Smart Computing and Information Security*, pp. 254-268, 2024.
[http://dx.doi.org/10.1007/978-3-031-58604-0_18]

[40] P. Gaba, A. Panwar, U. Sugandh, N. Pathak, and N. Sharma, "OptiCharge: A firefly algorithm-based approach for minimizing electric vehicle waiting time at charging stations", *Intell. Decis. Technol.*, pp. 1-14, 2024.

[http://dx.doi.org/10.3233/IDT-230619]

[41]   A.K. Dubey, A. Jain, A. Panwar, M. Kumar, H. Taneja, and P.S. Lamba, "Optimizing Emotion Recognition Through Weighted Averaging in Deep Learning Ensembles", *2023 International Conference on Communication, Security and Artificial Intelligence, ICCSAI 2023,* pp. 410-414, 2023. [http://dx.doi.org/10.1109/ICCSAI59793.2023.10421386]

[42]   A. Panwar, M. Khari, S. Misra, and U. Sugandh, "Blockchain in Agriculture to Ensure Trust, Effectiveness, and Traceability from Farm Fields to Groceries", *Future Internet,* vol. 15, no. 12, p. 404, 2023. [http://dx.doi.org/10.3390/fi15120404]

[43]   A.K. Dubey, A. Jain, A. Panwar, M. Kumar, H. Taneja, and P.S. Lamba, "UNet Segmentation based Effective Skin Lesion Detection using Deep Learning", *2023 International Conference on Communication, Security and Artificial Intelligence, ICCSAI 2023,* pp. 470-474, 2023. [http://dx.doi.org/10.1109/ICCSAI59793.2023.10421443]

[44]   U. Sugandh, M. Khari, and S. Nigam, *How Blockchain Technology Can Transfigure the Indian Agriculture Sector.* Handb. Green Comput. Blockchain Technol, 2021, pp. 69-88. [http://dx.doi.org/10.1201/9781003107507-6]

[45]   U. Sugandh, S. Nigam, and M. Khari, "Ecosystem of Technologies for Smart Agriculture to Improve the Efficiency and Profitability of Indian Farmers", *2023 10th International Conference on Computing for Sustainable Global Development (INDIACom), New Delhi, India,* pp. 1442-1449, 2023.

[46]   U. Sugandh, S. Nigam, and M. Khari, "Blockchain Technology in Agriculture for Indian Farmers: A Systematic Literature Review, Challenges, and Solutions", *IEEE Syst. Man. Cybern. Mag.,* vol. 8, no. 4, pp. 36-43, 2022. [http://dx.doi.org/10.1109/MSMC.2022.3197914]

[47]   U. Sugandh, S. Nigam, S. Misra, and M. Khari, "A Bibliometric Analysis of the Evolution of State-o--the-Art Blockchain Technology (BCT) in the Agrifood Sector from 2014 to 2022", *Sensors (Basel),* vol. 23, no. 14, p. 6278, 2023. [http://dx.doi.org/10.3390/s23146278] [PMID: 37514574]

[48]   U. Sugandh, S. Nigam, M. Khari, and S. Misra, "An Approach for Risk Traceability Using Blockchain Technology for Tracking, Tracing, and Authenticating Food Products", *Information (Basel),* vol. 14, no. 11, p. 613, 2023. [http://dx.doi.org/10.3390/info14110613]

[49]   S. Nigam, U. Sugandh, and M. Khari, "The integration of blockchain and IoT edge devices for smart agriculture: Challenges and use cases", In: *Advances in Computers.* vol. 127. Elsevier, 2022, pp. 507-537. [http://dx.doi.org/10.1016/bs.adcom.2022.02.015]

[50]   V. Shanmuganathan, H.R. Yesudhas, M.S. Khan, M. Khari, and A.H. Gandomi, "R-CNN and wavelet feature extraction for hand gesture recognition with EMG signals", *Neural Comput. Appl.,* vol. 32, no. 21, pp. 16723-16736, 2020. [http://dx.doi.org/10.1007/s00521-020-05349-w]

[51]   M. Khari, A.K. Garg, A.H. Gandomi, R. Gupta, R. Patan, and B. Balusamy, "Securing Data in Internet of Things (IoT) Using Cryptography and Steganography Techniques", *IEEE Trans. Syst. Man Cybern. Syst.,* vol. 50, no. 1, pp. 73-80, 2020. [http://dx.doi.org/10.1109/TSMC.2019.2903785]

[52]   Y. H. Robinson, S. Vimal, M. Khari, F. C. L. Hernández, and R. G. Crespo, "Tree-based convolutional neural networks for object classification in segmented satellite images", *Int. J. High Perform. Comput. Appl.,* 2020. [http://dx.doi.org/10.1177/1094342020945026]

[53]   V. Jain, M.S. Pillai, L. Chandra, R. Kumar, M. Khari, and A. Jain, "CamAspect: An Intelligent Automated Real-Time Surveillance System With Smartphone Indexing", *IEEE Sens. Lett.,* vol. 4, no.

10, pp. 1-4, 2020.
[http://dx.doi.org/10.1109/LSENS.2020.3019172]

[54]   H.M.R. Afzal, S. Luo, M.K. Afzal, G. Chaudhary, M. Khari, and S.A.P. Kumar, "3D Face Reconstruction From Single 2D Image Using Distinctive Features", *IEEE Access,* vol. 8, pp. 180681-180689, 2020.
[http://dx.doi.org/10.1109/ACCESS.2020.3028106]

[55]   N. S. Bhati, M. Khari, V. García-Díaz, and E. Verdú, "A Review on Intrusion Detection Systems and Techniques", *Int. J. Uncertain. Fuzziness Knowl.-Based Syst.,* vol. 28, no. Supp 02, pp. 65-91, 2020.
[http://dx.doi.org/10.1142/S0218488520400140]

[56]   A. Jain, R.G. Crespo, and M. Khari, *Smart Innovation of Web of Things.* CRC Press, 2020.
[http://dx.doi.org/10.1201/9780429298462]

CHAPTER 3

Influence of Wireless Sensor Network in Internet of Vehicles

Neha Sharma[1,2,*], **Vishal Gupta**[3] and **Jyoti Agarwal**[4]

[1] USICT, GGSIPU, New Delhi, India

[2] Bharati Vidyapeeth College of Engineering, Paschim Vihar, New Delhi, India

[3] NSUT East Campus (Formerly AIACT&R), New Delhi, India

[4] Graphic Era University, Dehradun, India

Abstract: The integration of Wireless Sensor Networks (WSNs) and the Internet of Vehicles (IoV) has emerged as an area of growing interest in recent years. WSNs provide an efficient means of gathering data from the environment, while the Internet of Vehicles empowers communication between vehicles, infrastructure, and among vehicles. However, the integration of WSNs and the Internet of Vehicles is challenging due to the high mobility of vehicles and the limited bandwidth of wireless communication. This bibliometric analysis examines the research trends and patterns in the area of Wireless Sensor Networks and metaheuristics for the Internet of Vehicles (IoV). Through a systematic analysis of publications in the Web of Science database, the study found that research on Wireless Sensor Networks for the Internet of Vehicles has been steadily increasing since 2010, with a peak in 2019. China was identified as the leading country in terms of research output, followed by the United States and India. The most common keywords associated with wireless sensor networks for IoV include "Internet of Things," "routing," "security," "energy efficiency," and "vehicle-to-vehicle communication." The analysis also revealed that the most popular research areas include routing protocols, energy efficiency, security, and vehicle-to-vehicle communication. This study provides valuable insights into the current state of research on WSNs for IoV and highlights the gaps between these two. Also, it shows the future research works done in this field discussing routing issues. Lens.org is used for data collection, and VoSviewer is used for data analysis.

Keywords: Mobility management, Data dissemination, Energy efficiency, Internet of vehicles, Metaheuristic, Quality of service, Security and privacy, Wireless sensor networks.

---

* **Corresponding author Neha Sharma:** USICT, GGSIPU, New Delhi, India and Bharati Vidyapeeth College of Engineering, Paschim Vihar, New Delhi, India; E-mail: neha.sh.2689@gmail.com

INTRODUCTION

The rapid progress in science and technology has prompted us to choose increasingly complex and unconventional techniques. In these cutting-edge technologies, the Internet of Things (IoT) is a standard bearer [1, 2]. We can sense and operate the required things remotely thanks to the Internet of Things [3]. A WSN is made up of several tiny, low-power sensor nodes that are limited in their bandwidth, computational capability, and energy supply but are nonetheless able to detect physical occurrences. WSNs are vulnerable to numerous assaults since they are typically installed in open, unprotected regions [4-6]. WSNs are vulnerable to several security vulnerabilities because of their self-organizing nature, constrained bandwidth, dispersed wireless operations, multi-hop traffic forwarding, and reliance on additional sensor nodes. A large number of intermediary nodes are used by wireless sensor nodes to transport data to the sink after processing it for improved performance [7-9]. These nodes work together to create a wire-free sensor network that can gather data and communicate it to the user upon request (sink). WSN may be used to gather data on the state of the environment, a target's location, a real-time event, *etc.* [10-14].

A wireless sensor network, or WSN, uses inexpensive, small sensor nodes to keep an eye on the outside world. In the field to be felt, hundreds to thousands of sensor nodes are randomly planted. Applications like environmental monitoring, weather forecasting, precision agriculture, natural catastrophe prevention, disaster management, border surveillance, smart cities, *etc.* all heavily rely on WSN [15, 16]. It is used to observe numerous physical characteristics in the actual world, including temperature, pressure, moisture content, gas, acoustics, vibrations, *etc.* [17-21]. In a WSN, the sensor node is composed of sensors, a microcontroller, a communication module, and a power source. The sensor unit keeps track of its surroundings, gathers data, analyses it, and sends it to other sensor nodes *via* a communication unit [22-29].

To create an energy-efficient WSN, many clustering and routing protocols with various elements have been established in the literature [30-35]. The clustering approach divides the network into clusters and organizes neighboring nodes into them. The remaining nodes are referred to as cluster members, and a leader named CH will be chosen from the group of nodes [36-38]. Equal clustering is the process of creating clusters in a network with the same number of nodes, whereas unequal clustering is the process of creating clusters with an uneven number of nodes [39-41]. A Cluster Head (CH) will be chosen from each cluster based on a set of requirements. Three tasks fall within the purview of the CH: collecting data from cluster members, aggregating it, and sending it to the BS. The CH also serves as a relay node for data transmission to BS from other CHs. Fig. (**1**) depicts the general system model of clustering. Only when the distribution of nodes is uniform can equal clustering be effective and yield superior outcomes. Uniform distribution is quite unlikely due to the nodes' haphazard placement. This causes the nodes to use energy inequitably, particularly CHs that are closest to the BS. When using multi-hop transmission, CHs closer to the base station (BS) serve as relays for remote CHs [42-49]. Therefore, CHs closer to BS exhaust their energy and pass away before their distance from BS.

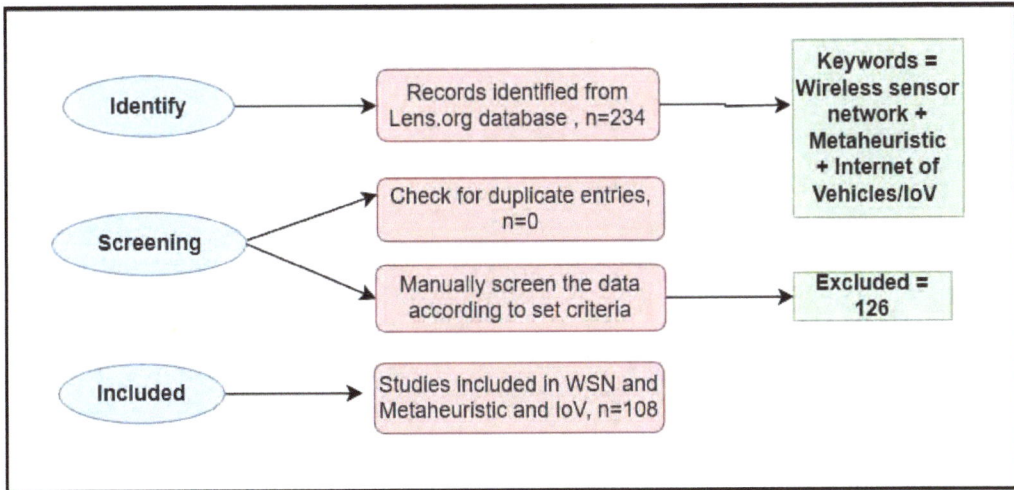

Fig. (1). Steps of publications retrieval.

Nodes in the WSN often communicate data to BS on a regular basis, making it ideal for applications that need periodic data monitoring [50-65]. Time-sensitive circumstances cause the physical environment to change suddenly and quickly, which results in multiple data transmissions and a considerable impact on energy usage. A reactive protocol, which transmits data when the threshold value is crossed [66-81], is introduced to solve this problem. Data will only be transmitted *via* the reactive protocol when the detected value is greater than the threshold value. Both hard and soft threshold values are included in the threshold value [82-85]. Following the selection of the CHs, it broadcasts to the other members of the cluster two threshold values (hard threshold and soft threshold values). The cluster members will broadcast the data to the CH when the detected value exceeds the hard threshold value [86-89]. By limiting the nodes' ability to broadcast to times when the detected value is within the range of interest, the hard threshold attempts to decrease the number of transmissions. By excluding any transmissions with a minimal or no change in the perceived value from the hard threshold value, the soft threshold significantly minimizes the number of transmissions [90-92]. The soft threshold can be changed depending on the intended application and how crucial the detected property is. At the cost of higher energy consumption, a smaller value of the soft threshold provides a more accurate representation of the network [93-95].

The potential applications of wireless sensor networks (WSNs), such as the Internet of Vehicles, have attracted a lot of interest in recent years. IoV stands for the Internet of Vehicles, which allows for communication between connected vehicles and other networked equipment. The present state of research in WSNs and the use of metaheuristics for IoV will be examined in this bibliometric analysis.

METHODOLOGY

From the scientometrics, one can trace the identity of the bibliometric analysis and the use of statistical tools for the analysis of the same. Bibliometric analysis is basically the tool for the analysis of research done in a particular field and its quantitative analysis depending on different fields. It is an advanced survey performed on the research done in that field. Researchers all over the globe are doing this analysis these days, whether it is marketing, electronics, physics, engineering, *etc.* The paper is analyzed from the following perspectives: citations, authors, co-authors, bibliographical coupling, universities, publications, co-occurrences, word cloud, *etc.*

The data for the analysis has been collected from "lens.org" database. A few of the analyses are performed on lens.org only and some analysis diagrams are drawn on VOS viewer. As the data is collected from lenses, the retrieved publications need to be screened so that publications that are irrelevant can be included and research articles that are not relevant to the topic will be excluded. There are 3 steps for finalizing publication retrieval:

- Identity: For identifying research articles, lens.org was searched and a total of 234 articles were selected. Now, the next thing is to select the articles which are related. The query used to search articles is
    - Query= Wireless (and) sensor (and) network (and) metaheuristic (and) internet of vehicles
- Screening: The selected articles need to be screened before analyzing them for bibliometric analysis. Few articles were excluded from the selected database. Two things were considered in the screening process:
    - Remove duplicate entries

○ Manually remove the articles that are not related to WSN, metaheuristics, and the Internet of Vehicles.

• Inclusion: After the exclusion of 126 articles, 108 articles were included in the analysis. Table **1** shows the inclusion criteria.

Table 1. Inclusion criteria.

Inclusion Criteria	Rationale for inclusion
Papers discussing Wireless sensor networks and metaheuristics and the Internet of vehicles	A proper review was performed to check the use of metaheuristic and WSN in Internet of Vehicles.
The paper title does not include WSN or Metaheuristics	The paper title does not include terms directly but the content of the paper discusses the same.

In the process, 126 articles were excluded. Table **2** shows the exclusion criteria.

Table 2. Exclusion criteria.

Exclusion Criteria	Rationale for inclusion
Papers not at all related to discussing Wireless sensor networks	The papers only including metaheuristics are excluded as the survey focuses on the use of metaheuristics in WSN.
Papers not at all related to discussing Metaheuristics	The papers only including WSN are excluded as the survey focuses on the use of metaheuristics in WSN.
Papers not at all related to the Internet of Vehicles	The papers only including the internet of vehicles are excluded as the survey focuses on the use of metaheuristics in WSN.
Papers related to only networks but not wireless or talking about sensors only	The term network only does not cover the scope, so such papers are excluded.
Papers only related to the internet of vehicles and metaheuristics but not related to WSN	The scope of the survey will not be covered.

Fig. (**1**) shows the steps of publication retrieval.

The search terms used for this study were "Wireless Sensor Networks" AND "Metaheuristics" AND "Internet of Vehicles" OR "IoV". The Web of Science database was used for the inquiry. In order to guarantee that the findings were up-to-date, the search was restricted to the years 2011 through 2023.

RESULTS AND DISCUSSION

Total 108 items in total were found through the search. After examining the papers, we discovered that there have been more publications in this area recently, most of which are in the engineering field. China, the USA, India, South Korea, and Turkey are the top five most prolific nations in this sector. The most fruitful publications in this field are computer networks, IEEE Internet of Things Journal, Journal of Network and Computer Applications, Sensors, and IEEE Transactions on Vehicular Technology. The majority of papers on WSNs and metaheuristics for IoV have been published in these journals.

The terms "Wireless Sensor Networks," "Internet of Vehicles," "Vehicular Ad Hoc Networks," "Routing Protocols," and "Energy Efficiency" were most commonly used in the articles. The present trends in this field of study are reflected in these keywords. The outcomes of bibliometric research are displayed using bibliometric diagrams. They can aid scholars in comprehending the patterns and trends within a specific area of study. Co-citation maps, bibliographic coupling maps, and term co-occurrence maps are a few examples of frequently used bibliometric diagrams [96-107]. Table **3** shows the list of the most productive authors, whereas Table **4** shows the list of the most influential universities. Also Table **5** shows the Most Influential Countries and Table **6** shows Name of Top Journals for the same.

Table 3. Most productive authors.

Authors	Total Publications
Xin-She Yang	9
Milan Tuba	5
Nebojsa Bacanin	9
Satvir Singh	9
Palvinder Singh Mann	8
Juan A Gómez-Pulido	7
Chun-Wei Tsai	6
Eva Tuba	6
Govind P Gupta	6
Jeng-Shyang Pan	6
Jose M Lanza-Gutierrez	6
Marko Beko	6
Miodrag Zivkovic	6
Albert Y S Lam	5
David Plets	5

Table 4. Most influential universities.

Universities	Total publications
University of Hong Kong	12

(Table 4) cont.....

Middlesex University	11
University of Nottingham	10
Polytechnic University of Catalonia	9
Punjab Technical University	9
Singidunum University	9
University of Extremadura	8
Ghent University	8
Islamic Azad University	8
National Institute of Technology, Raipur	7
Universiti Malaysia Pahang	7
Universiti Teknologi Malaysia	7

The relationships between two or more papers are visualized using co-citation maps based on how frequently they have been cited together. On the other hand, bibliographic coupling maps display the connections between two or more papers based on how many references they share. Based on how frequently they appear together in papers, keywords are related in maps of their co-occurrence.

The outcomes of this bibliometric analysis show that WSNs for IoV are a busy and expanding field. One can use bibliometric software like VOSviewer, CiteSpace, or Bibliometrix to generate bibliometric diagrams for WSNs and metaheuristics for IoV. These software tools can be used to analyze the bibliographic data and see the analysis's findings in various bibliometric graphs.

Table 5. Most influential countries.

Countries	Total Publications
United Kingdom	93
India	82
China	78
Spain	45
United States	42
Malaysia	31
France	25
Italy	24
Australia	23
Iran	16
Canada	14

(Table 5) cont....

Hong Kong	13
Serbia	13

Table 6. Name of top journals.

Publishers	Total Publications
Elsevier BV	94
IEEE	85
Institute of Electrical and Electronics Engineers (IEEE)	78
Springer Science and Business Media LLC	63
Multidisciplinary Digital Publishing Institute (MDPI)	36
Springer International Publishing	35
MDPI AG	21
Computers, Materials and Continua (Tech Science Press)	17
Springer Singapore	17

Fig. (**2**) depicts the authors by the field of study and analysis is done using lens.org. It shows the names of the authors who have worked in this field.

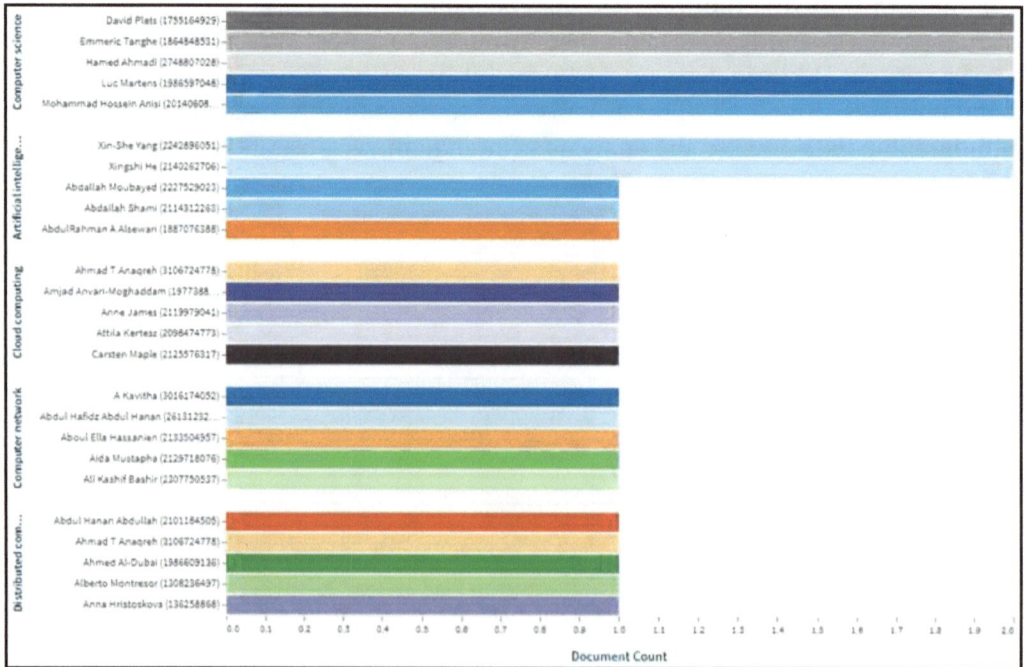

Fig. (2). Authors by the field of study.

Fig. (**3**) depicts the authors by institution. It categorizes the authors *via* institutions and provides an overview that Ghant University and the University of Teknologi are the universities, which have most of the authors working in this field.

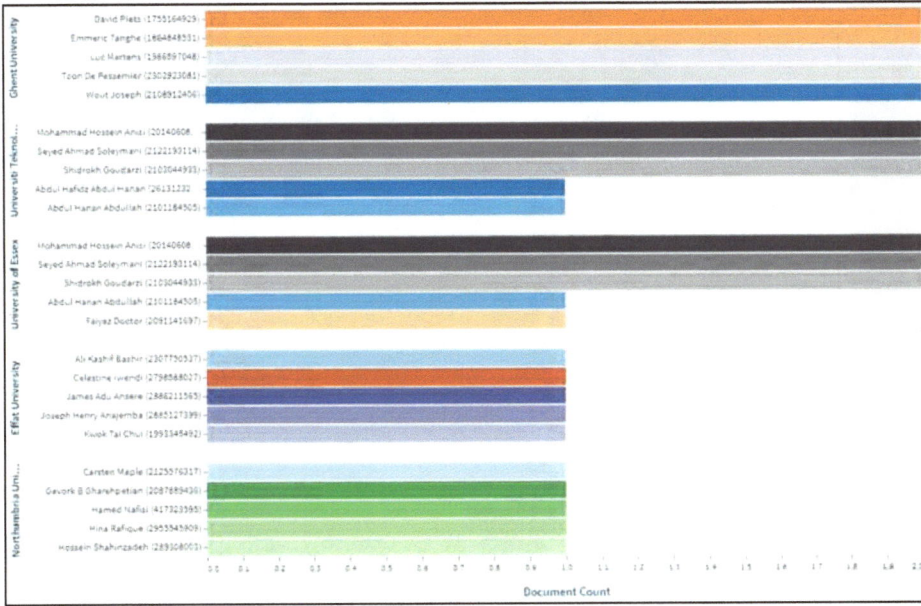

Fig. (3). Authors by institution.

Fig. (**4**) shows the data of collaborating authors. It depicts the collaborating authors with the count of documents in which they have worked.

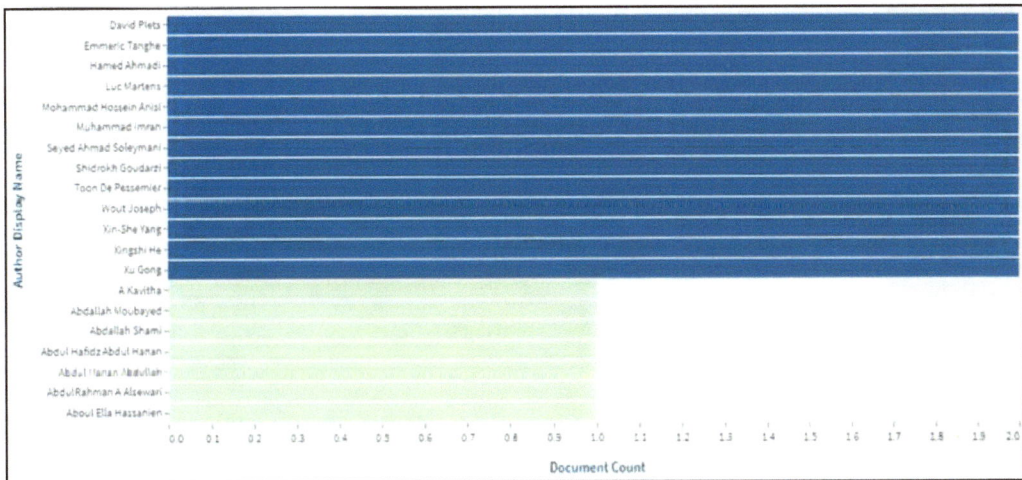

Fig. (4). Documents count of collaborating authors.

Fig. (**5**) shows the Institution's name and unique citing patent. It depicts which institution has the highest patent count. University College Dublin and the University of Oklahoma are one of the most influential universities in the field of patent in this field.

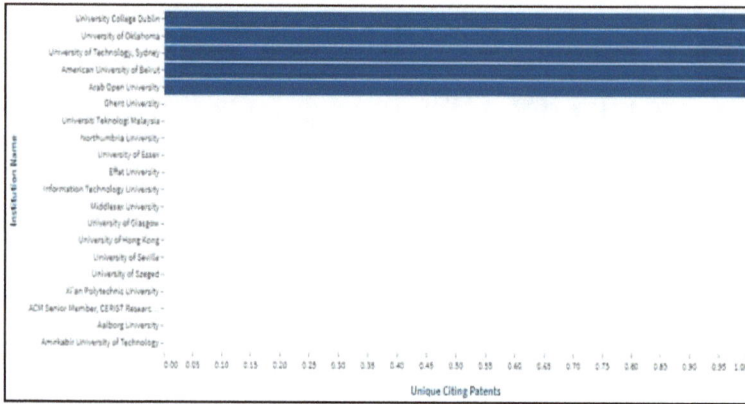

Fig. (5). Institution name and unique citing patent.

Fig. (**6**) depicts the institutions' names with country. The results show that the maximum number of institutions working in this field are from United Kingdom and China, whereas Fig. (**7**) depicts the Institution's names with the field of study.

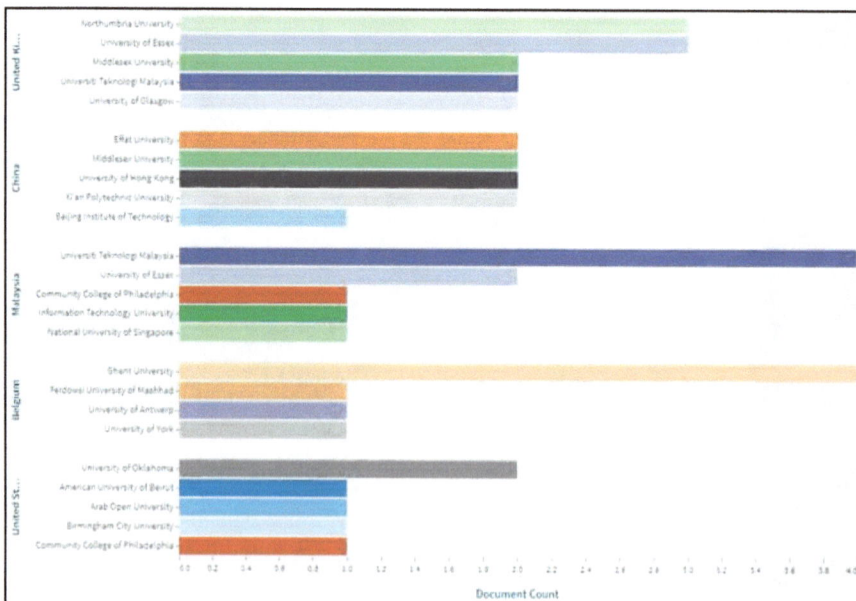

Fig. (6). Institution with country.

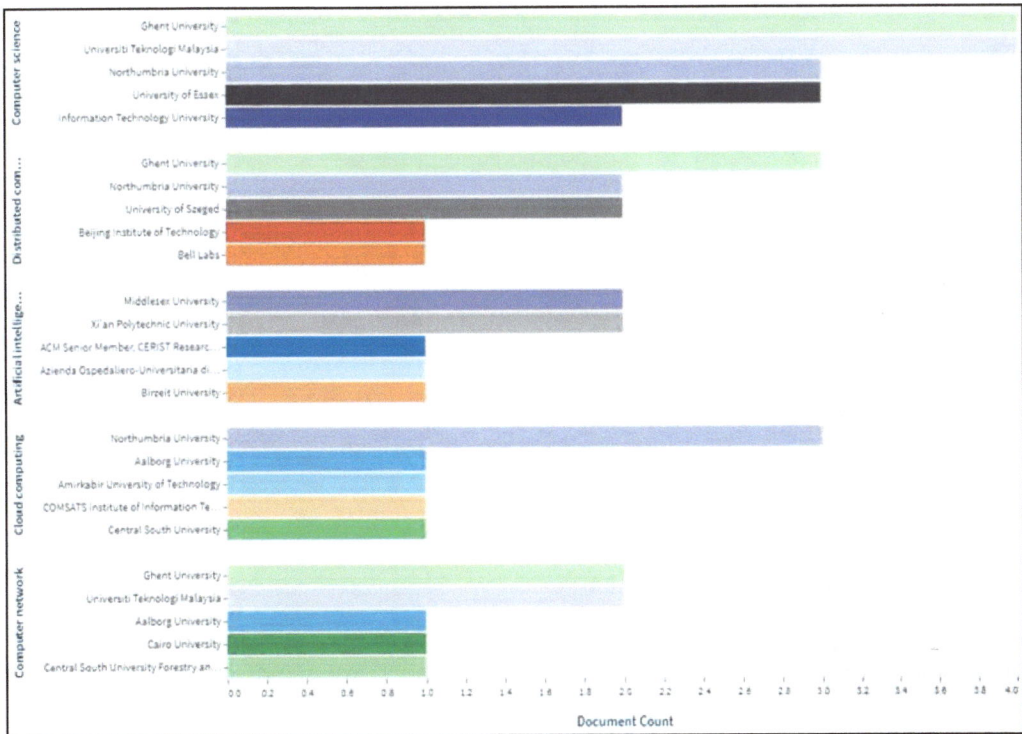

Fig. (7). Institution with the field of study.

A well-liked bibliometric software program for visualizing and analyzing bibliometric data is called VOSviewer. VOSviewer is a powerful tool for conducting citations and document analysis. It allows researchers to visualize and analyze bibliographic data to identify key trends, influential papers, authors, and collaborations. Co-authorship networks, co-citation networks, bibliographic coupling networks, and phrase co-occurrence networks are just a few of the different kinds of bibliometric diagrams that VOSviewer is capable of producing.

Bibliographic coupling with authors is an analysis that shows the papers that are frequently appearing together. VOSviewer is used for creating bibliographic coupling of the data collected from the lens.org. The analysis relates research articles which are potentially collaborated. Fig. (8) depicts the bibliographic coupling of the authors.

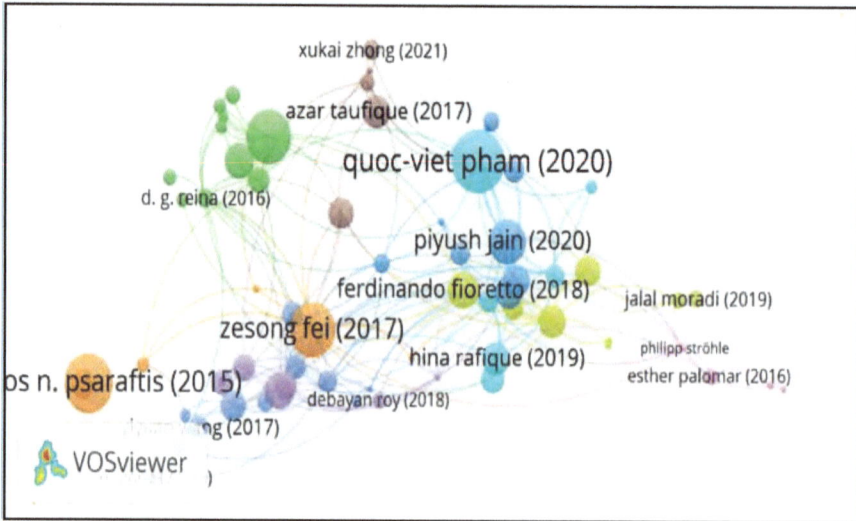

Fig. (8). Bibliographic coupling with authors using VOSviewer.

Citations and document analysis using VOSviewer involve examining the relationships between scientific publications based on their citations and other bibliographic data. VOSviewer is a software tool specifically designed for bibliometric analysis and visualization, enabling researchers to explore and understand patterns within large bibliographic datasets. Fig. (**9**) shows the citations and authors' analysis using VOSviewer whereas Fig. (**10**) shows the citations and documents' analysis using VOSviewer.

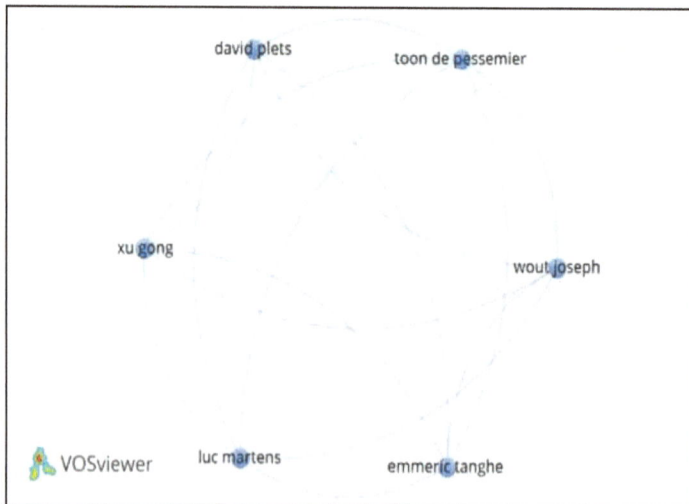

Fig. (9). Citations and authors VoSviewer.

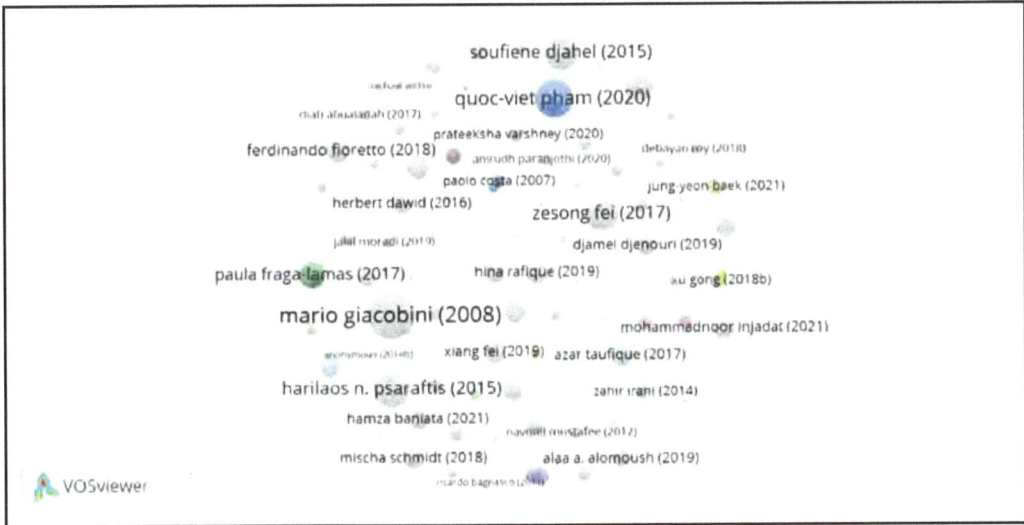

Fig. (10). Citations and documents VOSviewer.

The analysis identified key research topics within the field of WSNs for the IoV, including energy-efficient protocols, data aggregation techniques, security mechanisms, and applications in intelligent transportation systems and smart cities. These findings reflect the diverse challenges that researchers are addressing to enhance the performance, reliability, and security of WSNs in the IoV. In terms of metaheuristic algorithms, the analysis demonstrated the popularity and wide application of approaches such as genetic algorithms, particle swarm optimization, and ant colony optimization in the context of the IoV. Researchers have leveraged these algorithms to tackle optimization problems related to traffic management, routing efficiency, congestion control, and resource allocation in vehicular networks. Furthermore, the analysis provided insights into influential authors and institutions contributing to the field. These researchers have made significant contributions to the advancement of WSNs and metaheuristics for the IoV, indicating their expertise and leadership in the domain.

ROUTING ISSUES IN IOV USING WSN

Routing in the Internet of Vehicles (IoV) using Wireless Sensor Networks (WSN) is a complex challenge due to the dynamic and highly mobile nature of vehicles and the resource constraints of sensor nodes. The following solutions can be implemented for the routing issues in the above-mentioned collaboration.

Geographic Routing

In this case, one can rely on geographic routing algorithms that rely on the location information of vehicles and sensor nodes. These algorithms can efficiently forward data to nearby nodes and reduce communication overhead.

Adaptive Routing Protocols

Implement adaptive routing protocols that can dynamically adjust their behavior based on network conditions.

Vehicular Ad Hoc Networks (VANETs)

Leverage VANET-specific routing protocols designed for vehicle-to-vehicle communication. Protocols like AODV (Ad Hoc On-Demand Distance Vector) and DSR (Dynamic Source Routing) can be adapted for IoV-WSN scenarios.

Predictive Routing

Employ predictive routing mechanisms that anticipate the movement of vehicles and use predictive models to optimize route selection. Machine learning algorithms can aid in predicting vehicle trajectories.

Energy-Efficient Routing

Develop routing algorithms that consider the energy constraints of both sensor nodes and vehicles. Energy-efficient routing can prolong the lifetime of sensor nodes and reduce the impact on vehicle energy resources.

Multi-Hop and Relay Nodes

Implement multi-hop routing strategies when direct vehicle-to-vehicle communication is not feasible. Introduce relay nodes to extend the communication range and improve connectivity.

Solving routing issues in the IoV-WSN collaboration requires a holistic approach that considers the specific characteristics of vehicular networks, sensor nodes, and application requirements.

GAP IDENTIFICATION

Security and Privacy

Researchers need to develop robust encryption, authentication, and access control mechanisms to protect sensitive information.

Interoperability

Research should focus on standardization efforts and middleware solutions that facilitate communication between heterogeneous systems.

Real-Time Data Processing

The gap exists in developing edge computing and distributed analytics solutions that can handle the real-time data efficiently.

Regulatory Frameworks

The development of regulatory frameworks and policies to govern the use of collaborative WSNs and IoV is an evolving area. One can contribute to the formulation of guidelines and standards that ensure responsible and safe deployment.

Scalability and Reliability

As the scale of collaborative deployments grows, ensuring scalability and reliability becomes more challenging. Dynamic network management, fault tolerance, and load-balancing strategies can be improved.

FUTURE SCOPE

Autonomous and Connected Vehicles

The researchers can focus on developing reliable and high-performance sensor networks to support autonomous driving, enabling vehicles to communicate seamlessly with each other and with infrastructure.

Traffic Management and Optimization

In the future, one can explore advanced traffic management systems that leverage real-time data from WSNs and vehicles to optimize traffic flow, reduce congestion, and improve road safety. Intelligent traffic lights, dynamic route planning, and adaptive traffic signal control are promising areas.

Smart Cities and Urban Planning

Collaborative WSNs and IoV can significantly contribute to smart city initiatives. Researchers can work on integrating sensor data for improved city planning, resource management, and urban infrastructure development, such as smart lighting, waste management, and parking solutions.

Environmental Monitoring

The collaboration can enhance environmental monitoring efforts by leveraging WSNs and vehicle-based sensors to collect data on air quality, noise pollution, and other environmental factors. This data can inform policy decisions and help address urban environmental challenges.

Public Safety and Emergency Response

Future work can focus on enhancing public safety and emergency response systems by leveraging WSNs and IoV for early accident detection, rapid response coordination, and efficient evacuation strategies.

Energy-Efficiency and Sustainability

Researchers can explore how WSNs and IoV can contribute to energy-efficient transportation and reduce carbon emissions.

CONCLUSION

In conclusion, the bibliometric analysis conducted on Wireless Sensor Networks (WSNs) and the application of metaheuristic algorithms in the context of the Internet of Vehicles (IoV) using lens.org and VOSviewer provided valuable insights into the research landscape and trends in these domains. The analysis revealed a growing interest in both WSNs and metaheuristics for the IoV, as evidenced by the increasing number of publications over time. Researchers have recognized the significance of integrating WSNs with metaheuristic algorithms to optimize various aspects of the IoV, such as routing, resource allocation, scheduling, and data management. Overall, the bibliometric analysis using lens.org and VOSviewer allowed for a comprehensive understanding of the research landscape, emerging trends, and key contributors in the fields of WSNs and metaheuristics for the IoV. These findings can guide researchers, policymakers, and industry professionals in identifying research gaps, collaboration opportunities, and potential areas for further exploration and advancements in these domains.

REFERENCES

[1]   I. Mavromatis, A. Tassi, R.J. Piechocki, and A. Nix, "A City-Scale ITS-G5 Network for Next-Generation Intelligent Transportation Systems: Design Insights and Challenges", In: *Ad-hoc, Mobile, and Wireless Networks. ADHOC-NOW 2018.*, N. Montavont, G. Papadopoulos, Eds., vol. 11104. Springer: Cham, 2018. Lecture Notes in Computer Science.
[http://dx.doi.org/10.1007/978-3-030-00247-3_5]

[2]   A. Lima, F. Rocha, M. Völp, and P. Esteves-Veríssimo, "Towards safe and secure autonomous and cooperative vehicle ecosystems", *Proceedings of the 2nd ACM Workshop on Cyber-Physical Systems Security and Privacy*, pp. 59-70, 2016.

[http://dx.doi.org/10.1145/2994487.2994489]

[3]   M.A. Kafi, Y. Challal, D. Djenouri, M. Doudou, A. Bouabdallah, and N. Badache, "A study of wireless sensor networks for urban traffic monitoring: applications and architectures", *Procedia Comput. Sci.*, vol. 19, pp. 617-626, 2013.
[http://dx.doi.org/10.1016/j.procs.2013.06.082]

[4]   P. Porambage, J. Okwuibe, M. Liyanage, M. Ylianttila, and T. Taleb, "Survey on multi-access edge computing for internet of things realization", *IEEE Commun. Surv. Tutor.*, vol. 20, no. 4, pp. 2961-2991, 2018.
[http://dx.doi.org/10.1109/COMST.2018.2849509]

[5]   J. Santa, F. Pereñíguez, J.C. Cano, A.F. Skarmeta, C.T. Calafate, and P. Manzoni, "Comprehensive vehicular networking platform for V2I and V2V communications within the walkie-talkie project", *Int. J. Distrib. Sens. Netw.*, vol. 9, no. 7, p. 676850, 2013.
[http://dx.doi.org/10.1155/2013/676850]

[6]   C. Thomson, I. Wadhaj, Z. Tan, and A. Al-Dubai, "Mobility aware duty cycling algorithm (MADCAL) a dynamic communication threshold for mobile sink in wireless sensor network", *Sensors (Basel)*, vol. 19, no. 22, p. 4930, 2019.
[http://dx.doi.org/10.3390/s19224930] [PMID: 31726741]

[7]   R. Yu, Y. Zhang, S. Gjessing, W. Xia, and K. Yang, "Toward cloud-based vehicular networks with efficient resource management", *IEEE Netw.*, vol. 27, no. 5, pp. 48-55, 2013.
[http://dx.doi.org/10.1109/MNET.2013.6616115]

[8]   J.A. Sanguesa, M. Fogue, P. Garrido, F.J. Martinez, J.C. Cano, and C.T. Calafate, "A survey and comparative study of broadcast warning message dissemination schemes for VANETs", *Mob. Inf. Syst.*, vol. 2016, pp. 1-18, 2016.
[http://dx.doi.org/10.1155/2016/8714142]

[9]   H. Zhou, and Z. Zhang, "Differentiated statistical QoS guarantees for real-time CBR services in broadband wireless access networks", *2010 6th International Conference on Wireless Communications Networking and Mobile Computing (WiCOM), Chengdu, China*, pp. 1-4, 2010.
[http://dx.doi.org/10.1109/WICOM.2010.5601439]

[10]   W. Ejaz, M. Naeem, A. Shahid, A. Anpalagan, and M. Jo, "Efficient energy management for the internet of things in smart cities", *IEEE Commun. Mag.*, vol. 55, no. 1, pp. 84-91, 2017.
[http://dx.doi.org/10.1109/MCOM.2017.1600218CM]

[11]   Dhanalakshmi, and A. Ezil Sam Leni, "Instance vehicle monitoring and tracking with internet of things using Arduino", *Int. J. Smart Sensing Intell. Syst.*, vol. 10, no. 5, pp. 123-135, 2022.
[http://dx.doi.org/10.21307/ijssis-2017-240]

[12]   M. Cerchecci, F. Luti, A. Mecocci, S. Parrino, G. Peruzzi, and A. Pozzebon, "A low power IoT sensor node architecture for waste management within smart cities context", *Sensors (Basel)*, vol. 18, no. 4, p. 1282, 2018.
[http://dx.doi.org/10.3390/s18041282] [PMID: 29690552]

[13]   S.J. Cox, and S.J. Johnston, *Raspberry Pi Technology* MDPI, 2018.
[http://dx.doi.org/10.3390/books978-3-03842-580-9]

[14]   D. Patel, and M. Won, "Experimental study on low power wide area networks (LPWAN) for mobile Internet of Things", *2017 IEEE 85th Vehicular Technology Conference (VTC Spring), Sydney, NSW, Australia*, pp. 1-5, 2017.
[http://dx.doi.org/10.1109/VTCSpring.2017.8108501]

[15]   J. Sanguesa, J. Barrachina, M. Fogue, P. Garrido, F. Martinez, J.C. Cano, C. Calafate, and P. Manzoni, "Sensing traffic density combining V2V and V2I wireless communications", *Sensors (Basel)*, vol. 15, no. 12, pp. 31794-31810, 2015.
[http://dx.doi.org/10.3390/s151229889] [PMID: 26694405]

[16]   M. Antunes, J.P. Barraca, D. Gomes, P. Oliveira, and R.L. Aguiar, "Smart cloud of things: an evolved iot platform for telco providers", *J. Ambient. Wireless. Commun. Smart. Environ.,* vol. 1, no. 1, pp. 1-24, 2015.
[http://dx.doi.org/10.13052/ambientcom2246-3410.111]

[17]   M.K. Nasir, R.M. Noor, M. Iftikhar, M. Imran, A.W. Abdul Wahab, M.R. Jabbarpour, and R.H. Khokhar, "A framework and mathematical modeling for the vehicular delay tolerant network routing", *Mob. Inf. Syst.,* vol. 2016, pp. 1-14, 2016.
[http://dx.doi.org/10.1155/2016/8163893]

[18]   M. Hashem Eiza, T. Owens, and Q. Ni, "Secure and robust multi-constrained QoS aware routing algorithm for VANETs", *IEEE Trans. Depend. Secure Comput.,* vol. 13, no. 1, pp. 32-45, 2016.
[http://dx.doi.org/10.1109/TDSC.2014.2382602]

[19]   B. Mokhtar, and M. Azab, "Survey on security issues in vehicular ad hoc networks", *Alex. Eng. J.,* vol. 54, no. 4, pp. 1115-1126, 2015.
[http://dx.doi.org/10.1016/j.aej.2015.07.011]

[20]   T. Gao, G. Li, P. Wang, and C. Wang, "Camera detection through internet of video sensors", *Int. J. Multim. Intell. Secur.,* vol. 3, no. 1, pp. 51-62, 2013.
[http://dx.doi.org/10.1504/IJMIS.2013.056466]

[21]   M. Sharif-Yazd, M.R. Khosravi, and M.K Moghimi, "A survey on underwater acoustic sensor networks: Perspectives on protocol design for signaling, MAC and routing", *J. Comp. Commun.,* vol. 5, no. 5, 2017.
[http://dx.doi.org/10.4236/jcc.2017.55002]

[22]   M. Fazio, M. Paone, A. Puliafito, and M. Villari, "HSCLOUD: cloud architecture for supporting homeland security", *Int. J. Smart Sensing Intell. Syst.,* vol. 5, no. 1, pp. 246-276, 2012.
[http://dx.doi.org/10.21307/ijssis-2017-480]

[23]   S. Kapadia, B. Krishnamachari, and L. Zhang, "Data delivery in delay tolerant networks: A survey", *Mobile Ad-Hoc Networks: Protocol Design, InTech.* Jan. 30, 2011.
[http://dx.doi.org/10.5772/12944]

[24]   S. Najafzadeh, N.B. Ithnin, and S. Abd Razak, "Broadcasting in connected and fragmented vehicular ad hoc networks", *Int. J. Vehicular Technol.,* vol. 2014, pp. 1-15, 2014.
[http://dx.doi.org/10.1155/2014/969076]

[25]   Z. EL Khaled, and H. Mcheick, "Case studies of communications systems during harsh environments: A review of approaches, weaknesses, and limitations to improve quality of service", *Int. J. Distrib. Sens. Netw.,* vol. 15, no. 2, 2019.
[http://dx.doi.org/10.1177/1550147719829960]

[26]   D.E. Boyle, M.E. Kiziroglou, P.D. Mitcheson, and E.M. Yeatman, "Energy provision and storage for pervasive computing", *IEEE Perva. Comput.,* vol. 15, no. 4, pp. 28-35, 2016.
[http://dx.doi.org/10.1109/MPRV.2016.65]

[27]   C. Tripp-Barba, L. Urquiza-Aguiar, M. Igartua, D. Rebollo-Monedero, L. De la Cruz Llopis, A. Mezher, and J. Aguilar-Calderón, "A multimetric, map-aware routing protocol for VANETs in urban areas", *Sensors (Basel),* vol. 14, no. 2, pp. 2199-2224, 2014.
[http://dx.doi.org/10.3390/s140202199] [PMID: 24476683]

[28]   R. Hussian, S. Sharma, V. Sharma, and S. Sharma, "WSN applications: Automated intelligent traffic control system using sensors", *Int. J. Soft Comput. Eng,* vol. 3, no. 3, pp. 77-81, 2013. Corpus ID: 61208099

[29]   F.B. De Carvalho, W.T.A. Lopes, M.S. Alencar, and V.S. José Filho, "Cognitive vehicular networks: An overview", *Procedia. Comput. Sci.,* vol. 65, pp. 107-114, 2015.
[http://dx.doi.org/10.1016/j.procs.2015.09.086]

[30]   N. Correia, N. Carvalho, and G. Schütz, "Planning of vehicle routing with backup provisioning using

wireless sensor technologies", *Information (Basel),* vol. 8, no. 3, p. 94, 2017.
[http://dx.doi.org/10.3390/info8030094]

[31]   J. Huang, B. Zhu, and F. Lawal, "Public Safety Applications over WiMAX Ad-Hoc Networks", In: *Quality of Service and Resource Allocation in WiMAX.* IntechOpen, 2012.
[http://dx.doi.org/10.5772/29920]

[32]   J. Liu, J. Wan, D. Jia, B. Zeng, D. Li, C.H. Hsu, and H. Chen, "High-efficiency urban traffic management in context-aware computing and 5G communication", *IEEE Commun. Mag.,* vol. 55, no. 1, pp. 34-40, 2017.
[http://dx.doi.org/10.1109/MCOM.2017.1600371CM]

[33]   Y. Cao, Y. Miao, G. Min, T. Wang, Z. Zhao, and H. Song, "Vehicular-publish/subscribe (VP/S) communication enabled on-the-move EV charging management", *IEEE Commun. Mag.,* vol. 54, no. 12, pp. 84-92, 2016.
[http://dx.doi.org/10.1109/MCOM.2016.1600320CM]

[34]   A. Aliyu, A.H. Abdullah, N. Aslam, A. Altameem, R.Z. Radzi, R. Kharel, M. Mahmud, S. Prakash, and U.M. Joda, "Interference-aware multipath video streaming in vehicular environments", *IEEE. Access,* vol. 6, pp. 47610-47626, 2018.
[http://dx.doi.org/10.1109/ACCESS.2018.2854784]

[35]   H. Alawad, and S. Kaewunruen, "Wireless sensor networks: Toward smarter railway stations", *Infrastructures,* vol. 3, no. 3, p. 24, 2018.
[http://dx.doi.org/10.3390/infrastructures3030024]

[36]   V.W. Tang, Y. Zheng, and J. Cao, "An intelligent car park management system based on wireless sensor networks", *2006 First International Symposium on Pervasive Computing and Applications,* IEEE, pp. 65-70, 2006.
[http://dx.doi.org/10.1109/SPCA.2006.297498]

[37]   C. Velí, F. Solano, and Y. Donoso, "Routing optimization for delay tolerant networks in rural applications using a distributed algorithm", *Int. J. Comput. Commun. Control,* vol. 10, no. 1, pp. 100-111, 2015.
[http://dx.doi.org/10.15837/ijccc.2015.1.1569]

[38]   S.A. Putra, B.R. Trilaksono, M. Riyansyah, D.S. Laila, A. Harsoyo, and A.I. Kistijantoro, "Intelligent sensing in multiagent-based wireless sensor network for bridge condition monitoring system", *IEEE. Internet. Things. J.,* vol. 6, no. 3, pp. 5397-5410, 2019.
[http://dx.doi.org/10.1109/JIOT.2019.2901796]

[39]   A.O. Kotb, Y. Shen, and Y. Huang, "Smart parking guidance, monitoring and reservations: a review", *IEEE Intell. Transp. Syst. Mag.,* vol. 9, no. 2, pp. 6-16, 2017.
[http://dx.doi.org/10.1109/MITS.2017.2666586]

[40]   N. Bhutta, G. Ansa, E. Johnson, N. Ahmad, M. Alsiyabi, and H. Cruickshank, "Security analysis for delay/disruption tolerant satellite and sensor networks", *2009 International Workshop on Satellite and Space Communications,* IEEE, pp. 385-389, 2009.
[http://dx.doi.org/10.1109/IWSSC.2009.5286339]

[41]   B. Evans, M. Werner, E. Lutz, M. Bousquet, G.E. Corazza, G. Maral, and R. Rumeau, "Integration of satellite and terrestrial systems in future multimedia communications", *IEEE Wirel. Commun.,* vol. 12, no. 5, pp. 72-80, 2005.
[http://dx.doi.org/10.1109/MWC.2005.1522108]

[42]   W.J. Franz, R. Eberhardt, and T. Luckenbach, "Fleetnet-internet on the road", *In 8th World Congress on Intelligent Transport Systems,* 2001.

[43]   R.I. Meneguette, G.P.R. Filho, D.L. Guidoni, G. Pessin, L.A. Villas, and J. Ueyama, "Increasing intelligence in inter-vehicle communications to reduce traffic congestions: Experiments in urban and highway environments", *PLoS One,* vol. 11, no. 8, p. e0159110, 2016.
[http://dx.doi.org/10.1371/journal.pone.0159110] [PMID: 27526048]

[44]   Y. He, D. Zhai, R. Zhang, X. Du, and M. Guizani, "An anti-interference scheme for UAV data links in air–ground integrated vehicular networks", *Sensors (Basel),* vol. 19, no. 21, p. 4742, 2019.
[http://dx.doi.org/10.3390/s19214742] [PMID: 31683703]

[45]   B. Baron, P. Spathis, M. Dias de Amorim, Y. Viniotis, and M.H. Ammar, "Mobility as an alternative communication channel: A survey", *IEEE Commun. Surv. Tutor.,* vol. 21, no. 1, pp. 289-314, 2019.
[http://dx.doi.org/10.1109/COMST.2018.2841192]

[46]   C. Suthaputchakun, and Z. Sun, "Multihop broadcast protocol in intermittently connected vehicular networks", *IEEE Trans. Aerosp. Electron. Syst.,* vol. 54, no. 2, pp. 616-628, 2018.
[http://dx.doi.org/10.1109/TAES.2017.2761140]

[47]   A.A. Allahham, and M.A. Rahman, "A smart monitoring system for campus using Zigbee wireless sensor networks", *Int. J. Softw. Eng. Comput, Sys.,* vol. 4, no. 1, pp. 1-14, 2018. [IJSECS].
[http://dx.doi.org/10.15282/ijsecs.4.1.2018.1.0034]

[48]   K. Ashokkumar, B. Sam, R. Arshadprabhu, and Britto, "Cloud based intelligent transport system", *Procedia. Comput. Sci.,* vol. 50, pp. 58-63, 2015.
[http://dx.doi.org/10.1016/j.procs.2015.04.061]

[49]   M. Allegretti, and S. Bertoldo, "Cars as a diffuse network of road-environment monitoring nodes", *Wirel. Sens. Netw.,* vol. 6, no. 9, pp. 184-191, 2014.
[http://dx.doi.org/10.4236/wsn.2014.69018]

[50]   E.D. Likotiko, D. Nyambo, and J. Mwangoka, "Multi-agent based IoT smart waste monitoring and collection architecture", *Int. J. Comp. Sci. Eng. Inform. Technol.,* vol. 7, no. 5, 2017.
[http://dx.doi.org/10.5121/ijcseit.2017.7501]

[51]   R. Coppola, and M. Morisio, "Connected Car", *ACM Comput. Surv.,* vol. 49, no. 3, pp. 1-36, 2017. [CSUR].
[http://dx.doi.org/10.1145/2971482]

[52]   C. Cambra, S. Sendra, J. Lloret, and L. Parra, "Ad hoc network for emergency rescue system based on unmanned aerial vehicles", *Network Protocols and Algorithms,* vol. 7, no. 4, pp. 72-89, 2016.
[http://dx.doi.org/10.5296/npa.v7i4.8816]

[53]   M. Asgari, M. Ismail, and R. Alsaqour, "Reliable contention-based beaconless packet forwarding algorithm for vanet streets", *Procedia. Technol.,* vol. 11, pp. 1011-1017, 2013.
[http://dx.doi.org/10.1016/j.protcy.2013.12.288]

[54]   M.C. Peng, and H. Lu, "The information security scheduling method of vehicle self-organising system for wireless sensor", *Int. J. Internet Manuf. Serv.,* vol. 7, no. 1/2, pp. 36-49, 2020.
[http://dx.doi.org/10.1504/IJIMS.2020.105035]

[55]   R. Fotohi, "Securing of Unmanned Aerial Systems (UAS) against security threats using human immune system", *Reliab. Eng. Syst. Saf.,* vol. 193, p. 106675, 2020.
[http://dx.doi.org/10.1016/j.ress.2019.106675]

[56]   C. D. McDermott, and A. Petrovski, "Investigation of computational intelligence techniques for intrusion detection in wireless sensor networks", *Int. J. Comp. Network. Commun.,* vol. 9, no. 4, 2017.
[http://dx.doi.org/10.5121/ijcnc.2017.9404]

[57]   A. Venčkauskas, N. Morkevicius, K. Bagdonas, R. Damaševičius, and R. Maskeliūnas, "A lightweight protocol for secure video streaming", *Sensors (Basel),* vol. 18, no. 5, p. 1554, 2018.
[http://dx.doi.org/10.3390/s18051554] [PMID: 29757988]

[58]   S. C. Shah, "Recent Advances in Mobile Grid and Cloud Computing", *Intell. Automat. Soft Comput.,* vol. 24, no. 2, pp. 285-298, 2018.
[http://dx.doi.org/10.1080/10798587.2017.1280995]

[59]   K.N. Qureshi, A.H. Abdullah, and R.W. Anwar, "Wireless sensor based hybrid architecture for vehicular ad hoc networks", *TELKOMNIKA (Telecommunication Computing Electronics and*

Control), vol. 12, no. 4, pp. 942-949, 2014.
[http://dx.doi.org/10.12928/telkomnika.v12i4.537]

[60] C. Zhang, L. Zhu, C. Xu, X. Du, and M. Guizani, "A privacy-preserving traffic monitoring scheme *via* vehicular crowdsourcing", *Sensors (Basel),* vol. 19, no. 6, p. 1274, 2019.
[http://dx.doi.org/10.3390/s19061274] [PMID: 30871229]

[61] J. B. Villalba, "Using Ontologies and Intelligent Systems for Traffic Accident Assistance in Vehicular Environments", Universitat Politècnica de València. [Tesis doctoral], 2014.
[http://dx.doi.org/10.4995/Thesis/10251/39004]

[62] N. Zingirian, and M. Dalla Via, "Vehicular sinks over wide area wireless sensor networks for telemetry applications in logistics", *2019 7th International Conference on Future Internet of Things and Cloud (FiCloud), Istanbul, Turkey,* pp. 96-101, 2019.
[http://dx.doi.org/10.1109/FiCloud.2019.00021]

[63] P. Asuquo, H. Cruickshank, J. Morley, C.P.A. Ogah, A. Lei, W. Hathal, S. Bao, and Z. Sun, "Security and privacy in location-based services for vehicular and mobile communications: An overview, challenges, and countermeasures", *IEEE. Internet. Things. J.,* vol. 5, no. 6, pp. 4778-4802, 2018.
[http://dx.doi.org/10.1109/JIOT.2018.2820039]

[64] J. Pillmann, B. Sliwa, C. Kastin, and C. Wietfeld, "Empirical evaluation of predictive channel-aware transmission for resource efficient car-to-cloud communication", *2017 IEEE Vehicular Networking Conference (VNC),* IEEE, pp. 235-238, 2017.
[http://dx.doi.org/10.1109/VNC.2017.8275635]

[65] J. Vera-Pérez, D. Todolí-Ferrandis, S. Santonja-Climent, J. Silvestre-Blanes, and V. Sempere-Payá, "A joining procedure and synchronization for TSCH-RPL wireless sensor networks", *Sensors (Basel),* vol. 18, no. 10, p. 3556, 2018.
[http://dx.doi.org/10.3390/s18103556] [PMID: 30347821]

[66] G. Soni, and R. Sudhakar, "A L-IDS against dropping attack to secure and improve RPL performance in WSN aided IoT", *2020 7th International Conference on Signal Processing and Integrated Networks (SPIN), Noida, India,* pp. 377-383, 2020.
[http://dx.doi.org/10.1109/SPIN48934.2020.9071118]

[67] A. Vaibhav, D. Shukla, S. Das, S. Sahana, and P. Johri, "Security challenges, authentication, application and trust models for vehicular ad hoc network-a survey", *Int. J. Microw. Wirel. Technol.,* vol. 7, no. 3, pp. 36-48, 2017.
[http://dx.doi.org/10.5815/ijwmt.2017.03.04]

[68] F. Chen, Z. Zhao, G. Min, W. Gao, J. Chen, H. Duan, and P. Yang, "Speed control of mobile chargers serving wireless rechargeable networks", *Future Gener. Comput. Syst.,* vol. 80, pp. 242-249, 2018.
[http://dx.doi.org/10.1016/j.future.2016.12.011]

[69] C. Wu, T. Yoshinaga, Y. Ji, and Y. Zhang, "Computational intelligence inspired data delivery for vehicle-to-roadside communications", *IEEE Trans. Vehicular Technol.,* vol. 67, no. 12, pp. 12038-12048, 2018.
[http://dx.doi.org/10.1109/TVT.2018.2871606]

[70] Q. Liu, S. Kumar, and V. Mago, "Safernet: Safe transportation routing in the era of internet of vehicles and mobile crowd sensing", In: *14th IEEE Annual Consumer Communications & Networking Conference (CCNC)* IEEE, 2017, pp. 299-304.
[http://dx.doi.org/10.1109/CCNC.2017.7983123]

[71] T.M. Deng, and Y.Y. Sha, "Network Characteristics Analysis of Ad hoc Network for APTS", *Procedia Eng.,* vol. 29, pp. 3049-3053, 2012.
[http://dx.doi.org/10.1016/j.proeng.2012.01.438]

[72] R.O. Schoeneich, and P. Sadło, "Delay Tolerant Networks over Near Field Communications: The Automatic Multi-packet Communication", *Int. J. Comput. Commun. Control,* vol. 12, no. 5, pp. 704-714, 2017.

[http://dx.doi.org/10.15837/ijccc.2017.5.2942]

[73]   S. Zhang, Y. Liu, S. Li, Z. Tan, X. Zhao, and J. Zhou, "Fimpa: A fixed identity mapping prediction algorithm in edge computing environment", *IEEE Access,* vol. 8, pp. 17356-17365, 2020.
[http://dx.doi.org/10.1109/ACCESS.2020.2966399]

[74]   S.H. Ahmed, A.K. Bashir, and W. Guibene, "Introduction to the special section on emerging technologies for connected vehicles and ITS networks", *Comput. Electr. Eng.,* vol. 75, pp. 309-311, 2019.
[http://dx.doi.org/10.1016/j.compeleceng.2019.02.019]

[75]   D. Ludicke, and A. Lehner, "Train communication networks and prospects", *IEEE Commun. Mag.,* vol. 57, no. 9, pp. 39-43, 2019.
[http://dx.doi.org/10.1109/MCOM.001.1800957]

[76]   D. Gutiérrez-Reina, V. Sharma, I. You, and S. Toral, "Dissimilarity metric based on local neighboring information and genetic programming for data dissemination in vehicular ad hoc networks (VANETs)", *Sensors (Basel),* vol. 18, no. 7, p. 2320, 2018.
[http://dx.doi.org/10.3390/s18072320] [PMID: 30018267]

[77]   S. Vavassori, J. Soriano, D. Lizcano, and M. Jiménez, "Explicit context matching in content-based publish/subscribe systems", *Sensors (Basel),* vol. 13, no. 3, pp. 2945-2966, 2013.
[http://dx.doi.org/10.3390/s130302945] [PMID: 23529118]

[78]   M.A. Bernal, W.S. Cortés, and M.Á. Leguizamón, "MANET: Advantages, challenges and applications for education", *Sistemas y Telemática,* vol. 15, no. 43, pp. 45-63, 2017.
[http://dx.doi.org/10.18046/syt.v15i43.2764]

[79]   M.D. Phung, T.H. Dinh, and Q.P. Ha, "System architecture for real-time surface inspection using multiple UAVs", *IEEE Syst. J.,* vol. 14, no. 2, pp. 2925-2936, 2019.
[http://dx.doi.org/10.1109/JSYST.2019.2922290]

[80]   K. Sathish, R. Cv, M.N. Ab Wahab, R. Anbazhagan, G. Pau, and M.F. Akbar, "Underwater Wireless Sensor Networks Performance Comparison Utilizing Telnet and Superframe", *Sensors (Basel),* vol. 23, no. 10, p. 4844, 2023.
[http://dx.doi.org/10.3390/s23104844] [PMID: 37430763]

[81]   V.N. Soares, F. Farahmand, and J.J. Rodrigues, "A layered architecture for vehicular delay-tolerant networks", *2009 IEEE Symposium on Computers and Communications,* 2009pp. 122-127
[http://dx.doi.org/10.1109/ISCC.2009.5202332]

[82]   C. Chang, S.N. Srirama, and R. Buyya, "Mobile cloud business process management system for the internet of things: a survey", *ACM Comput. Surv.,* vol. 49, no. 4, pp. 1-42, 2017. [CSUR].
[http://dx.doi.org/10.1145/3012000]

[83]   R. Silva, and R. Iqbal, "Ethical implications of social internet of vehicles systems", *IEEE Internet Things J.,* vol. 6, no. 1, pp. 517-531, 2019.
[http://dx.doi.org/10.1109/JIOT.2018.2841969]

[84]   J.A. Stankovic, I. Lee, A. Mok, and R. Rajkumar, "Opportunities and obligations for physical computing systems", *Computer,* vol. 38, no. 11, pp. 23-31, 2005.
[http://dx.doi.org/10.1109/MC.2005.386]

[85]   E. De Poorter, P. Becue, I. Moerman, and P. Demeester, "Exploring a boundary-less cooperation approach for heterogeneous co-located networks", *2011 IEEE International Conference on Communications (ICC),* IEEE, pp. 1-6, 2011.
[http://dx.doi.org/10.1109/icc.2011.5963028]

[86]   Y. Geng, and C.G. Cassandras, "A new "smart parking" system infrastructure and implementation", *Procedia Soc. Behav. Sci.,* vol. 54, pp. 1278-1287, 2012.
[http://dx.doi.org/10.1016/j.sbspro.2012.09.842]

[87]   C. Westphal, "Opportunistic routing in dynamic ad hoc networks: The OPRAH protocol", *2006 IEEE*

International Conference on Mobile Ad Hoc and Sensor Systems, IEEE, pp. 570-573, 2006.
[http://dx.doi.org/10.1109/MOBHOC.2006.278612]

[88]   I.A. Rahardjo, R. Anggoro, and F.X. Arunanto, "Studi Kinerja 802.11 P pada Protokol Ad Hoc On-Demand Distance Vector (AODV) di Ling kungan Vehicular Ad Hoc Network (VANET) Menggunakan Network Simulator 2 (NS-2)", *J. Teknik ITS,* vol. 6, no. 1, pp. A50-A55, 2017.
[http://dx.doi.org/10.12962/j23373539.v6i1.21994]

[89]   N.E.H.B. Youssef, Y. Barouni, S. Khalfallah, J.B.H. Slama, and K.B. Driss, "Evaluating content-centric communication over power line communication infrastructure for smart grids", *Procedia Comput. Sci.,* vol. 73, pp. 217-225, 2015.
[http://dx.doi.org/10.1016/j.procs.2015.12.015]

[90]   I. Harris, Y. Wang, and H. Wang, "ICT in multimodal transport and technological trends: Unleashing potential for the future", *Int. J. Prod. Econ.,* vol. 159, pp. 88-103, 2015.
[http://dx.doi.org/10.1016/j.ijpe.2014.09.005]

[91]   V.J. Hodge, S. O'Keefe, M. Weeks, and A. Moulds, "Wireless sensor networks for condition monitoring in the railway industry: A survey", *IEEE Trans. Intell. Transp. Syst.,* vol. 16, no. 3, pp. 1088-1106, 20145, 2015.
[http://dx.doi.org/10.1109/TITS.2014.2366512]

[92]   A.H. Alahmadi, "Always Best Connected Mobile Sensor Network to Support High Accuracy Internet of Farming", *Comp. Eng. Appl. J.,* vol. 6, no. 2, pp. 51-58, 2017.
[http://dx.doi.org/10.18495/comengapp.v6i2.202]

[93]   M. Erritali, O.M. Reda, and B.E. Ouahidi, "A Contribution to Secure the Routing Protocol Greedy Perimeter Stateless Routing Using a Symmetric Signature-Based AES and MD5 Hash", *Int. J. Distributed. Parallel. System (IJDPS),* vol. 2, no. 5, 2011.
[http://dx.doi.org/10.5121/ijdps.2011.2509]

[94]   S.V. Ragavan, K. Haider, and M. Shanmugavel, "Healthcare telematics service implementation using OSGi framework", *Procedia Comput. Sci.,* vol. 42, pp. 168-174, 2014.
[http://dx.doi.org/10.1016/j.procs.2014.11.048]

[95]   R.A. Osman, X.H. Peng, and M.A. Omar, "Adaptive cooperative communications for enhancing QoS in vehicular networks", *Phys. Commun.,* vol. 34, pp. 285-294, 2019.
[http://dx.doi.org/10.1016/j.phycom.2018.08.008]

[96]   Y. Cao, O. Kaiwartya, N. Aslam, C. Han, X. Zhang, Y. Zhuang, and M. Dianati, "A trajectory-driven opportunistic routing protocol for VCPS", *IEEE Trans. Aerosp. Electron. Syst.,* vol. 54, no. 6, pp. 2628-2642, 2018.
[http://dx.doi.org/10.1109/TAES.2018.2826201]

[97]   T. Qiu, X. Liu, K. Li, Q. Hu, A.K. Sangaiah, and N. Chen, "Community-aware data propagation with small world feature for internet of vehicles", *IEEE Commun. Mag.,* vol. 56, no. 1, pp. 86-91, 2018.
[http://dx.doi.org/10.1109/MCOM.2018.1700511]

[98]   S.Y. Huang, S.S. Chen, M.X. Chen, Y.C. Chang, and H.C. Chao, "The Efficient Mobile Management Based on Metaheuristic Algorithm for Internet of Vehicle", *Sensors (Basel),* vol. 22, no. 3, p. 1140, 2022.
[http://dx.doi.org/10.3390/s22031140] [PMID: 35161884]

[99]   T. Kayarga, and A.K. S, "Improving QoS in Internet of Vehicles Integrating Swarm Intelligence Guided Topology Adaptive Routing and Service Differentiated Flow Control", *Int. J. Adv. Comput. Sci. Appl.,* vol. 14, no. 4, 2023.
[http://dx.doi.org/10.14569/IJACSA.2023.0140448]

[100] I. De la Iglesia, U. Hernandez-Jayo, E. Osaba, and R. Carballedo, "Smart bandwidth assignation in an underlay cellular network for internet of vehicles", *Sensors (Basel),* vol. 17, no. 10, p. 2217, 2017.
[http://dx.doi.org/10.3390/s17102217] [PMID: 28953256]

[101] F. Aadil, W. Ahsan, Z.U. Rehman, P.A. Shah, S. Rho, and I. Mehmood, "Clustering algorithm for internet of vehicles (IoV) based on dragonfly optimizer (CAVDO)", *J. Supercomput.,* vol. 74, no. 9, pp. 4542-4567, 2018.
[http://dx.doi.org/10.1007/s11227-018-2305-x]

[102] G.K. Ijemaru, L.M. Ang, and K.P. Seng, "Swarm Intelligence Internet of Vehicles Approaches for Opportunistic Data Collection and Traffic Engineering in Smart City Waste Management", *Sensors (Basel),* vol. 23, no. 5, p. 2860, 2023.
[http://dx.doi.org/10.3390/s23052860] [PMID: 36905062]

[103] D. Gupta, and R. Rathi, "A Novel Metaheuristic Approach for Efficient Data Dissemination based on Ideal Decision in VANET", *2023 6th International Conference on Information Systems and Computer Networks (ISCON), Mathura, India,* pp. 1-7, 2023.
[http://dx.doi.org/10.1109/ISCON57294.2023.10112005]

[104] C.M. Chen, Z. Li, S. Kumari, G. Srivastava, K. Lakshmanna, and T.R. Gadekallu, "A provably secure key transfer protocol for the fog-enabled Social Internet of Vehicles based on a confidential computing environment", *Vehicular Communications,* vol. 39, p. 100567, 2023.
[http://dx.doi.org/10.1016/j.vehcom.2022.100567]

[105] F. Miri, A. Javadpour, F. Ja'fari, A.K. Sangaiah, and R. Pazzi, "Improving resources in internet of vehicles transportation systems using markov transition and TDMA protocol", *in IEEE Transactions on Intelligent Transportation Systems,* vol. 24, no. 11, pp. 13050-13067, 2023.

[106] H.H. Cho, W.C. Chien, F.H. Tseng, and H.C. Chao, "Artificial-Intelligence-Based Charger Deployment in Wireless Rechargeable Sensor Networks", *Future. Internet.,* vol. 15, no. 3, p. 117, 2023.
[http://dx.doi.org/10.3390/fi15030117]

[107] P.S. Mann, S.D. Panchal, and S. Singh, "Energy-efficient clustering protocol for IoT-based unmanned aerial vehicles", In: *Intelligent Green Communication Network for Internet of Things.* CRC Press, 2023, pp. 141-153.
[http://dx.doi.org/10.1201/9781003371526-9]

CHAPTER 4

Federated Learning in Secure and Reliable Systems for IoVs

Umang Kant[1,*] and **Prachi Dahiya**[2]

[1] *Department of CSE-AIML, KIET Group of Institutions, Ghaziabad, UP, India*

[2] *Department of CSE, Delhi Technological University, Delhi, India*

Abstract: The Internet of Vehicles (IoV) is an emerging technology that allows vehicles to communicate with each other and with the infrastructure around them. This technology has the potential to revolutionize the transportation industry, but it also raises concerns about the security of the data that is shared among vehicles, with their base stations and infrastructure.

In this context, secure data-sharing methodologies are essential to protect sensitive information, such as location, driving patterns, data of the people travelling in the vehicle, and protection of shared data from malicious factors. This chapter explores some of the methods that can be used for secure data sharing in the IoV. One approach is to use encryption and decryption techniques to protect data in transit and at rest. This method involves encoding the data in a way that only authorized parties can access it, and decoding it when it reaches its destination. Another approach is to use blockchain technology, which provides a decentralized and immutable ledger that can be used to store and verify data. Additionally, access control mechanisms, such as role-based access control, can be used to limit the access of different users to specific data sets. This method ensures that only authorized parties can access sensitive data.

In conclusion, secure data-sharing methodologies are crucial for the successful implementation of the IoV. Encryption and decryption, blockchain technology, and access control mechanisms are some of the methods that can be used to protect sensitive information and maintain the privacy and security of the data.

Keywords: Blockchain, Heterogeneity, Internet of things, Machine learning, Scalability.

INTRODUCTION

Federated learning is a machine learning technique that enables multiple devices to collaboratively train a shared model while keeping their data decentralized and

* **Corresponding author Umang Kant:** Department of CSE-AIML, KIET Group of Institutions, Ghaziabad, UP, India; E-mail: umang.kant@gmail.com

Shelly Gupta, Puneet Garg, Jyoti Agarwal, Hardeo Kumar Thakur & Satya Prakash Yadav (Eds.)

private. In this approach, the data remains on individual devices, and only model updates are shared with a central server as shown in Fig. (**1**). Federated learning has gained a lot of attention in recent years as it offers several benefits, including privacy-preserving machine learning, reduced data transfer, and increased scalability. In the context of the Internet of Vehicles (IoVs), federated learning can be used to build intelligent systems that enable vehicles to learn from the data collected from various sources, including sensors, cameras, and other IoT devices. IoVs can generate vast amounts of data, and the ability to learn from this data can significantly improve the performance of vehicles, such as better routing, energy efficiency, and driver assistance [1, 2].

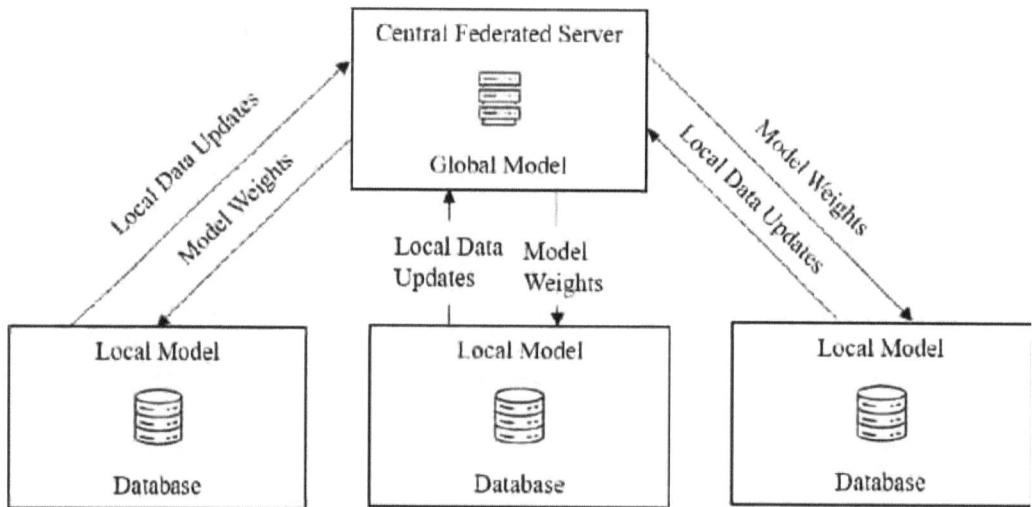

Fig. (1). Collaborated model training using federated learning.

One of the key benefits of federated learning in the context of IoVs is that it allows multiple vehicles to train a shared model while preserving the privacy of their data. This can be especially useful in scenarios where data privacy is critical, such as location tracking, driving behavior analysis, and accident prediction. By enabling vehicles to learn from each other's data without sharing it directly, federated learning can help create more intelligent and efficient systems while ensuring the privacy of individuals' data. The Internet of Vehicles (IoV), as shown in Fig. (**2**), refers to the interconnectedness of vehicles, road infrastructure, and other entities in the transportation system [3]. With the growing number of connected vehicles, the need for secure and reliable systems is becoming increasingly important. The reason is that insecure and unreliable systems in IoV can lead to accidents, loss of life, and financial losses. For example, hackers could compromise the system and gain control of a vehicle, resulting in an accident [4, 5].

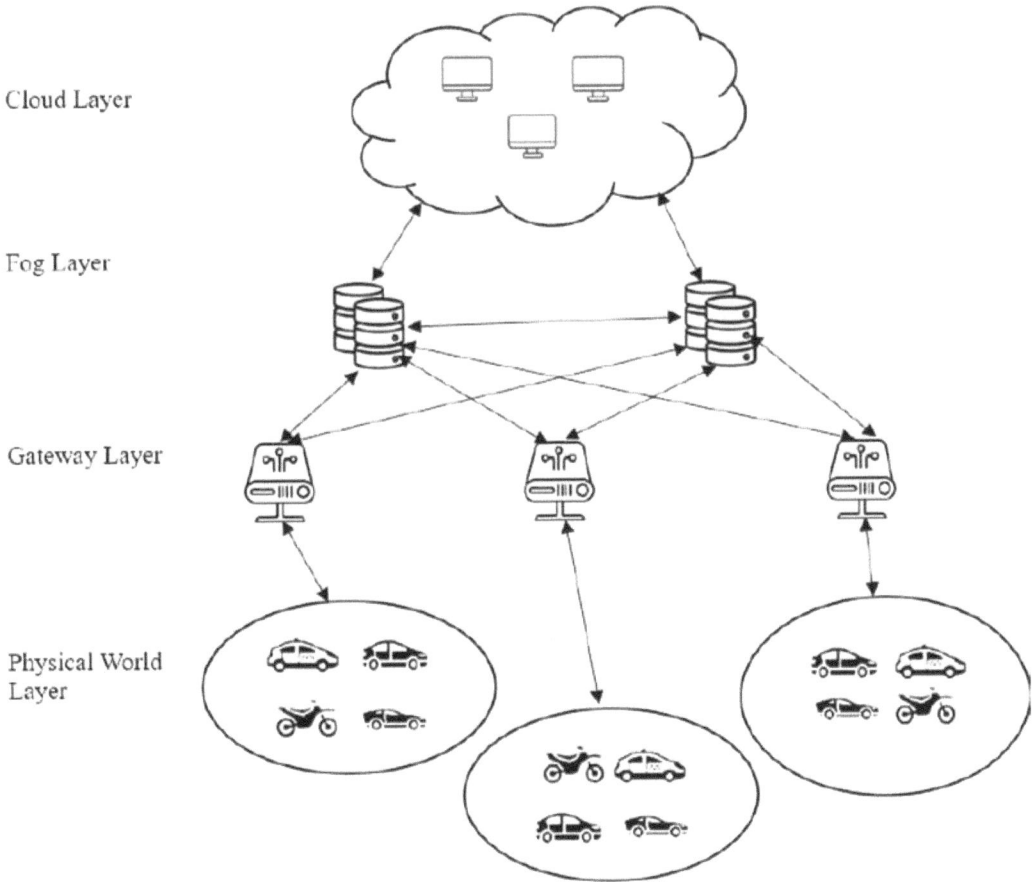

Fig. (2). IoV architecture.

Federated learning is a technique used in machine learning that allows multiple parties to train a shared model without sharing their data. Instead of sending data to a central server for processing, data remains on local devices and is only used to update the shared model. This approach can help address the security and privacy concerns in IoV systems. By using federated learning, the data remains on local devices, reducing the risk of data breaches. Additionally, since data is not being sent to a central server, there is less risk of a single point of failure that could compromise the entire system. Furthermore, federated learning allows the system to learn from multiple sources, resulting in a more accurate and robust model [6, 7].

Federated Learning has emerged as a viable solution to address the privacy concerns associated with traditional machine learning techniques, such as Automated Machine Learning. While these advanced technologies offer numerous benefits to organizations across sectors, the adoption of such approaches often requires granting third-party access to valuable business ecosystems and databases, raising significant privacy considerations. This obstacle has led many companies to hesitate when considering outsourcing machine learning tasks. However, Federated Learning presents a potential remedy to these concerns. Conventional machine learning methods typically rely on a centralized data centre or server where local datasets are uploaded for training models. In contrast, Federated Learning enables multiple entities to collaboratively construct a robust machine learning model while retaining their training data on their respective servers. Essentially, Federated Learning allows for model training without necessitating the sharing of data with a central computational node. Consequently, companies can create a shared model that mitigates critical issues surrounding data privacy, security, and access rights [8].

By employing Federated Learning, organizations can retain control over their data and avoid transmitting sensitive information to a central location. This decentralized approach minimizes the risks associated with data breaches and unauthorized access. As the raw data remains locally stored, privacy and security concerns are significantly reduced. Moreover, Federated Learning also provides a resolution to challenges related to data access rights. In situations where legal or contractual obligations restrict data sharing, Federated Learning enables collaborative model development without violating data governance rules. Participants can implement their access controls, deciding which parts of the model or aggregated information are shared. Federated Learning facilitates collaboration and knowledge sharing in machine learning tasks by amalgamating the collective knowledge of multiple actors while preserving data privacy. It opens up possibilities for organizations across various sectors to harness the power of machine learning while upholding the confidentiality of their data [9, 10]. However, it is important to acknowledge that Federated Learning is not a universally applicable solution. It introduces its own set of challenges, including communication overhead, data heterogeneity, and ensuring fairness among participants. Nonetheless, ongoing research and advancements in Federated Learning techniques aim to address these challenges, enhancing the effectiveness and efficiency of this approach.

This chapter covers the basic fundamentals of federated learning in the introduction section, as discussed above. Further sections of the chapter can be divided into the benefits and limitations of federated learning. The role of federated learning in providing a secure and reliable system of IoV along with various use cases is discussed in detail. A case study on federated learning on anomaly detection in autonomous vehicles is presented. The last section covers the conclusion and future scope of the study.

FEDERATED LEARNING: FUNDAMENTALS AND CHALLENGES

As discussed in the above section, federated learning is a distributed machine learning approach that allows multiple parties to collaboratively train a model without sharing their data [11]. Instead of sending data to a central server for processing, the data remains on local devices and is only used to update the shared model. Federated learning works as follows (Fig. **3**).

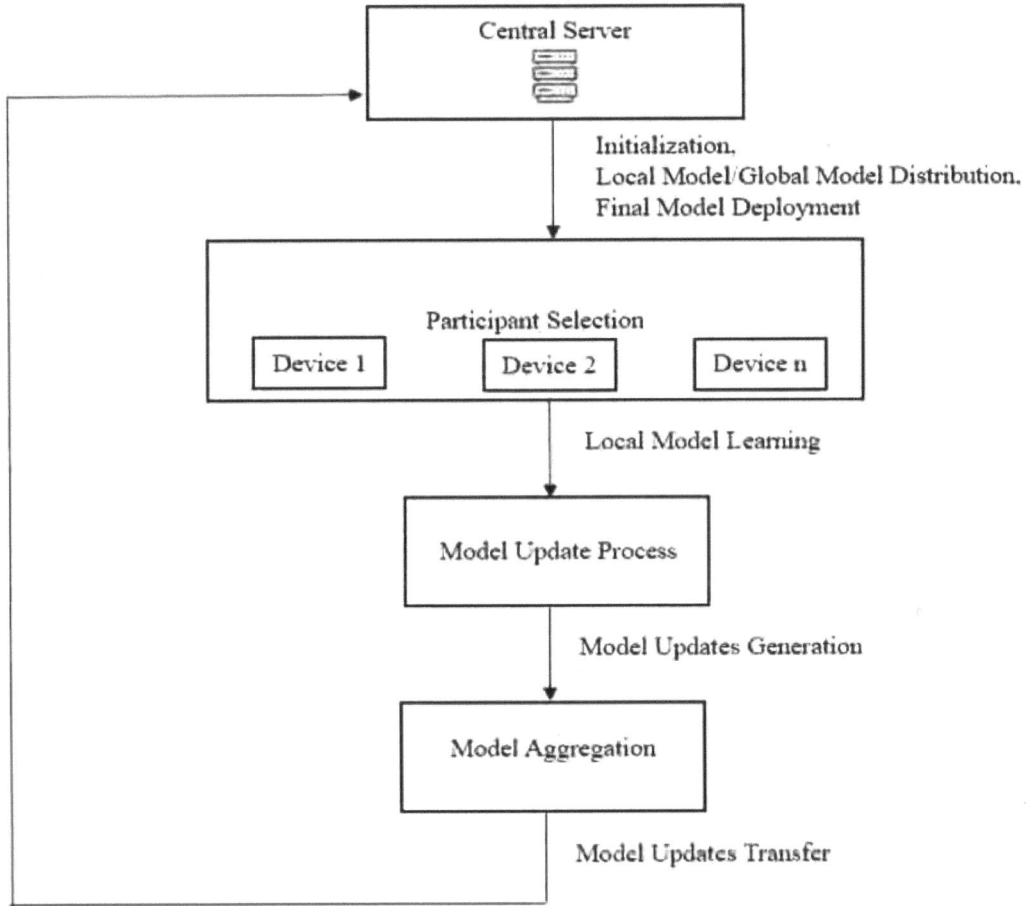

Fig. (3). Fundamentals of federated learning.

Initialization

A central server or coordinator initializes the Federated Learning process by defining the architecture of the model to be trained. This can be a neural network or any other machine learning model suitable for the task at hand.

Participant Selection

The central server selects a set of participants, which can be individual devices (*e.g.*, smartphones, IoT devices) or organizations, that will contribute to the training process. These participants typically have local datasets that they want to use for the model.

Local Model Training

Each participant downloads the initial model from the central server and performs local model training using their local dataset. The training process can follow any conventional machine-learning technique specific to the participant's data.

Model Update

Once local training is complete, participants generate a model update by fine-tuning the initial model using their local dataset. The update consists of the changes made to the model's parameters based on the participant's training data.

Model Aggregation

The participants securely send their model updates (not the raw data) back to the central server. The server then aggregates these updates, typically through techniques like weighted averaging or federated averaging, to create a consolidated global model.

Iterative Training

The central server distributes the updated global model to the participants, who repeat the process of local model training and generating model updates. This iterative training process continues for a defined number of rounds or until convergence is achieved.

Model Deployment

Once the training is completed, the final global model is obtained. It can be used by the central server for downstream tasks or distributed to participants for deployment on their local devices or systems.

Federated Learning ensures that the raw data remains on the local devices or servers of participants, addressing privacy and security concerns. Only model updates or aggregated information are shared, minimizing the risk of exposing sensitive data [12]. Additionally, privacy-preserving techniques like encryption and differential privacy can be employed to further enhance data security during the model aggregation process. By leveraging the collective knowledge of multiple participants while preserving data privacy, Federated Learning allows organizations to benefit from collaborative machine learning without compromising sensitive data training. The working of federated learning, as shown in Fig. (**3**) is also depicted in Fig. (**4**) in section 5.

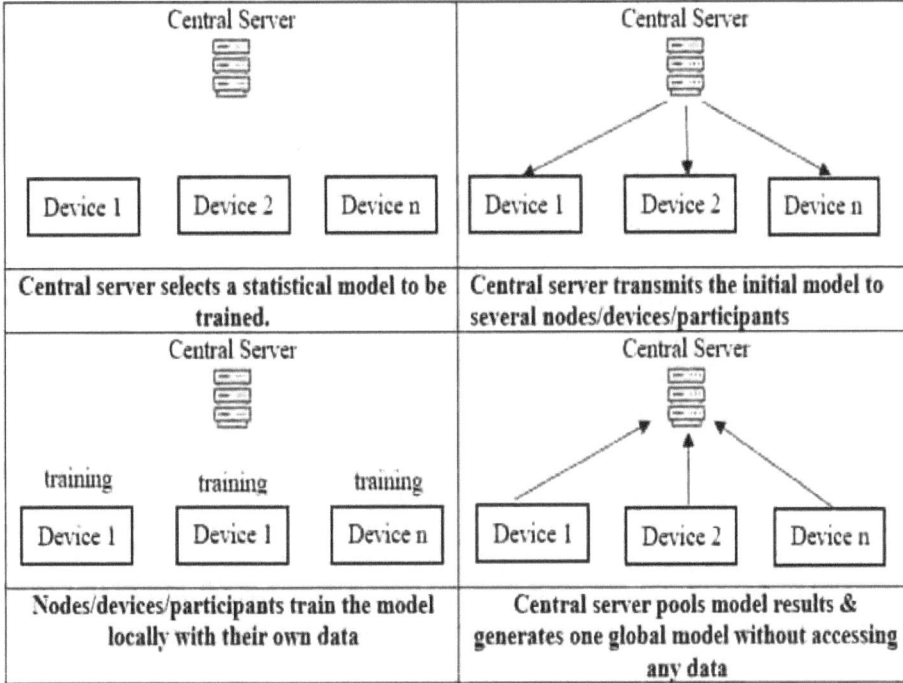

Central Server	Central Server
Device 1 Device 2 Device n	Device 1 Device 2 Device n
Central server selects a statistical model to be trained.	**Central server transmits the initial model to several nodes/devices/participants**
Central Server	Central Server
training training training Device 1 Device 1 Device n	Device 1 Device 2 Device n
Nodes/devices/participants train the model locally with their own data	**Central server pools model results & generates one global model without accessing any data**

Fig. (4). Working of Federated Learning.

Advantages of Federated Learning

Privacy

Since data remains on local devices, federated learning reduces the risk of data breaches and preserves user privacy.

Efficiency

Federated learning allows models to be trained on distributed data, reducing the need for large amounts of centralized computing resources.

Scalability

Federated learning can scale to large numbers of devices, making it suitable for IoT and edge computing applications.

Robustness

Federated learning can improve the robustness of machine learning models by learning from diverse data sources.

Limitations of Federated Learning

Communication Overhead

Federated learning requires devices to communicate with the server, which can be a bottleneck for large numbers of devices or slow network connections.

Heterogeneous Data

Federated learning assumes that data on all devices is representative of the same distribution. However, if the data is highly heterogeneous, it can negatively impact model performance.

Security

Federated learning relies on trusting the participating devices to accurately train the model, which can be a challenge in adversarial settings.

Federated Learning is particularly useful in the context of the Internet of Vehicles (IoVs), where a large number of devices with diverse data sources are connected to the Internet. However, there are several challenges and issues associated with implementing federated learning in IoVs:

Data Heterogeneity

IoVs are composed of a wide range of devices that produce different types of data, such as images, videos, and sensor readings. This data heterogeneity can make it challenging to develop a model that can accurately capture the patterns in the data from all devices. Additionally, some devices may have limited computational resources, which can affect the quality of the local models and slow down the training process [13].

Privacy Concerns

Privacy is a critical concern in IoVs since many of the data collected by these devices are highly sensitive, such as location data and personal information. Federated learning addresses this issue by allowing local devices to keep their data on their own devices, but there is still the potential for privacy breaches.

For example, a malicious actor could potentially intercept the communication between the local devices and the central server and gain access to sensitive data.

Communication Overhead

Federated learning involves a significant amount of communication between the local devices and the central server. This communication overhead can be a major bottleneck, particularly in IoVs, where devices may be connected to the internet through low-bandwidth, high-latency connections. Additionally, the communication overhead can consume a significant amount of energy, which can drain the batteries of the devices.

Model Aggregation

The central server needs to aggregate the local models from all devices to create a global model. However, this process can be challenging since the local models may have different statistical properties and require different weighting to achieve optimal performance. Additionally, the central server needs to ensure that the aggregated model is secure and not susceptible to malicious attacks [14].

While federated learning has the potential to enable collaborative training of machine learning models in IoVs, several challenges and issues need to be addressed to ensure that the approach is effective and secure as discussed above. Addressing these challenges will require significant research and development efforts from the scientific community. Table **1** below discusses the comparison of recent federated learning techniques.

Table 1. Comparison of recent federated learning techniques.

Refs No.	Title	Description	Merits	Demerits
[15]	Security of Internet of Things (IoT) using federated learning and deep learning — Recent advancements, issues and prospects	It discusses the traffic flow prediction with the help of spatio-temporal correlation. The data is trained locally and a mechanism called federated graph convolutional network (FedGCN) is used here on the server side of the model. The average of the local models is estimated in this and then the results are shown.	A budget for privacy loss is already set at the start of the training of the model with increased data privacy .	Enhanced data privacy is the goal of the proposed model is there.

(Table 1) cont.....

Refs No.	Title	Description	Merits	Demerits
[16]	Real-time End-to-End Federated Learning: An Automotive Case Study.	Federated learning is used as a training model over here which helps in increasing the vehicle acceleration feature. Here, federated learning is compiled with a real-time model aggregation protocol. Different functions of the vehicle are explored here like steering wheel angle prediction and several other approaches that can be used here.	Proposed model has strength, better prediction accuracy and performance, ;less communication overhead along with high efficiency. Cost-effectiveness is there.	This is a time-consuming model as the training of datasets takes time, and prediction also takes time.
[17]	Federated Learning for improved prediction of failures in Autonomous Guided Vehicles	This paper works on signal prediction accuracy with an improved federated learning model that is used in autonomous vehicles. Global prediction models are used along with real time datasets provided by different companies. It works on distributed datasets and information along with an operational environment. The decentralized approaches are used here that prove to be good in synchronization environments with real data.	The proposed model provides better efficiency and better signal prediction accuracy is there.	The real-time datasets are used here, not publicly available ones so it becomes difficult to see the recent trends and changes in the data. Enlarged datasets are not used here.
[18]	A Decentralized Federated Learning Approach for Connected Autonomous Vehicles	Bloackchain-based federated learning system is used here for data privacy and vehicular network communication is used here. Vehicle Machine Learning (oVML) models are used here which work without a centralized dataset. Parameters like transmission limit, the performance of the system, block size, *etc.* are used here. End-to-end delay is to be eliminated here by the usage of oVML systems.	Optimal block arrival rates with communication, consensus delays, *etc.* are the advantages here along with efficient communication.	Only centralized datasets are used here with only a certain number of parameters as compared to other techniques.

(Table 1) cont.....

Refs No.	Title	Description	Merits	Demerits
[19]	Towards Federated Learning in UAV-Enabled Internet of Vehicles: A Multi-Dimensional Contract-Matching Approach	This paper proposes an enhanced Deep Learning and Artificial Intelligence model as a collaborative learning scheme for the Internet of Vehicles (IoVs). Service providers for such models are based on data collection for Drones As A Service (DaaS) which is a term developed in recent years. A multi-dimensional model is formed such that the UAVs with the lowest cost are assigned to the different sub regions.	This is a low-cost model and provides efficient results as compared to different prevalent techniques. Privacy-preservasion of the dataset is done through collaborative models.	Adoption of wireless techniques is still required in such models which preserve energy. Wireless charging services need to be considered along with the mobility of the vehicles in the subregions.

SECURITY AND PRIVACY CONCERNS IN IOV

This section aims to highlight the security and privacy concerns with respect to IoV. There is a need to focus on these aspects [20] so that a secure system can be achieved.

Threats and Vulnerabilities in IoV Systems

IoV systems face various threats and vulnerabilities that can compromise their security. Some common threats include:

Vehicle-to-vehicle (V2V) and Vehicle-to-infrastructure (V2I) Attacks

Attackers can exploit communication channels between vehicles and infrastructure to intercept, manipulate [21], or forge messages. This can lead to malicious actions like false traffic information, unauthorized access to vehicles, or even causing accidents.

Malware and Remote Attacks

Malicious software can infect the IoV ecosystem through compromised devices, such as infotainment systems or telematics units. These attacks can result in unauthorized control of vehicles, data theft, or disruptions to critical systems.

Data Integrity and Authenticity

The integrity and authenticity of data exchanged within IoV systems can be compromised, leading to false information propagation, unauthorized access [22] to sensitive data, or tampering with safety-critical functions.

Physical Attacks

Physical tampering with vehicles or infrastructure components can also pose security risks. For example, attackers can physically connect to a vehicle's diagnostic port to manipulate its functionalities.

Privacy Concerns and Data Protection in IoV

Privacy is a significant concern in IoV systems due to the collection and processing of vast amounts of personal data. Some key privacy considerations include:

Location Privacy

IoV systems collect location information, which can be used to track individuals' movements and habits [23]. This raises concerns about unauthorized surveillance and potential misuse of personal information.

Personal Identifiable Information (PII)

IoV systems gather PII, such as driver profiles, contact details, and vehicle identification numbers. The storage, transmission, and access control of this data need to be carefully managed to prevent unauthorized access and identity theft.

Data Sharing and Aggregation

IoV systems often involve sharing data among multiple entities, such as service providers [24], manufacturers, and infrastructure operators. Ensuring proper consent, anonymization, and secure data-sharing mechanisms is crucial to protect privacy.

User Consent and Transparency

Users should have clear visibility into the data collected by IoV systems, how it is used, and the ability to provide informed consent for data processing activities.

Secure Communication Protocols for IoV

Secure communication protocols are essential for protecting the integrity, confidentiality, and authenticity of data transmitted [25] within IoV systems. Some considerations include:

Authentication and Access Control

Robust authentication mechanisms should be in place to verify the identities of communicating entities, including vehicles, infrastructure components, and remote servers. Access control mechanisms should restrict unauthorized access to sensitive functionalities.

Encryption and Secure Channels

Data exchanged in IoV systems should be encrypted using strong encryption algorithms. Secure channels, such as Transport Layer Security (TLS), should be utilized to prevent eavesdropping and data manipulation.

Intrusion Detection and Prevention Systems

Implementing intrusion detection and prevention systems can help detect and mitigate potential attacks in real time, ensuring the security of the communication channels.

Over-the-air Updates

Secure protocols should be employed for over-the-air updates of vehicle software and firmware to prevent tampering and ensure the integrity of updates.

Secure Messaging and Event Logging

Secure messaging protocols and robust event logging mechanisms enable traceability and forensic analysis in case of security incidents or breaches.

These considerations form the foundation for addressing security and privacy concerns in IoV systems. Implementing appropriate security measures [26], including encryption, authentication, access control, and intrusion detection, is vital to ensure the safety and trustworthiness of IoV environments while protecting the privacy of users' data.

SECURE AND RELIABLE SYSTEMS FOR IOVS

IoV (Internet of Vehicles) is a rapidly growing field that aims to connect vehicles to the Internet and create a network of vehicles that can communicate with each other and with other devices. However, with this increased connectivity comes an increased [27] risk of security threats and the need for secure and reliable systems. Here are the key features of secure and reliable systems for IoVs:

Data Encryption

Data encryption is the process of converting plaintext data into ciphertext, which can only be decrypted using a secret key. Data encryption is an essential feature of secure and reliable systems for IoVs, as it helps to protect sensitive information from unauthorized access or theft.

Access Control

Access control is the process of controlling who has access to a system or a particular piece of data. Access control is crucial for IoVs, as it helps to ensure that only authorized users can access sensitive information and perform certain actions.

Fault Tolerance

Fault tolerance is the ability of a system to continue operating even in the presence of faults or errors. In the context of IoVs, fault tolerance is essential to ensure that the system can continue to operate even if a particular vehicle or device fails.

Reliability

Reliability is the ability of a system to consistently perform a given task without failure. In the context of IoVs, reliability is critical to ensure that the system can perform its functions accurately and consistently.

Secure and reliable systems for IoVs must include data encryption, access control, fault tolerance, and reliability to ensure the safety and security of the network and its users.

Federated learning is a machine learning technique used in IoVs that enables multiple vehicles to collaborate and share data to build a shared machine learning model. However, this approach poses several challenges in terms of privacy, security, and performance. The key features of secure and reliable systems can help address these challenges and enhance the performance and security of federated learning in IoVs. In summary, the key features of secure and reliable systems can help address the challenges of federated learning in IoVs by enhancing the privacy, security, and performance of the system. By using data encryption, access control, fault tolerance, and reliability, the system can be designed to be more secure, reliable, and effective, making it an ideal solution for IoVs.

ARCHITECTURE AND COMPONENTS OF FEDERATED LEARNING IN IOV

This section elaborates on the architecture and components of federated learning in the Internet of Vehicles [28] (IoV):

The high-level architecture of a federated learning system for IoV typically consists of the following components:

Edge Devices

Edge devices in IoV, such as vehicles or roadside units, act as data sources and participate in the federated learning process. They collect and preprocess data from various sensors, such as cameras, lidar, GPS, and vehicle diagnostics. Edge devices have computational capabilities to perform local model training and contribute to the federated learning process.

Central Server

The central server acts as the coordinating entity in the federated learning system. It manages the overall federated learning process, including model distribution, aggregation, and coordination of edge devices' participation. The central server maintains the global model, facilitates secure model updates, and coordinates the training process across multiple edge devices.

Data Aggregation

Data aggregation is a critical step in federated learning. Edge devices train local models using their respective [29] data and send the model updates to the central server for aggregation. Aggregation techniques such as federated averaging or secure aggregation are applied to merge the model updates from multiple devices into a global model, which is then shared back with the edge devices.

In Fig. (**4**) shown above, the central server is depicted at the top, maintaining the global model. The edge devices (Device 1, Device 2, Device 3, up to Edge Device n) are connected to the central server. Each edge device has its own local model and collects data from various sensors in the IoV environment. During the federated learning process, the edge devices train their local models using their respective data. These devices are the data sources in IoV systems, equipped with sensors and computational capabilities. They collect data from various sources, preprocess it, and train local models using federated learning techniques. Edge devices play a crucial role in preserving data privacy since data typically remains on the device, and only model updates are shared. The central server coordinates the federated learning process. It receives local model updates from edge devices, aggregates them to create a global model, and distributes the updated global model back to the devices. The central server ensures synchronization, manages the training process, and applies appropriate security measures for secure model updates. The trained local models are then sent to the central server as model updates. The central server applies aggregation techniques, such as federated averaging or secure aggregation, to combine the model updates and generate an updated global model. Data aggregation techniques are used to merge local model updates from edge devices into a global model. Federated averaging is a commonly used technique where model updates are weighted and averaged to create a new global model. Secure aggregation techniques, such as secure multi-party computation (MPC) or homomorphic encryption, are employed to preserve data privacy during the aggregation process. This updated global model is then shared back with the edge devices, and the process continues iteratively. This architecture enables collaborative learning while preserving data privacy since the data remains on edge devices, and only model updates are exchanged. The central server acts as the coordinator, managing the training process, aggregating [30] the models, and facilitating secure model updates.

Further, communication protocols and data exchange mechanisms play a vital role in federated learning for IoV. Some of the protocol considerations include:

Secure Communication

Secure communication protocols, such as Transport Layer Security (TLS), are used to ensure secure and encrypted communication between edge devices and the central server. This protects against eavesdropping and tampering of data during transmission.

Data Exchange Mechanisms

Data exchange mechanisms should be designed to minimize the transmission of raw data while enabling the sharing of model updates. Differential privacy techniques can be employed to add noise to the local model updates, preserving privacy while still allowing useful information to be shared.

Synchronization and Timing

Efficient synchronization and timing mechanisms are crucial in federated learning for IoV. Edge devices need to coordinate their training cycles with the central ser ver to ensure timely model updates and avoid disruptions to the overall federated learning process.

These components, along with secure communication protocols [31] and efficient data exchange mechanisms, form the foundation of a federated learning system for IoV. The architecture enables collaboration between edge devices and the central server while preserving data privacy and ensuring secure and reliable model updates for improved performance and intelligence in the IoV ecosystem.

FEDERATED LEARNING IN SECURE AND RELIABLE SYSTEMS FOR IOVS: USE CASES

Use cases are methodologies that help various federated learning techniques to identify, analyse, organize the data provided by the different system requirements provided in a particular application. The use cases develop the sequences of different interactions set up among users and systems in an autonomous environment related to an oblique set of goals in the future. These use cases make [32] and create a document that describes the steps that are taken by the user in order to reach the desired goal. Use cases also maintain the planning system requirements, software prototypes, training and testing, validating the testing software and creating an outline for the user help manual. These manuals developed by the use cases help the users to understand and identify the errors present in the software prototype that can occur during the implementation phase and to resolve them as soon as possible.

Some criteria are formed in order to select adequate use cases for the proper usage of datasets through federated learning. Some are given below:

Right Data for an Efficient Model

Before implementing the model, one should know the type of data to be used and analysed in order to improve the model. There should be a way in order to eliminate the biased data and as with the biased data, to reach the right solution is quite impossible. Hence, diverse datasets must be chosen which can easily represent the diverse and big population.

Federated Learning Use Case

Personalized datasets [33] should be used for machine learning practices depending upon the application, software, and business products to be used, in healthcare. This is why the personalization of the datasets are important for machine learning.

Not Enough Datasets for a Model

Sometimes, the personalized data that is provided for a model is not enough to get the desired output and objectives and hence, this data provided by the use case is not accurate for goals. At times, accurate data is important for a model.

Hence, a project should meet each and every requirement [34] mentioned above for the federated learning. There are different use cases in federated learning in IoVs. Some of them are discussed below:

Steering Wheel Angle Prediction Use Case

Road images and videos are used in order to predict the steering wheel angle along with the pixel information which shows that a neural network is able to predict the wheel position by using image pixel values. Advanced methods [35] like convolutional long short-term memory (C-LSTM), use both visual and dynamic dependencies of the driving of vehicles. Deep learning neural networks directly predict the steering wheel angles and monitor the steering wheel prediction which captures human behaviour and it gave the concept of end-to-end learning in federated learning. This kind of model uses the real time behaviour of the factors of federated learning taken into account. No new information of the traffic or of the vehicle route or the road marking detection, semantic analysis, *etc.* are required by the convolutional network in order to predict the position of the steering wheel. A robust model is required in order to enhance the model prediction and detection accuracy. A two part stream model is required to make the model robust and this model uses lower training cost as compared to traditional methods. Federated learning is used to accelerate the speed of the training, which boosts the model quality and spreads global awareness among all the vehicles.

Predictive Maintenance of the Vehicle Use Case

In IoVs, sensitive data of the vehicles is collected from the sensors present in the vehicle like camera, temperature, speed, location, *etc.* for the need of associative analysis. A lot of decisions can be taken with the data generated from these sensors for efficient path decision, traffic prediction or autonomous driving, *etc.* The traditional methods of federated learning require a central server system [36] and a lot of machine learning and deep learning techniques to train the model and to analyse the data. As the data is increasing day by day and it becomes difficult to collect and organise all the data at the central server of the model. Data security, low bandwidth issues, and asymmetric computation power issues are also there while collecting the data.

Above mentioned are the limitations for vehicle maintenance for which different federated learning methods are proposed by different researchers to address the transmission problems, and security concerns and ensure that the proper security is provided for the data along with less overhead. Learned gradients are used in different approaches so that the security of data is ensured as these approaches do not use actual data but a copy which reduces the amount of data also that is to be shared. Multilayer perceptron is used for training and testing of data in federated learning. Some techniques utilize new Mobile Edge Computing (MEC), which uses different resource-sharing techniques to use them in an efficient manner in edge computing for IoVs. The central server system uses its cloud in order to process the data and takes on necessary decisions on the complete processing of the data. Higher communication capabilities are required in order to collect the whole data and to perform in global standard situations.

Google uses a fresh approach in order to deal with a large amount of data in federated learning and there is a data security requirement of generated data. Multiple participants can easily participate in and contribute to data in the developing model and the participants can share the data which will help in resolving [37] the privacy issue of the data. Unexplored data can also be accessed by the participants. Federated learning provides an experience of distributed learning to all the participants. They can train their individual data and parameters in the neural network which improves security as well as the privacy of the system and data. This will help in the modelling of a pseudo centralized system which will help in the training of neural networks along with its security improvement and privacy. At times, it becomes hard for federated learning to implement generated data with limitations in computation and communication.

A lot of problems can be resolved using federated learning such as the communication overhead is reduced. Dynamic variations are observed in vehicular traffic and that is the reason federated learning is used. Vehicles have high mobility speed, prediction is also dynamic, weather events [38] are unpredictable at times and all these conditions lead to the dynamic behaviour of the traffic. These kinds of challenges are faced by researchers and that is why federated learning comes into play. Gradient component computation is required as the processing power of the vehicles is very slow and that is the reason federated learning is required to increase the computation overhead on the end of the vehicle. An ideal situation is that a model is trained with centralized nodes, which update the global nodes in the asynchronous mode of learning and the updated model is being broadcasted to all the nodes connected with it. The important thing is that the actual data is not shared among the nodes while only learned parameters are shared or gradients are shared only.

Traffic Forecasting Use Case

Good planning and right management arerequired while one talks about traffic monitoring and forecasting. Mobile traffic is one of the most important aspects of IoVs and it needs to be managed and mobile networks require efficient and smart planning. The main drawback is that there is limited information present on the base station. Training methods are required in order to generate accurate and efficient predictions in order to generalize the observations for different parties. Data is collected from different base stations when traditional methods come into play and are sent to the central base station and then different machine learning methods are implemented upon the collected and received data in order to search or predict certain decisions. There are different limitations in the data dissemination such as performance issues, quality concerns, confidentiality and privacy issues, and application of machine learning techniques. These issues are addressed by various machine learning methods but still up to no heed.

Effectiveness of federated learning is analyzed for time series forecasting in traffic prediction. Different types of neural network architectures are being used which have collected different data for the traffic prediction [39] and Smart 5G prediction which is in itself quite a challenge. Some of the results show that the new federated learning architectures have set a standard for least prediction error, pre-processing methods and techniques that lead to high level prediction accuracy along with the state-of-art techniques that outperform different traditional approaches.

Deep learning models used in federated learning have shown great numbers as gathered by different organizations. Different challenges are still faced by the federated learning-based techniques. There is a term called 'isolated islands', data privacy, and security issues, which are becoming more important and significant in the coming up times. A model is given in order to address some of the above given challenges, which predict the traffic flow and differs from traditional methods in a lot of ways. It updates the central learning model by providing several aggregators and parameters mechanisms rather than sharing the data to different organizations. In this way, this model called FedGRU (Federated Learning Based Gated Recurrent Unit Neural Network) prevents the data from leaking here and there and ensures efficient data security. An algorithm is used that controls the overhead communication [40] that is used in parameter communication. Hence, this extensive averaging federated algorithm provides much better results than the traditional methods along with the security, and privacy of the data that is to be communicated.

Privacy-Preserving Traffic Prediction Use Case

Deep learning frameworks have made effective traffic prediction and have achieved enormous success with their efficient capability. Distributed datasets can easily be trained by using federated learning and it eliminates data privacy and security in every field. Data privacy is compromised at times when federated learning comes into play for efficient communication and a robust model. A robust model comprises correlation data with various parameters and these comprise training of traffic data. The spatial correlation of the correlated traffic data can be easily proposed. Federated learning-based techniques work upon differential privacy schemes for the protection and preservation of the data. The data is trained in the local usage area on the client side. Federated convolutional networks [41] are used here in order to find the average trained models. The results show that the convolutional networks based federated learning techniques provide much better results than all the other traditional algorithms and techniques. Privacy loss is hence removed or eliminated in this model. Table **2** as shown below discusses the use-cases in the field of federated learning.

Table 2. Use cases in federated learning.

Sr. No.	Use Case	Technique	Challenges	Remedies
1.	Steering Wheel Angle Prediction	Advanced methods like convolutional long short-term memory (C-LSTM) use both visual and dynamic dependencies of the driving of vehicles. Deep learning neural networks directly predict the steering wheel angles and monitor the steering wheel prediction, which gave the concept of end-to-end learning in federated learning.	Enhancement in the model prediction and detection accuracy is required.	A robust model is required, which uses lower training cost as compared to traditional mechanisms. Speed acceleration is done through federated learning which boosts the overall model quality.
2.	Predictive Maintenance of the Vehicle	Sensitive data of the vehicles is collected from the sensors present in the vehicle like camera, temperature, speed, location, *etc.* for the need of associative analysis. A lot of decisions can be taken with the data generated from these sensors for efficient path decision, traffic prediction or autonomous driving, *etc.*	Data security, low bandwidth issues, asymmetric computation power issues are also there while collecting the data.	A new technique based on federated learning is required such that proper security is provided for the collected data, which also has a less overhead and solves the overall issues.

(Table 2) cont.....

Sr. No.	Use Case	Technique	Challenges	Remedies
3.	Traffic Forecasting	Mobile traffic is one of the most important aspects of IoVs and it needs to be managed and mobile networks require efficient and smart planning. Different types of neural network architectures are being used which have collected different data for traffic prediction and Federated learning architectures have set standards for least prediction error, and pre-processing methods along with state-o--art techniques that outperform different traditional approaches.	The main drawback is that there is limited information present on the base station. Limitations in data dissemination such as performance issues, quality concerns, confidentiality and privacy issues, *etc.* are there.	Learned gradients are used in different approaches so that the security of data is ensured. Multilayer perceptron is used for training and testing of data in federated learning. Some techniques utilize new Mobile Edge Computing (MEC), which uses different resource-sharing techniques to use them in an efficient manner in edge computing for IoVs.
4.	Privacy-Preserving Traffic Prediction	Deep learning frameworks have made effective traffic predictions and have achieved enormous success with their efficient capability. Distributed datasets can easily be trained by using federated learning and it eliminates the data privacy and security in every field.	Data privacy is compromised at times when federated learning comes into play.	A robust model uses correlation data with various parameters in the training of traffic data. The spatial correlation of the correlated traffic data can be easily proposed.

SECURITY MECHANISMS, RELIABILITY, AND FAULT TOLERANCE FOR FEDERATED LEARNING IN IOV

Security Mechanism

Secure Model Aggregation Techniques

Federated Averaging

Federated averaging is a commonly used technique for model aggregation in federated learning. It involves weighting and averaging the local model updates received from the edge devices to create a new global model. To enhance security, secure aggregation protocols can be employed to protect the privacy of individual model updates during the aggregation process.

Secure Multi-Party Computation (MPC)

MPC is a cryptographic technique that allows multiple parties (in this case, the central server and edge devices) to jointly compute a function while keeping their respective inputs private [42]. In the context of federated learning, MPC can be used to perform secure model aggregation without revealing the individual model updates.

Privacy-preserving Methods for Data Sharing in Federated Learning

a. Differential Privacy: Differential privacy techniques add controlled noise to the local model updates to protect the privacy of individual data samples. By introducing randomness, differential privacy prevents adversaries from inferring sensitive information about specific data points while still allowing useful information to be shared for model training.

Secure Data Aggregation

Secure data aggregation protocols, such as secure multi-party computation or homomorphic encryption, can be employed to perform data aggregation in a privacy-preserving manner. These techniques allow for the computation of aggregate statistics or model parameters without exposing individual data samples.

Local Data Processing

In federated learning, edge devices perform local model training using their own data without sharing the raw data. By keeping the data on the edge devices and only sharing the model updates, privacy is preserved since the sensitive data remains localized.

Authentication and Access Control Mechanisms for Federated Learning in IoV

Device Authentication

Robust device authentication mechanisms are essential in federated learning for IoV. Each edge device should be authenticated before participating in the federated learning process to ensure that only trusted devices contribute to the model training. Techniques such as digital certificates, secure keys, or biometric authentication can be employed for device authentication.

Access Control

Access control mechanisms ensure that only authorized edge devices have access to participate in the federated learning process [43]. Role-based access control or attribute-based access control can be implemented to define and enforce access policies based on device credentials, trust levels, or other relevant factors.

Secure Communication Channels

Secure communication protocols, such as Transport Layer Security (TLS), should be employed to establish secure and encrypted channels between the edge devices and the central server. This protects against eavesdropping, data tampering, and unauthorized access to the communication channel.

Secure Model Updates

When edge devices send their model updates to the central server, secure mechanisms such as encryption or digital signatures can be used to ensure the integrity and authenticity of the updates. This prevents unauthorized modifications to the model updates during transmission.

These security mechanisms help protect the privacy of data, ensure the authenticity and integrity of model updates, and establish a trusted environment for federated learning in IoV systems. By incorporating these mechanisms, the overall security of the federated learning process is enhanced, enabling secure and privacy-preserving collaboration among edge devices and the central server prevents unauthorized modifications to the model updates during transmission.

Reliability

Robust Communication

Reliable communication is crucial for federated learning in IoV. The communication channels between edge devices and the central server should be reliable and have low latency to ensure timely transmission of model updates and coordination. Robust communication protocols and error-handling mechanisms can be employed to handle network disruptions, packet losses, or connection failures.

Resilient Edge Devices

Edge devices in IoV should be designed to be resilient and capable of handling various operating conditions. They should have sufficient computational resources, storage capacity, and power backup mechanisms to ensure reliable participation in the federated learning process.

Data Synchronization

To ensure reliable synchronization, edge devices need to have well-defined synchronization protocols with the central server [44]. This ensures that all devices are operating on the same version of the global model, minimizing inconsistencies and convergence issues.

Fault Tolerance

Redundancy and Replication

To achieve fault tolerance, redundancy and replication techniques can be employed. This involves deploying multiple instances of the central server or utilizing distributed computing approaches to distribute the workload and handle failures. Redundancy also helps in minimizing single points of failure and ensures continuous operation in the event of server failures.

Model Checkpoints

Regular model checkpoints can be created to save the progress of the federated learning process. These checkpoints allow for quick recovery in case of failures or interruptions [45]. If a failure occurs, the process can resume from the latest checkpoint, reducing the need to start the training process from scratch.

Fault Detection and Recovery

Fault detection mechanisms can be implemented to identify and diagnose failures in the federated learning system. This can include monitoring the health and performance metrics of edge devices, central servers, and communication channels. Automatic recovery mechanisms, such as restarting failed processes or reassigning tasks to alternative devices, can help maintain the continuity of the federated learning process.

Data Integrity and Error Correction

Data integrity and error correction techniques, such as error-correcting codes or checksums, can be employed to detect and correct errors during data transmission or storage. This helps to maintain the accuracy and reliability of the data used in federated learning.

Robustness Testing

Comprehensive testing and validation of the federated learning system can help identify and address potential vulnerabilities or weaknesses. Robustness testing involves simulating various failure scenarios and stress testing the system to ensure its resilience and fault tolerance.

By considering reliability and fault tolerance in federated learning for IoV, the system can withstand failures, maintain continuous operation, and recover gracefully from disruptions. These measures help ensure the reliability, availability, and resilience of the federated learning process [46], ultimately contributing to improved performance and effectiveness in IoV environments.

CASE STUDY: FEDERATED LEARNING FOR ANOMALY DETECTION IN AUTONOMOUS VEHICLES

This section discusses different case studies for federated learning that have happened in the recent years to provide a better intake at how anomaly detection is done through federated learning in IoVs. Some of them are discussed below.

Some authors [17] talk about the Autonomous Guided Vehicles (AGVs), their handling, their maintenance, and their operational activities, which have become a major component in IoVs these days. Machine Learning is a powerful tool that can help detect the anomalies through various signals and data as collected by IoT edge devices. Appropriate signals, accuracy in predictions is required in order to detect the anomalies accurately which is based upon multiple sensor readings and prediction of selected signals in the data. Federated Learning uses a new multi round approach for building better models and global prediction models for the detection of anomalies through collecting data over a distributed environment. It is seen that federated learning provides better results through centralized approaches and performs better than the traditional approaches in such cases. Constant and frequent synchronization of data is a key factor in federated learning for better prediction quality.

The experimental results of the federated learning shows the effectiveness of the algorithm for the experiences collected by the AGVs. It also improves the overall performance of the signal prediction which makes it easier for the algorithm to detect the anomalies effectively and provides much better results with some significant variations while collecting the data from signals. The experimental results shown in this type of learning are given by performing around 8 rounds of the model averaging technique along with the synchronization based upon the MSE (Mean Square Errors) values that can easily be obtained from the local synchronised data collected and trained by the federated learning techniques. The results in the proposed algorithm are 19% more effective than the traditional algorithms like LSTM.

Several methods are compared in the above discussion in which one method tried to reduce the number of defects present in a model which eventually depletes the percentage also through federated learning and leads to an advantageous side over the neural networks and recurrent neural networks close to by 5% of the overall accuracy. The proposed approach provides a better viewpoint through federated learning in gaining good prediction performance and also increases the data security.

[18] discusses an autonomous blockchain anomaly through federated learning techniques which is privacy efficient in vehicle communication and networking where the updation is done by on vehicle machine learning model (oVML). It updates and exchanges the given and required information in a distributed format. Blockchain based federated learning also called as BFL enables the working over a non centralised form of training data and the coordination is done according to the consensus mechanism of the blockchain technology. Different BFL parameters are developed and looked into through different mathematical calculations and frameworks over a controllable network. Different parameters addressed in this approach can be block size, frame size, retransmission rate, block arrival rate, *etc.* they can easily impact the performance of the model as well as the prediction accuracy. A rigorous analysis can quantify the end to end delays and provides helpful insights to the developed model through communication and the delays.

[19] talks about the mixture of federated learning and deep learning when combined together can provide better results to the analogies present in the IoVs. Enhanced computational capabilities can be provided by the IoVs and their components that enable and are effective through Artificial Intelligence (AI) methods and techniques. In recent times, UAVs (Unmanned Aerial Vehicles) are the talk of the town and are increasing rapidly with different service providers available for data collection. DaaS (Drones As A Service) is becoming quite popular in the coming times, still they have regulations over them but it is a growing community. Adoption of the federated learning for the privacy preserving in the drone community and traffic management during the flight are important aspects. There are a lot of problems in drone data which is inconsistency, asymmetry, multi-dimensionality, incentive mismatches, *etc.* these all problems need to be resolved with evolving times. Self revealing properties of federated learning for multi-dimensional data comes into play which perform several activities like transmission costs, computation costs, *etc.* Gale-Shapley algorithm is used here to match the lowest cost of all the subregions. This kind of

simulation validates the results, their compatibility, efficiency and hence guarantees the maximum profit that can be obtained through this model.

[46] discuss the data sharing mechanisms of Internet of Vehicles (IoVs) through collaborative techniques of federated learning and Internet of Things (IoT) which will in turn improve the driving speed and traffic prediction as well as the driving experience and the service quality of the product. There are a lot of issues that need to be addressed such as data sharing, bandwidth issues, privacy in data, data security, sharing access of the data which is collaborated by a lot of data providers. At times, due to unreliable communication, mismanagements, reliability issues, data sharing needs to be enhanced further. A new federated learning-based architecture is being proposed for privacy in transmission load provided to the service providers. In order to enhance the security of the model parameters, federated learning is combined with a hybrid blockchain model architecture which is enhanced by Direct Acyclic Graph (DAG). An asynchronous federated learning along with the reinforcement learning are combined for better node selection and improves the efficiency also. Different learned models are integrated with the blockchain technique which executes a two-step verification which also ensures the privacy of the shared data. The numerical results provide that the proposed algorithm has high accuracy in learning from the training data and a very fast convergence as compared to the previously proposed algorithms.

[47] talks about the federated learning-based techniques that help in intelligent transportation through IoVs and it uses the 6G technologies that have the abilities of low latency rate, fast data rate, ultra-dense network systems that help in Vehicle-to-everything or V2X communication. Distributed machine learning techniques are in demand in today's world that have advantages over the heterogeneous data collected by different devices over a massive interconnected circuit of the devices. A federated learning model of two layers is proposed here that takes all the advantages of heterogeneous data and the distributed end-edge cloud data in a 6G environment. It is a method that achieves accurate and efficient learning of the data along with privacy protection and reduction in the communication overheads. Intelligent object detection which is a very critical challenge which is addressed through a context aware distributed machine learning mechanism in transportation systems that contain different autonomous vehicles. The implementation results show that the proposed method provides better accuracy results with an improved precision and recall values in the confusion matrix and in the end, it outperforms all the traditional algorithms. It provides better convergence results in large numbers.

[48] discusses the challenges present in IoT in the current times and how a security framework is required with adequate data sharing techniques is the need

of the hour which may help in eliminating some adversarial attacks happening in the model. A dynamic security model with distributed data sharing techniques is required for IoT with IoVs as the main aspect of the application-based aspect. Federated learning is an important aspect of ML and it is increasing rapidly in the field of IoVs and hence, it prevents any kind of data leakages which may occur in the model. Conventional methods in ML may not provide the adequate results that are required in today's times and hence, federated learning plays an important role. FL modes basically maintain the security and privacy of devices as well as the data while sharing with other models and devices. The experimental results and summarizations show that federated learning-based approaches provide better results as compared to deep learning-based approaches. Federated learning models overcome all the drawbacks that are present in the conventional machine learning models as mentioned above.

Federated learning identifies a lot of security threats as well as the potential threats that can occur in IoVs and it provides a robust security system model that can fight against the malicious activities that are occurring in the system and network. These malicious activities include malware, spyware, ransomware, confidentiality issues in data, authentication issues and attacks. These all kinds of threats are handled and managed by federated learning approaches and work in the heterogeneity of the devices in a constrained nature. Layer wise attacks on the IoVs are detected through federated learning to protect the system and then these algorithms provide a robust solution against all the attacks. The federated learning-based security model must be formed according to the specifications of the IoVs and hence, it is important to see all the aspects and functionalities of the IoV system architecture.

[49] discusses the collaborative environment of IoVs which are characterized by computing, processing, data sensing, *etc.* which consists of different emerging technologies such as Artificial Intelligence (ML), Big Data Analytics tools (BDA), *etc.* Due to the involvement of these emerging technologies, there is a significant advantage of efficiency of knowledge accumulation and sharing processes. Conventional processes and AI algorithms cannot work properly on the IoV systems in a distributed network. This work basically proposes a blockchain based network with a hierarchical federated learning mechanism which works on knowledge sharing where the vehicles or devices learn through the environment in a format of reinforcement learning and then share the learned knowledge with the other devices. This is a robust blockchain network with hierarchies for separate layers of the IoV network that solves feasibility issues of vehicular networks. The distributed pattern of data and the privacy issues of the data is resolved through this federated learning architecture. The data or knowledge is modelled such that regular patterns can be shared and noted down by the model and behavioral

patterns can be processed in the model for different multi-player or multilevel or multi-leader games. This hierarchical algorithm can increase the efficiency of the model that has come to a threshold through the traditional algorithms and enhances the learning ability of the model. And further, this model also deals with the different security attacks in an efficient manner.

APPLICATIONS OF FEDERATED LEARNING

Federated learning helps a lot of devices connected over a particular network to learn in a collaborative manner as data is collected from different edge devices as they work upon the same shared model. Once all the data is collected, it regularly updates the model through the central server such that every connected device can look for the changes presented in the model. The cloud of the system is updated and it is notified to every device connected to the central server. This cloud safely protects the data that is sent to the individual device by keeping all the data in local format. This encrypted communication of data with the server, with the connected devices ensures the efficiency of the system and the model's services towards the devices. A collective shared learning model is there among the connected devices while the training data of every device is kelp local such that other devices are not able to see some of the private information regarding a device and it is not uploaded or stored anywhere else. This can be said that federated learning is a decentralized machine learning algorithm, which can also be termed as collaborative learning [50] as it is discussed in the previous sections. It basically takes the input from a wide range of datasets as provided so that more experience can be gained. These datasets are there at different locations and thus reduce the infrastructural hardware and software.

Apart from the IoV sector discussed in this chapter, there are a lot of applications of federated learning and some of them will be discussed in this section as there are a variety of sectors in which federated learning has its applications. Fig. (5) shows the basic diagram of federated learning applications in which it plays a major role in different functionalities that are performed over the data and the overall security of the framework.

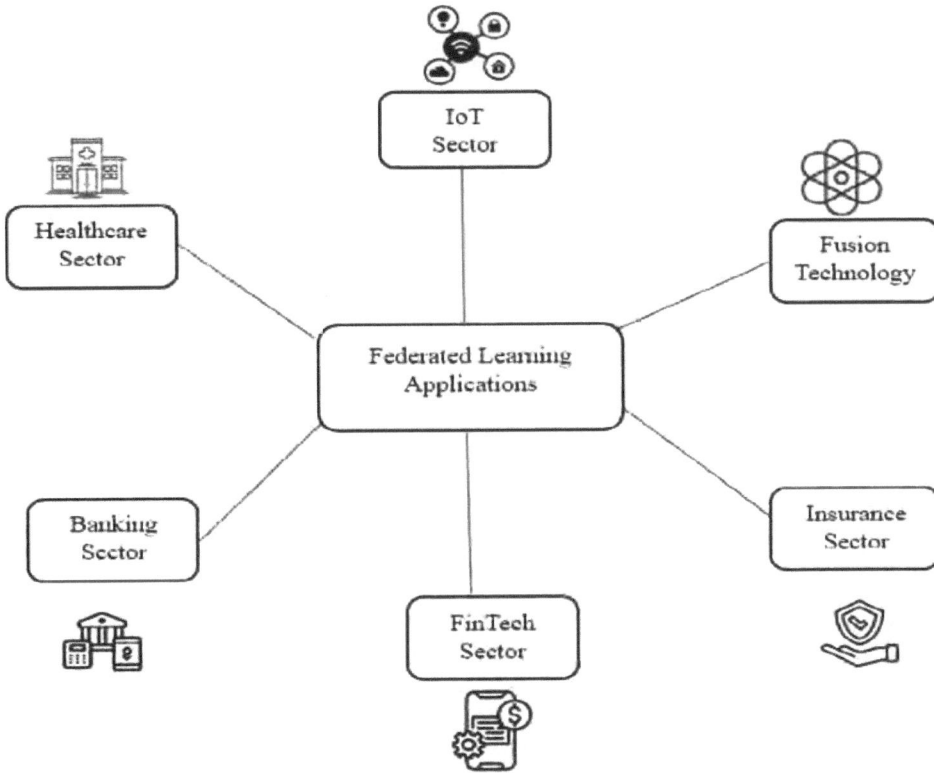

Fig. (5). Applications of Federated Learning.

Applications in Healthcare Industry

The healthcare sector is very difficult to deal with and that is the reason why federated learning can play a major role in this as the data with the healthcare departments is less and it becomes difficult at times to train and test the data. The resources are scarce and the time is also very limited so this technology is to be used. During the pandemic situations also, the healthcare sector was in use at its peak level and the professionals of this sector will have to depend on the technology. The vast datasets, modelling, and training of the algorithm, *etc.* are the tasks required to get better results through federated learning, which is a very long and tiring process. These datasets contain the health-related personal information of the patients which they do nt want to share with public. Participation in federated learning comes at this place where the patient data is treated as the local data and it is trained through the algorithm. Following this, the analysis and research are performed on that basis. An in-house data pool kind of cloud is created for the proper training of the data.

Different healthcare institutions can enjoy these federated learning algorithms that may provide help and access to different sets of regulations that can help with the data provided by the patients. They can work around these algorithms and can get several useful insights from the varied data collected through edge devices in the healthcare institute. A pool of several activities and utilities can be made in the healthcare sector with the help of federated learning. Hence, federated learning is a recent approach that has been developed under the umbrella term of machine learning and it has immense power and potential to transform the face of the healthcare sector. It has much more benefits than the other machine learning algorithms and can help healthcare professionals in a big way. In fact, it does not want to replace the professionals with machines but it wants to help them in an efficient way.

Applications in FinTech

FinTech is basically a combination of finance and technology, it deals with the ventures of the financial operations and functions collaborated with the technology. Federated learning plays a big role catering to the needs of the clients as well as the server businesses and all. Data protection laws are very prevalent in today's time and this allows the people or consumers or clients to trust one another in a secure network phase where their data is protected and they can share their personal information with the edge devices and to remote central servers. This ensures the trust, security and safety of the people with financial practices and functionalities. The financial sector faces a lot of data sharing, data security issues, malware issues, *etc.* that can harm the system and this can also include lawful consent for data sharing, getting clearance [51] for several sharing activities, preservation of data that is being stored for several years and is important to the company database, the time and cost constraints in the financial business evaluations. Collecting and transferring data over the whole network is a whole different aspect of federated learning in financial technology.

Federated learning provides different security solutions by maintaining the data in the local body training it there and then testing it at a global model level. This local data is there with all the edge devices and this is done with the help of edge computations and several other tools. Federated learning is a kind of distributed machine learning technique that works in an encrypted manner as it works on the decentralized kind of data where all the connected devices are not required to request for the transmission of the data and that is the reason a joint training machine is used in federated learning.

There are various benefits of federated learning that can help in resolving the problems present in the finance sector and can provide efficient security solutions for FinTech. Account Takeover is a term used for a data breach where the data of the user is being taken from them and federated learning can help search that data and secure it in an efficient manner. Other benefits include the credit score analysis in which learning is done through the user's footprint which basically prevents fraudulent activities.

Practices like getting the KYC on time by the users without even transferring their data to the third party and getting your work done in an efficient manner are also fruitful. Preventing the risks that can happen inside the FinTech model is the goal that needs to be achieved, which requires some innovative approaches that are to be used by their clients. This enables in making of a new concept that is tried and tested by the users for their business and other finance related activities. This basically generated a sense of trust as well as security between the two parties. This gives rise to an enhanced relationship with different consumers of the model as well as the trusted third parties and the makers of the model that deal with everything.

Applications in the Insurance Sector

The insurance sector is one of the major sectors that use federated learning practices in order to secure data in one form or another and it has been a vital part of the country's industry since its making decades ago. It has been rising globally since the day it was formed and since then it has aided all the kinds of mishaps that occur in the world which is due to the boom of this technology. An increase in the investments that are happening all over the world are basically made in order to provide support to the insured person if, at any time, they face any kind of mishap that may happen due to some unforeseen event happening in their life. Still, with all the security, there are some drawbacks as well as boundaries of the insurance-giving companies that assist the user in the form of monetary benefits. When an insured person or consumer violates any kind of rule or boundaries as set by the insurance firm and then breaches the company's trust through false claims as ensured by the company which is the owner of the security framework in one form or another, such people or the insured businesses are subject to fraudulent activities and illicit behavioral activities.

A considerable amount of insurance data is present with these companies of the users and businesses. This data can be in the form of health insurance, business insurance, vehicle insurance, housing insurance, *etc*. This data is associated with a lot of people and companies in different places. So, one needs machine learning algorithms that are to be designed such that this unsorted data can be put in place as this data is collected from a lot of datasets that cannot be easily shared with third parties and even to different locations. Instead of traditional machine learning algorithms, federated learning resolves such data issues that occur in these insurance companies. Federated learning helps an insurance company to find out the user's or their client's patterns in one way or another without letting the client know what is happening and without violating any kind of rules or data clauses. Hence, with the help of federated learning, people do not violate any kind of rules by doing some kind of wrong activity, or any type of fraud is not reported. These algorithms are designed, modelled and trained and govern the data and ensure the client's safety and security of their data, as well as the violations, are not made which ensures confidentiality.

Applications in IoT

The Internet of Things is a major technology emerging in today's world and is significantly increasing with the growing information along with an increase in devices. With increasing information, there is an increase in security and privacy concerns about devices and information which need to be protected. A lot of organizations using IoT are basically adopting federated learning algorithms in order to secure the data by training the obtained data from different datasets and without exchanging any kind of data with any third parties. The main aim of federated learning is to collect the data from various datasets which makes the data decentralized as it is collected from different devices through different mediums. Without letting any device know, FL collects all the data and keeps it secure, keeping it local and vital for important studies, research, and for performing analysis. Federated learning provides an in-house or on-device machine learning technique to provide security solutions for the collected data without transferring the data to some other device as this is the user's data that needs to be secured and hence, each and every analysis and manipulation happens at the central server of the system.

Hence, a sense of personalization can be achieved by federated learning and it also enhances the performance of the IoT devices and in turn, makes the IoT applications more advanced as compared to other devices. Hence, data personalization, advanced technologies, and enhanced performances can be achieved by using federated learning in IoT devices.

Applications in the Baking Sector

Federated learning also helps out in the banking sector as there are a lot of things that need to be taken care of. People trust these banks with their money, their private information regarding the money, their account details, and bank lockers where they keep their precious items and hence, these all tasks are very important and need to be secured. Hence, banks contain a lot of confidential information regarding different individuals, their families, companies, *etc.* Their information is collected and secured by the concerned bank by using federated learning.

Application in Fusion with Technologies

There are a lot of technologies that can be fused with federated learning such that one gets the best results possible. One application can be that of predictive keyboards that are used today on online websites in the form of keyboards such as Google's Android keyboard used in all of its applications. It basically takes the input of the past data of the user and then predicts the coming up text or words on its own depending upon the past data. Apple also uses federated learning to improve some of its devices as Apple Watch uses FL in order to improve the voice recognition of Siri and this is done by collecting the user's data.

Another kind of application that uses federated learning is blockchain technology for getting updates in several models of the applications and to keep their data and, their model safe and to secure their organization and privacy of the data. In cyber-security also, federated learning plays an important role as it preserves the data on the device and only shares the updates with the connected networks.

CONCLUSION AND FUTURE DIRECTIONS

The key findings from this chapter come out to be that federated learning is the need of the hour in IoVs and this type of machine learning algorithm will help in giving the right kind of results with efficiency, which will provide the best type of security solutions. It will bring a significant change in the evolution of the IoV systems and hence, it will be a way better solution for security purposes of the IoV systems. Federated learning as well as IoVs are both emerging technologies in computer science and hence, they will be the future of tomorrow and thus, this chapter provides the much-needed contributions.

The first section of this chapter gives a brief introduction after the abstract. It provides an overview of what is federated learning and how it can be incorporated into the IoVs such that the security issues of IoVs and other kinds of issues like DoS, data sharing, homogeneity, *etc.*, can be resolved. The data security is also a big issue in IoVs as information is collected from several devices that are connected over the Internet and hence, that needs to be resolved. This section also discusses how collaborative learning can be done when we have a number of devices and a model is trained and collaborative data is collected and tested. The next section discusses the pros and cons of federated learning and how it can help with the emerging technologies. Some of the challenges discussed in the chapter for federated learning are the heterogeneous form of data, security of devices, data sharing and other things connected over the network in an application, communication overhead issues in the framework, *etc.* Some of the positive sides of federated learning are given as privacy solutions, reliability, robustness, scalability solutions, *etc.*, which actually provide better results when applied to

IoV systems.

The third section discusses the privacy and security considerations of the IoVs along with federated learning. It basically discusses some major security considerations that are needed to be taken care of while the fusion of both federated learning and IoVs is done and implemented. This includes vehicle-to-vehicle attacks, vehicle-to-infrastructure attacks and activities happening over it. Other kind is the malware attacks or the malicious attack taking place inside the system when it is in operation such as spam, ransomware, trojan horses, worm, *etc.* These all malwares take one way or another to capture the data from users and they try to overpower the system. Systems need to adopt some methodologies that can overcome such security threats. Different types of protocols are to be followed such as encryption-decryption algorithms, security protocols, access control protocols, authentication protocols, intrusion detection protocols and systems, message control protocols, *etc.* Section 4 discusses the security and reliability of the IoV systems, which are important concerns as data is to be secured, access control should be authenticated along with data encryption mechanisms, fault tolerance in the actual data shared, *etc.*

Section 5 talks about the architecture and framework of the IoV systems, which discuss different components and working of the IoV systems. The architecture has three components which are edge devices, the central server and the data aggregation process. Data is collected from different edge-based devices and then that data is trained through the learning models that are basically done through federated learning and then sent to the central server where updates are done in the data. The model is updated according to the data and a new global model is formed through data aggregation. Communication between devices is important, data exchange mechanisms are used here, which transfer and update the data and that is why synchronization and data timings are very important in the model of an IoV system. Section 6 discusses different methodologies and use cases of federated learning used in the IoVs to make them more secure and reliable such that better results can be obtained which are efficient, productive, less time-consuming, *etc.* There are a lot of challenges that need to be addressed and hence, federated learning deals with them in a very efficient manner. Data aggregation, reliability, and not enough datasets for edge devices are some of them that are dealt with. This section mentions a lot of use cases, which are named as Steering Wheel Angle Prediction Use Case, Predictive Maintenance of the Vehicle Use Case, Traffic Forecasting Use Case, and Privacy-Preserving Traffic Prediction Use Case. All these different kinds of use cases are presented in the section and they have different purposes in an IoV system and are used in different applications.

Section 7 gives different security mechanisms, reliability issues, and fault tolerance issues that are present in the IoV systems. After this, one of the important sections is section 8 which provides different case studies of federated learning in IoVs. It basically presents a kind of literature survey discussing different research papers that have shown key features and results in the IoVs. Different types of federated learning used in different ways in different applications are discussed in this section. Different kinds of technologies are incorporated along with federated learning such that one can get the best results possible. Section 9 discusses different kinds of applications where federated learning can play a major role apart from the IoVs.

Hence, federated learning is an evolving technology that is changing the face of computer science, it has its own sets of challenges and limitations that need to be overcome but still, it is a game-changing machine learning technique and can help in multiple aspects of the industry. Hence, FL is making significant progress in major areas around the world, and scientists and researchers are keen to implement this technology in various areas with reduced costs and efficient results. FL will have to deal with several consumer changing behaviors and increased infrastructure costs in order to survive in today's fast-growing world. Hence, FL is a booming technology that can help major industries achieve higher benefits.

REFERENCES

[1]   P. Garg, A. Dixit, and P. Sethi, "Ml-fresh: novel routing protocol in opportunistic networks using machine learning", *Comput. Syst. Sci. Eng.,* vol. 40, no. 2, pp. 703-717, 2022.
[http://dx.doi.org/10.32604/csse.2022.019557]

[2]   P.S. Yadav, S. Khan, Y.V. Singh, P. Garg, and R.S. Singh, "A Lightweight Deep Learning-Based Approach for Jazz Music Generation in MIDI Format", *Comput. Intell. Neurosci.,* vol. 2022, pp. 1-7, 2022.
[http://dx.doi.org/10.1155/2022/2140895] [PMID: 36035841]

[3]   T.A. Butt, R. Iqbal, S.C. Shah, and T. Umar, "Social Internet of Vehicles: Architecture and enabling technologies", *Comput. Electr. Eng.,* vol. 69, pp. 68-84, 2018.
[http://dx.doi.org/10.1016/j.compeleceng.2018.05.023]

[4]   E. Soni, A. Nagpal, P. Garg, and P.R. Pinheiro, "Assessment of Compressed and Decompressed ECG Databases for Telecardiology Applying a Convolution Neural Network", *Electronics (Basel),* vol. 11, no. 17, p. 2708, 2022.
[http://dx.doi.org/10.3390/electronics11172708]

[5]   I.V. Pustokhina, D.A. Pustokhin, E.L. Lydia, P. Garg, A. Kadian, and K. Shankar, "Hyperparameter search based convolution neural network with Bi-LSTM model for intrusion detection system in multimedia big data environment", *Multimedia. Tools. Appl.,* vol. 81, pp. 1-18, 2021.
[http://dx.doi.org/10.1007/s11042-021-11271-7]

[6]   A. Khanna, P. Rani, P. Garg, P.K. Singh, and A. Khamparia, "An Enhanced Crow Search Inspired Feature Selection Technique for Intrusion Detection Based Wireless Network System", *Wirel. Pers. Commun.,* vol. 127, pp. 1-18, 2021.
[http://dx.doi.org/10.1007/s11277-021-08766-9]

[7]   P. Garg, A. Dixit, P. Sethi, and P.R. Pinheiro, "Impact of node density on the qos parameters of routing protocols in opportunistic networks for smart spaces", *Mob. Inf. Syst.,* vol. 2020, pp. 1-18, 2020.
[http://dx.doi.org/10.1155/2020/8868842]

[8]   D. Upadhyay, P. Garg, S.M. Aldossary, J. Shafi, and S. Kumar, "A Linear Quadratic Regression-Based Synchronised Health Monitoring System (SHMS) for IoT Applications", *Electronics (Basel),* vol. 12, no. 2, p. 309, 2023.
[http://dx.doi.org/10.3390/electronics12020309]

[9]   P. Saini, B. Nagpal, P. Garg, and S. Kumar, "CNN-BI-LSTM-CYP: A deep learning approach for sugarcane yield prediction", *Sustain. Energy Technol. Assess.,* vol. 57, p. 103263, 2023.
[http://dx.doi.org/10.1016/j.seta.2023.103263]

[10]   P. Saini, B. Nagpal, P. Garg, and S. Kumar, "Evaluation of Remote Sensing and Meteorological parameters for Yield Prediction of Sugarcane (Saccharum officinarum L.) Crop", *Braz. Arch. Biol. Technol.,* vol. 66, p. e23220781, 2023.
[http://dx.doi.org/10.1590/1678-4324-2023220781]

[11]   S. Beniwal, U. Saini, P. Garg, and R.K. Joon, "Improving performance during camera surveillance by integration of edge detection in IoT system", *Int. J. E-Health Med. Commun.,* vol. 12, no. 5, pp. 84-96, 2021.
[http://dx.doi.org/10.4018/IJEHMC.20210901.oa6]

[12]   R. Rani, K.K. Yogi, and S.P. Yadav, "Detection of Cloned Attacks in Connecting Media using Bernoulli RBM_RF Classifier (BRRC)", *Multimed Tools Appl,* vol. 83, pp. 77029-77060, 2024.
[http://dx.doi.org/10.1007/s11042-024-18650-w]

[13]   V.K. Kanaujia, A. Kumar, and S.P. Yadav, "Advancements in Automatic Kidney Segmentation Using Deep Learning Frameworks and Volumetric Segmentation Techniques for CT Imaging: A Review", *Arch Computat Methods Eng.,* vol. 31, pp. 3151-3169, 2024.
[http://dx.doi.org/10.1007/s11831-024-10067-w]

[14]   J. Kang, Z. Xiong, D. Niyato, Y. Zou, Y. Zhang, and M. Guizani, "Reliable Federated Learning for Mobile Networks", *IEEE Wirel. Commun.,* vol. 27, no. 2, pp. 72-80, 2020.
[http://dx.doi.org/10.1109/MWC.001.1900119]

[15]   S. Lonare, and R. Bhramaramba, "Federated Approach for Privacy Preserving Traffic Prediction Using Graph Convolutional Network", *J. Shanghai Jiaotong Univ. (Sci.),* vol. 29, pp. 509-517, 2021.
[http://dx.doi.org/10.1007/s12204-021-2382-5]

[16]   H. Zhang, J. Bosch, and H. Olsson, "Real-time End-to-End Federated Learning: An Automotive Case Study", *45th Annual Computers, Software, and Applications Conference (COMPSAC),* pp. 459-468, 2021.
[http://dx.doi.org/10.1109/COMPSAC51774.2021.00070]

[17]   B. Shubyn, D. Kostrzewa, P. Grzesik, P. Benecki, T. Maksymyuk, V. Sunderam, J. Syu, J. Chun-Wei Lin, and D. Mrozek, "Federated Learning for improved prediction of failures in Autonomous Guided Vehicles", *J. Comput. Intell.,* vol. 69, Elsevier, p. 101956, 2023.
[http://dx.doi.org/10.1016/j.jocs.2023.101956]

[18]   S. Raj, and J. Choi, "A Decentralized Federated Learning Approach for Connected Autonomous Vehicles", In: *IEEE Wireless Communications and Networking Conference Workshops. WCNCW,* 2020.
[http://dx.doi.org/10.1109/WCNCW48565.2020.9124733]

[19]   Bryan Lim W., Huang J., Xiong Z., Kang J., ; Dusit Niyato; Hua X., Leung C. and Miao C, "Towards Federated Learning in UAV-Enabled Internet of Vehicles: A Multi- Dimen-sional Contract-Matching Approach", In: *IEEE Transactions on Intelligent Transportation Systems IEEE.* vol. 22. , 2021, no. 8, pp. 5140-5154.
[http://dx.doi.org/10.1109/TITS.2021.3056341]

[20]   Y. Liu, J. Peng, J. Kang, A.M. Iliyasu, D. Niyato, and A.A.A. El-Latif, "A Secure Federated Learning Framework for 5G Networks", *IEEE Wirel. Commun.*, vol. 27, no. 4, pp. 24-31, 2020.
[http://dx.doi.org/10.1109/MWC.01.1900525]

[21]   H. Moudoud, S. Cherkaoui, and L. Khoukhi, "Towards a Secure and Reliable Federated Learning using Blockchain", *IEEE Global Communications Conference (GLOBECOM), Madrid, Spain*, pp. 01-06, 2021.
[http://dx.doi.org/10.1109/GLOBECOM46510.2021.9685388]

[22]   Y. Zheng, S. Lai, Y. Liu, X. Yuan, X. Yi, and C. Wang, "Aggregation Service for Federated Learning: An Efficient, Secure, and More Resilient Realization", *IEEE Trans. Depend. Secure Comput.*, vol. 20, no. 2, pp. 988-1001, 2023.
[http://dx.doi.org/10.1109/TDSC.2022.3146448]

[23]   W. Liu, Y. Zhang, and G. Han, "Secure and Efficient Smart Healthcare System Based on Federated Learning", In: *Comp. Commun.* vol. 195. Wiley Online Library, 2023, pp. 346-361.
[http://dx.doi.org/10.1155/2023/8017489]

[24]   O. Aouedi , G. Yenduri , K. Piamrat, M Alazab ,S.Bhattacharya, P. K. R. Maddikunta , and T.R. Gadekallu, "Federated Learning for Intrusion detection system: Concepts, challenges and future directions. 195", In: *Comp. Commun.* vol. 195. , 2022, pp. 346-361.
[http://dx.doi.org/10.1016/j.comcom.2022.09.012]

[25]   B. Ghimire, and D.B. Rawat, "Recent Advances on Federated Learning for Cybersecurity and Cybersecurity for Federated Learning for Internet of Things", *IEEE. Internet. Things. J.*, vol. 9, no. 11, pp. 8229-8249, 2022.
[http://dx.doi.org/10.1109/JIOT.2022.3150363]

[26]   G. Xu, H. Li, and K. Liu, "VerifyNet: Secure and Verifiable Federated Learning", *in IEEE Transactions on Information Forensics and Security*, vol. 15, pp. 911-926, 2020.
[http://dx.doi.org/10.1109/TIFS.2019.2929409]

[27]   J. Posner, L. Tseng, M. Aloqaily, and Y. Jararweh, "Federated Learning in Vehicular Networks: Opportunities and Solutions", *IEEE Netw.*, vol. 35, no. 2, pp. 152-159, 2021.
[http://dx.doi.org/10.1109/MNET.011.2000430]

[28]   V.P. Chellapandi, L. Yuan, C.G. Brinton, S.H. Żak, and Z. Wang, "Federated Learning for Connected and Automated Vehicles: A Survey of Existing Approaches and Challenges", *IEEE Trans. Intell. Veh.*, vol. 9, no. 1, pp. 119-137, 2024.
[http://dx.doi.org/10.1109/TIV.2023.3332675]

[29]   H. Zhang, J. Bosch, and H. H. Olsson, "End-to-End Federated Learning for Autonomous Driving Vehicles", *2021 International Joint Conference on Neural Networks (IJCNN), Shenzhen, China*, pp. 1-8, 2021.
[http://dx.doi.org/10.1109/IJCNN52387.2021.9533808]

[30]   A. M. Elbir, B. Soner, S. Çöleri, D. Gündüz and M. Bennis, "Federated Learning in Vehicular Networks", *2022 IEEE International Mediterranean Conference on Communications and Networking (MeditCom), Athens, Greece*, pp. 72-77, 2022.
[http://dx.doi.org/10.1109/MeditCom55741.2022.9928621]

[31]   H. Xiao, J. Zhao, Q. Pei, J. Feng, L. Liu, and W. Shi, "Vehicle Selection and Resource Optimization for Federated Learning in Vehicular Edge Computing", *IEEE Trans. Intell. Transp. Syst.*, vol. 23, no. 8, pp. 11073-11087, 2022.
[http://dx.doi.org/10.1109/TITS.2021.3099597]

[32]   L.U. Khan, E. Mustafa, J. Shuja, F. Rehman, K. Bilal, Z. Han, and C.S. Hong, "Federated Learning for Digital Twin-Based Vehicular Networks: Architecture and Challenges", *IEEE Wirel. Commun.*, vol. 31, no. 2, pp. 156-162, 2024.
[http://dx.doi.org/10.1109/MWC.012.2200373]

[33]   U. Kant, M. Singh, S. Mishra, and V.M. Srivastava, "Internet of Things and Artificial Intelligence", In: *Visual Surveillance to Internet of Things.* Chapman and Hall/CRC, 2019, pp. 111-120. [http://dx.doi.org/10.1201/9780429297922-8]

[34]   U. Kant, and V. Kumar, "Introduction to Emerging Technologies in Computer Science and Its Applications", *Emerging Technologies in Computing,* 2021. [http://dx.doi.org/10.1201/9781003121466-1]

[35]   U. Kant, and V. Kumar, "IoT Network Used in Fog and Cloud Computing", In: *Internet of Things: Security and Privacy in Cyberspace.* Springer Nature Singapore: Singapore, 2022, pp. 165-187. [http://dx.doi.org/10.1007/978-981-19-1585-7_8]

[36]   U. Kant, M. Singh, and V.M. Srivastava, "Internet of things and Cloud computing", In: *From Visual Surveillance to Internet of Things.* Chapman and Hall/CRC, 2019, pp. 97-110. [http://dx.doi.org/10.1201/9780429297922-7]

[37]   D.M. Manias, and A. Shami, "Making a Case for Federated Learning in the Internet of Vehicles and Intelligent Transportation Systems", *IEEE Netw.,* vol. 35, no. 3, pp. 88-94, 2021. [http://dx.doi.org/10.1109/MNET.011.2000552]

[38]   B. Brik, A. Ksentini, and M. Bouaziz, "Federated Learning for UAVs-Enabled Wireless Networks: Use Cases, Challenges, and Open Problems", *IEEE Access,* vol. 8, pp. 53841-53849, 2020. [http://dx.doi.org/10.1109/ACCESS.2020.2981430]

[39]   A. Renda, P. Ducange, F. Marcelloni, D. Sabella, M.C. Filippou, G. Nardini, G. Stea, A. Virdis, D. Micheli, D. Rapone, and L.G. Baltar, "Federated Learning of Explainable AI Models in 6G Systems: Towards Secure and Automated Vehicle Networking", *Information (Basel),* vol. 13, no. 8, p. 395, 2022. [http://dx.doi.org/10.3390/info13080395]

[40]   S. Banabilah, M. Aloqaily, E. Alsayed, N. Malik, and Y. Jararweh, "Federated learning review: Fundamentals, enabling technologies, and future applications", *Inf. Process. Manage.,* vol. 59, no. 6, p. 103061, 2022. [http://dx.doi.org/10.1016/j.ipm.2022.103061]

[41]   S.R. Pokhrel, and J. Choi, "Federated Learning With Blockchain for Autonomous Vehicles: Analysis and Design Challenges", *IEEE Trans. Commun.,* vol. 68, no. 8, pp. 4734-4746, 2020. [http://dx.doi.org/10.1109/TCOMM.2020.2990686]

[42]   L. Barbieri, S. Savazzi, M. Brambilla, and M. Nicoli, "Decentralized federated learning for extended sensing in 6G connected vehicles", *Vehicular Communications,* vol. 33, no. January, p. 100396, 2022. [http://dx.doi.org/10.1016/j.vehcom.2021.100396]

[43]   S. Doomra, N. Kohli, and S. Athavale, "Turn Signal Prediction: A Federated Learning Case Study", *arXiv,* 2012. [http://dx.doi.org/10.48550/arXiv.2012.12401]

[44]   X. Zhou, W. Liang, J. She, Z. Yan, and K. Wang, "Two-Layer Federated Learning With Heterogeneous Model Aggregation for 6G Supported Internet of Vehicles", *IEEE Trans. Vehicular Technol.,* vol. 70, no. 6, pp. 5308-5317, 2021. [http://dx.doi.org/10.1109/TVT.2021.3077893]

[45]   D. Jallepalli, N. C. Ravikumar, P. V. Badarinath, S. Uchil and M. A. Suresh, "Federated Learning for Object Detection in Autonomous Vehicles", *2021 IEEE Seventh International Conference on Big Data Computing Service and Applications (BigDataService), Oxford, United Kingdom,* pp. 107-114, 2021. [http://dx.doi.org/10.1109/BigDataService52369.2021.00018]

[46]   Y. Lu, X. Huang, K. Zhang, S. Maharjan and Y. Zhang, "Blockchain Empowered Asynchronous Federated Learning for Secure Data Sharing in Internet of Vehicles", *in IEEE Transactions on Vehicular Technology,* vol. 69, no. 4, pp. 4298-4311, 2020. [http://dx.doi.org/10.1109/TVT.2020.2973651]

[47]   X., Liang W., She J., Yan Z. and Wang K, "Two-Layer Federated Learning With Het-erogeneous Model Aggregation for 6G Supported Internet of Vehicles", *In IEEE Transactions on Vehicular Technology,,* vol. 70, no. 6, pp. 5308-5317, 2021.
[http://dx.doi.org/10.1109/TVT.2021.3077893]

[48]   V. Gugueoth, S. Safavatv, and S. Shetty, "Security of Internet of Things (IoT) using federated learning and deep learning — Recent advancements, issues and prospects", *ICT. Express.,* vol. 9, no. 5, pp. 941-960, 2023.
[http://dx.doi.org/10.1016/j.icte.2023.03.006]

[49]   H. Chai, S. Leng, Y. Chen, and K. Zhang, "A Hierarchical Blockchain-Enabled Federated Learning Algorithm for Knowledge Sharing in Internet of Vehicles", *IEEE Trans. Intell. Transp. Syst.,* vol. 22, no. 7, pp. 3975-3986, 2021.
[http://dx.doi.org/10.1109/TITS.2020.3002712]

[50]   D.C. Nguyen, M. Ding, P.N. Pathirana, A. Seneviratne, J. Li, and H. Vincent Poor, "Federated Learning for Internet of Things: A Comprehensive Survey", *IEEE Commun. Surv. Tutor.,* vol. 23, no. 3, pp. 1622-1658, 2021.
[http://dx.doi.org/10.1109/COMST.2021.3075439]

[51]   L. Khan, Y.K. Tun, and M. Alsenwi, "A Dispersed Federated Learning Framework for 6G-Enabled Autonomous Driving Cars", *IEEE Trans. Netw. Sci. Eng.,* 2022.
[http://dx.doi.org/10.1109/TNSE.2022.3188571]

CHAPTER 5

Adaptive Solutions for Data Sharing in IoVs

Virendra Singh Kushwah[1], **Apurva Jain**[2], **Jyoti Parashar**[2,*], **Lokesh Meena**[2] and **Nisar Ahmad Malik**[3]

[1] *VIT Bhopal University, Sehore, India*

[2] *Dr. Akhilesh Das Gupta Institute of Technology & Management, New Delhi, India*

[3] *Govt Degree College Kulgam, J&K, India*

Abstract: With the rapid growth of the Internet of Vehicles (IoV), there is an increasing need for effective and secure data sharing among vehicles, infrastructure, and other entities within the IoV ecosystem. However, traditional data-sharing mechanisms face numerous challenges, such as heterogeneity of data formats, privacy concerns, and scalability issues. In this study, we propose adaptive solutions for data sharing in IoVs, which aim to address these challenges and facilitate efficient and secure data exchange. Our approach leverages adaptive techniques to dynamically adjust data-sharing mechanisms based on the context and requirements of the IoV environment. We present a comprehensive overview of the proposed solutions, including data format transformation, privacy-preserving techniques, and scalable data-sharing protocols. We also discuss the potential benefits and limitations of our approach and provide insights into future research directions in the field of data sharing in IoVs

Keywords: Adaptive, Accessibility, Centralized, IoV, Security.

INTRODUCTION

Because it permits real-time communication between diverse entities such as automobiles, handheld devices carried by pedestrians, and roadside units, the Internet of Vehicles (IoVs) makes it feasible to control traffic in a manner that is both safer and more effective. Because IoV is superior to other technologies, academic research into the Internet of Vehicles applications such as autonomous driving, vehicle management, high-definition (HD) maps, and big data awareness has proven to be fruitful. It stands to reason that the protection of this information as it is shared among IoV participants should be considered an essential compo-

---

* **Corresponding author Jyoti Parashar:** Dr. Akhilesh Das Gupta Institute of Technology & Management, New Delhi, India; E-mail: jyoti.parashar123@gmail.com

Shelly Gupta, Puneet Garg, Jyoti Agarwal, Hardeo Kumar Thakur & Satya Prakash Yadav (Eds.)

nent of IoV infrastructure given that the Internet of Vehicles applications rely heavily on vast amounts of data collected from vehicles [1, 2].

Existing IoV systems, on the other hand, have shortcomings that could put the safety of the data-sharing paradigm in automobiles at risk.

- The security of all information and systems. The Client-Server (CS) paradigm, on which the great majority of IoV systems are built, introduces a potential single point of failure and invites malevolent attacks such as Distributed Denial of Service (DDoS) attacks and Sybil attacks, both of which have the potential to render the entire IoV system unusable [3]. This is due to the fact that the CS model includes a client that acts as both a server and a client. The information pertaining to vehicles and RSUs that are stored in the centralized database is susceptible to being manipulated by adversaries, who might use this information to create havoc on the streets.
- Keeping one's identity a secret from others. Analyzing patterns in data acquired from vehicles, such as driving track data, which is exchanged wirelessly, allows attackers to discover the identities of automobiles. This type of data includes driving track data. People's enthusiasm for sharing vehicle data is dampened as a result of the possibility of disclosure of their identity, which in turn slows down the real implementation of IoV systems [4, 5].

In order to solve these problems, Horng and colleagues came up with a method for secure data sharing in car networks that is based on the identification of the user. However, because their architecture is dependent on dependable cloud computing nodes, it contains a single point of failure, which is a significant weakness. It is possible that frequent modifications to the group members could place a large computational load on the group manager. This is because the group manager serves as a trusted arbiter in the BBS04 group signature-based privacy-preserving vehicular communication technique that was developed by Wei *et al.* In the linkable location-based services system proposed by Yadav *et al.*, which is based on a modified Linkable Spontaneous Anonymous Group (LSAG) [6] ring signature approach, the trusted parties, also known as RSUs, are required to serve as signature proxies. This is the case even if the LSAG ring signature technique was modified. Constructing decentralized and zero-trust vehicular networks ought to be seen as a fashionable security alternative in future IoV systems, as such centralized approaches are no longer sufficient to deal with the sophistication of today's cyberattacks. This is because the Internet of Vehicles (IoV) is a network of vehicles [7, 8].

The development of blockchain technology has captured a significant amount of people's interest in recent years. There is a reason to believe that blockchain technology, which possesses beneficial characteristics such as decentralization, trustworthy execution, and tamper resistance, may be able to assist with the aforementioned problems. One such concept for assuring the trustworthy exchange of data in IoV networks comes from the research conducted by Chen *et al.*, who propose for a quality-driven incentive system based on consortium blockchains. This particular proposal can be found in the work of Chen *et al.* To make the exchange of confidential information easier, Zhou and his colleagues developed LVBS, a condensed blockchain optimized for automobiles [9, 10]. These solutions do not take into account the fact that disclosing cars' identity could potentially compromise their privacy, despite the fact that a decentralized fabric makes the system more secure. In addition, the capabilities of the currently available blockchains are unable to satisfy the demand for high throughput as well as the mobility of IoV systems. As a consequence of this, new challenges have arisen as a direct consequence of the incorporation of IoV into blockchain-based infrastructures:

The first challenge is to maintain the confidentiality of identifiers under specific circumstances. When it comes to the protection of drivers' personal information, the blockchain presents a potential security issue because it is a publicly distributed ledger. This means that anybody who has access to the internet can view its data. Even if pseudonym accounts on a blockchain can "anonymize" the identification of a vehicle, an attacker could still discover the car's true identity by monitoring and analyzing the transactions linked with it. Due to the ineffective anonymity method implemented by the blockchain, consumers are unlikely to provide information about their vehicles to the IoV systems. Despite the anonymity protections they provide, Trusted Authorities (TAs) should nevertheless be held responsible for revealing the identities of malicious nodes and penalizing them. This is the case even while TAs protect users' privacy. Therefore, IoV systems that are based on blockchain technology require a strategy that protects users' privacy when it comes to conditional identifiers [11].

Another challenging area is the capacity for rapid expansion in response to changing conditions. Due to the fact that it utilizes a large number of cutting-edge technologies, the blockchain suffers from scalability problems and speed constraints [12]. The number of consensus nodes can have a direct impact on the convergence speed of the blockchain, which in turn has an effect on the performance of the blockchain. As a result, the vast amounts of data and transactions involved in IoV systems are currently beyond the capability of the blockchain as it is.

In this study, we present a multi-sharding blockchain-based system that may be used to exchange data pertaining to vehicles in a manner that is confidential to the users of the system. We provide a system for sharing of data that is both anonymous and capable of being audited by utilizing the Zero-Knowledge Proof (ZKP) technology as the basis for privacy protection and the ability to disclose the identities of potentially hazardous cars to Tas [13]. We design an efficient multi-sharding blockchain protocol for IoV to lower blockchain communication costs without harming the security of the blockchain. This allows us to bridge the gap between the poor performance of blockchains and the high mobility of IoV systems [14]. Currently, blockchains are unable to keep up with the high mobility of IoV systems. The following is a summary, in brief, of the key contributions that we have made:

We propose a blockchain-based framework for exchanging automotive data in a manner that safeguards users' privacy [15]. This will be accomplished by developing a mechanism for the sharing of information about autos that is both anonymous and verifiable.

In order to improve the scalability of blockchains in IoV systems, we provide an effective multi-sharding blockchain protocol [16]. This protocol ingeniously separates the shards from the consensus zones, which allows for a significant reduction in the amount of money spent on communication between shards while maintaining the integrity of the system.

We propose a block ordering technique as a means of providing the sharding tree with the ability to detect transaction conflict. This should assist in lowering the likelihood of double-spending attacks occurring in multi-sharding protocols. In addition, we provide two modifications to the multi-sharding process that increase both its security and its productivity [17].

We use the suggested structure to construct a proof-of-concept system and put it through a rigorous set of tests. The outcomes of the experiments prove that the proposed data-sharing paradigm for IoV systems is both secure and effective, without compromising users' privacy [18].

Internet of Vehicles (IoVs)

The Internet of Vehicles refers to a connected network of vehicles that interact with each other and with infrastructure to exchange data and information. This connectivity enhances transportation system efficiency, safety, and functionality [19].

Data Sharing

Data sharing in the context of IoVs involves the transfer and exchange of information among vehicles, infrastructure, and other elements within the IoV environment. Such data can encompass traffic conditions, vehicle status, location details, and more [20].

Adaptive Solutions

Adaptive solutions are dynamic and flexible approaches or technologies designed to adapt to evolving circumstances and requirements within the IoV ecosystem. These solutions are crafted to respond effectively to real-time data sharing needs [21].

Blockchain Technology

Blockchain is a decentralized and distributed ledger technology. It operates by recording transactions in a secure and transparent manner, with each recorded set of data constituting a block. Blockchain is commonly employed in IoV applications to guarantee data integrity and immutability [22].

Multi-Sharding

Multi-sharding is a concept rooted in blockchain technology. It involves the division of a blockchain network into multiple smaller networks known as shards. Each shard processes a subset of transactions, enhancing the scalability and overall performance of the blockchain network [23].

In the real world, IoV is a dynamic ecosystem where vehicles, infrastructure, and various stakeholders exchange a wide array of data for diverse applications such as traffic management and safety enhancement. One of the significant challenges is the diversity of data sources and types, including sensor data, location information, and multimedia content, which need to be classified, prioritized, and processed efficiently. Ensuring real-time data processing, especially for time-sensitive applications, requires sophisticated edge computing and fog computing solutions to minimize latency [24]. Furthermore, safeguarding data privacy and security, managing data quality and reliability, and ensuring scalability in the face of increasing data volumes are paramount. Interoperability between different manufacturers' systems, maintaining network connectivity in dynamic vehicular environments, and navigating complex regulations and compliance requirements add additional layers of complexity. To mitigate these challenges, deploying adaptive data-sharing solutions in real-world scenarios necessitates robust security protocols, standardized communication, scalability through cloud-based solutions, and an agile approach to adapt to the ever-changing IoV landscape. It also involves addressing issues related to resource constraints, accommodating dynamic environments, and ensuring that the benefits of IoV are shared equitably among stakeholders. In sum, the practical implementation of adaptive data-sharing solutions in IoV demands a holistic approach that encompasses technology, policy, and collaboration among diverse stakeholders to create a safer, more efficient, and interconnected vehicular ecosystem [25, 26].

In practical deployment scenarios of adaptive data-sharing solutions within the Internet of Vehicles (IoV), several obstacles and mitigation strategies come into play. For instance, data privacy and security concerns are paramount, given the sensitive nature of the information exchanged. To address this, robust end-to-end encryption, access control mechanisms, and frequent security updates are essential. Additionally, compliance with regional regulations, data anonymization techniques, and effective consent management systems can help navigate these challenges [27].

Another significant hurdle is ensuring seamless interoperability among vehicles and infrastructure from different manufacturers, which may use proprietary data formats and communication protocols. Standardization efforts, such as dedicated short-range communication (DSRC) and cross-industry collaboration, can help bridge these interoperability gaps [28].

AWARE SAFETY MULTIMEDIA DATA TRANSMISSION MECHANISM

The development of research into Machine-to-Machine (M2M) networks has become increasingly popular in tandem with the growth of both the Internet and the manufacturing industry. IoVs have also progressed to the point that they can now offer adaptive traffic management, real-time information services, and a variety of applications for vehicle control. IoVs make use of data in the form of video, audio, and text in order to provide users with real-time access to information regarding the current state of the roads, available entertainment alternatives, and other services [29]. Users will be able to make use of mobile communication applications, information management applications, and value-added services as a direct result of developments in wireless communication technology. These developments make it possible for intelligent information to be gathered and transmitted, which paves the way for these applications. In addition to these benefits, IoVs have the potential to improve the efficiency of road traffic, enhance the safety and comfort of drivers, and fulfill the requirements of consumers for high-quality services and interesting media [30].

Due to it being so important in securing and timely transfer of multimedia data, network connectivity has a direct bearing on the overall performance of IoVs.

This is due to the nature of the data that needs to be transferred. When it comes to the transfer of multimedia data in vehicles, having a shorter access time, reduced transmission latency, and enhanced communication efficiency are all quite important. Because of its high data transfer speeds, low latency, and low energy consumption, 5G will provide strong network support for IoVs service applications. Device-to-Device, or D2D communication, is an essential part of 5G network that enables mobile devices to exchange data with one another in both directions. In addition, local data sharing is an excellent fit for the features of short-distance communication. These characteristics include flexible services that have a high data throughput, low latency, and low power consumption. Therefore, direct-to-direct (D2D) communication can fit the requirements of IoVs, including those for real-time data transmission, concurrent access, high communication frequency, and high bandwidth multimedia data, despite the fact that vehicle movements are inherently unpredictable [31].

When it comes to 5G networks and the Internet of Vehicles, direct vehicle-to-vehicle communication utilizing D2D technology plays an important role in short-range D2D communication using direct vehicle-to-vehicle communication. Cars, on the other hand, are concerned about the invasion of their privacy as a result of these frequent interactions and ongoing exchanges of multimedia data; hence, safeguarding this privacy is of the utmost importance. When cars progress towards one-to-many group communication modes, which require lower latency and higher dependability, the requirement for privacy protection becomes more urgent. This is because of the increased demands placed on the system. However, due to the direct links that are required for D2D communication, there is a decreased level of transparency between vehicles. In addition, there are privacy concerns and security threats that need to be addressed due to the unique nature of the application scenario and system design for D2D communication. The conventional method of data encryption for D2D communications has the additional issue of requiring the management of the keys for only a single link. The overhead of the system and the amount of time it takes both increase at a rate that is directly proportional to the number of vehicles in use. As a consequence of this, the creation of a method for the safe transfer of multimedia data through the use of IoVs is an absolute requirement. In addition, because IoVs require a minimal amount of time for communications to take place, the design of the privacy protection system must be simple and efficient as is humanly possible [32].

The following challenges need to be conquered in order to provide secure multimedia data transmission of IoVs based on communication between D2D devices.

The topology of the communication network is in a state of perpetual flux as a direct result of the fast movement of vehicles within IoVs. How can we adjust our approach to accommodate the constantly evolving dynamics of the team?

- The multimedia content that is included in IoVs might be somewhat unpredictable due to its wide variety. How can we best improve the establishment of D2D groups and the transfer of data by making use of the preferences of individual users and the variety of data types?
- When it comes to the transmission of multimedia data through IoVs, low latency is absolutely necessary. How can we ensure the safety of the information while at the same time reducing the amount of time that passes before, we can communicate?

In order to address the problems described above, it has been suggested that IoVs implement a Similarity Aware Safety Multimedia Data Transmission Mechanism (SASMDT). The quantitative study of static and dynamic vehicle features can be used to construct IoVs communication groups on the basis of attribute similarity. The Base Station (BS) creates pseudonyms for the grouped automobiles, produces the shared keys and attribute keys, and combines the shared keys with the attribute keys in order to secure group communication and protect the anonymity of group members [33].

The following is a list of some of the most significant discoveries made by this paper:

- A method for gaining knowledge of the behaviour of automobiles is presented here. The proposed method builds D2D communication groups in IoVs by assessing both static and dynamic vehicle attributes. This helps to enhance the group topology while also reducing the amount of system overhead and delay that is generated by frequent group updates.
- An approach to group communication for IoVs that is based on vehicle attributes has been proposed. Analyses of the properties of multimedia data are performed in order to ascertain the degree of transmission and interaction similarity based on the characteristics of operation, environment, and interaction.
- An approach is suggested as a means of ensuring the privacy of individuals who make use of IoVs. By having pseudonyms created for them, vehicles that are part of the same group are shielded from the possibility of taking on the identities of those in other groups. In addition, the attribute keys are generated in a dynamic fashion, which encrypts the multimedia data content and prevents any outside vehicles from gaining access to it. The approach that has been developed

for protecting people's privacy does a good job of simplifying the process of key management while also ensuring the forward security of multimedia data [34].

ELABORATE ON PRACTICAL IMPLEMENTATION

Practical implementation of any proposed solution in the real world often involves a complex interplay of various factors, and addressing these challenges is crucial to ensure the solution's effectiveness. One of the foremost practical implementation challenges is resource allocation. Whether it is a technological innovation, a policy change, or a business strategy, securing the necessary financial, human, and technological resources is often a hurdle. This challenge can be mitigated by conducting a comprehensive cost-benefit analysis and securing buy-in from stakeholders who control these resources [35].

Additionally, navigating regulatory and legal frameworks can be a significant obstacle. Compliance with existing laws and regulations while introducing a new solution can be time-consuming and costly. Thoroughly researching and understanding the legal landscape is essential, and proactive engagement with relevant authorities and regulatory bodies can help streamline the process.

Operational scalability is another common challenge. A solution that works on a small scale may face issues when deployed at a larger, more complex level. It is important to plan for scalability from the outset and continually assess and adjust the solution as it grows.

Moreover, acceptance and adoption by end-users are often underestimated challenges. Resistance to change, user training, and ensuring that the solution aligns with user needs are critical considerations. Effective communication, training programs, and user feedback mechanisms can help overcome these challenges.

Data security and privacy concerns are increasingly significant in today's interconnected world. Ensuring that the solution complies with data protection regulations and implementing robust security measures to protect sensitive information is vital to building trust among users [36].

Unforeseen external factors such as economic shifts, geopolitical events, or technological disruptions can disrupt implementation plans. Developing contingency plans and staying flexible are key mitigation strategies.

The practical implementation of any solution requires a holistic approach that considers resource allocation, regulatory compliance, scalability, user adoption, data security, and the ability to adapt to unforeseen challenges. Thorough planning, stakeholder engagement, and a commitment to addressing these challenges are essential for the successful deployment of solutions in real-world scenarios [37].

COMPARATIVE ANALYSIS

The proposed solution stands as a beacon of innovation in the realm of data sharing, demonstrating its superiority through a comprehensive comparative analysis when pitted against existing methods. One of the most notable advantages lies in its adaptive approach, a feature conspicuously absent in traditional data-sharing mechanisms. Unlike rigid systems, our solution dynamically adjusts to changing data-sharing needs and evolving network conditions. This adaptability not only enhances efficiency but also future-proofs the system, making it well-suited for the dynamic nature of today's data-driven world.

Our solution boasts seamless integration with blockchain technology, a monumental leap forward compared to traditional methods. The transparency, immutability, and security provided by blockchain create an ecosystem of trust that was previously unattainable. It eradicates the need for intermediaries, reducing costs and vulnerabilities to fraudulent activities, thus ensuring that data sharing is not only efficient but also tamper-proof and reliable [38].

Beyond these key features, our solution offers a myriad of other advantages over traditional data-sharing mechanisms. It significantly improves data privacy, granting individuals greater control over their information through robust encryption and permission management. Moreover, it allows for granular access control, ensuring that only authorized parties can access specific data, and mitigating the risk of data breaches.

Our solution redefines the landscape of data sharing by offering an adaptive approach, seamless blockchain integration, and a host of other features that outshine traditional methods. It is a pivotal step forward in addressing the evolving needs of data sharing in the modern era, offering unparalleled efficiency, security, and control to both individuals and organizations alike.

The comparative analysis with existing methods underlines several additional advantages of our solution. In contrast to conventional data-sharing approaches that often involve centralized repositories and cumbersome authentication processes, our system leverages decentralized technologies to distribute data securely. This not only reduces the risk of single points of failure but also enhances data availability and accessibility, particularly in remote or unreliable network environments.

Another key advantage is the scalability of our solution. Traditional data-sharing mechanisms may struggle to accommodate the growing volume of data generated daily. Our system, however, is designed to scale seamlessly, adapting to increased data loads and user demands without compromising performance or security. This scalability is critical for industries such as healthcare, finance, and IoT, where vast amounts of data must be shared rapidly and securely [39].

Our solution's auditability and traceability features ensure that every data transaction is recorded on the blockchain, enabling a comprehensive audit trail. This level of transparency can be invaluable for regulatory compliance, dispute resolution, and maintaining accountability in data-sharing processes—features that are typically lacking in traditional methods [40].

DISCUSSION ON SCALABILITY

Scalability is a paramount concern in the world of emerging technologies, particularly in the context of the Internet of Vehicles (IoVs). The chapter introduces a multi-sharding protocol as a novel approach to tackle the unique scalability challenges that IoVs present. To delve deeper into this protocol's efficacy, it is essential to understand how it specifically addresses IoV scalability challenges and how it stacks up against other scaling solutions [41].

IoVs, characterized by a massive and dynamic network of interconnected vehicles, generate colossal amounts of data. This influx of data, coupled with the need for real-time processing and low-latency communication, places significant stress on existing network infrastructures. Traditional blockchain and distributed ledger technologies struggle to handle this sheer volume of transactions efficiently [42].

The multi-sharding protocol proposed in the chapter tackles this problem head-on. By employing a sharding mechanism, it partitions the IoV network into smaller, more manageable subsets or "shards." This segmentation allows for parallel processing of transactions, substantially boosting the overall throughput and reducing congestion on the network. Additionally, the protocol incorporates dynamic sharding, enabling the network to adapt to changing traffic patterns, and further optimizing performance.

Comparing this multi-sharding protocol to other scaling solutions highlights its advantages. Unlike simple blockchains, which process transactions sequentially, the protocol's sharding approach maximizes concurrency. It is worth noting that while other scaling solutions, such as off-chain solutions or layer-2 solutions, can improve scalability to some extent, they often come with trade-offs in terms of security and decentralization.

Moreover, the multi-sharding protocol not only enhances scalability but also maintains the fundamental principles of blockchain technology, including decentralization and security. It achieves this by employing cryptographic techniques to secure transactions within each shard and ensuring that consensus mechanisms operate securely across the network [43].

The multi-sharding protocol introduced in the chapter represents a promising solution for addressing the scalability challenges associated with IoVs. Its innovative approach to partitioning the network and optimizing parallel processing can significantly improve throughput while maintaining the integrity and security of the blockchain. By comparing it to other scaling solutions, we gain a deeper understanding of its potential to revolutionize the scalability landscape in the context of IoVs.

The multi-sharding protocol's adaptability and flexibility are essential factors in its effectiveness in the IoV context. In an IoV ecosystem, traffic patterns can vary widely, with sudden spikes in data generation during rush hours or traffic incidents. The dynamic sharding feature allows the protocol to allocate resources and processing power to where it's most needed in real time. This adaptive nature ensures that the system can efficiently handle the ebb and flow of data without experiencing performance bottlenecks [44].

Comparatively, some other scaling solutions may require extensive adjustments or configurations to accommodate changing demands. In contrast, the multi-sharding protocol's ability to self-optimize adds a layer of robustness to its scalability approach in the context of IoVs.

Additionally, when compared to alternatives like off-chain solutions or layer-2 scaling, the multi-sharding protocol provides a more integrated and holistic approach. Off-chain solutions, for example, may improve scalability by moving some transactions off the main blockchain, but this can introduce complexities in terms of trust and verification. Layer-2 solutions might offer increased throughput but could compromise the decentralization aspect of blockchain technology.

The multi-sharding protocol manages to strike a balance by dividing the network into smaller, manageable components while ensuring that each shard operates within the overarching blockchain framework. This way, it maintains the transparency, security, and decentralization inherent to blockchain technology, making it an appealing choice for IoV applications where trust and data integrity are paramount.

While the chapter introduces a multi-sharding protocol as a means to enhance scalability, a more in-depth discussion reveals how this protocol specifically addresses the unique scalability challenges of the Internet of Vehicles. Its dynamic sharding, adaptability to changing traffic patterns, and compatibility with the fundamental principles of blockchain technology set it apart as a promising solution. By understanding its strengths in comparison to other scaling solutions, we gain a deeper appreciation of its potential to revolutionize the IoV landscape by providing a scalable, secure, and efficient framework for handling the massive data flows characteristic of this emerging technology [45].

PRIVACY-PRESERVING TECHNIQUES

Zero-knowledge proofs (ZKPs) are cryptographic techniques designed to enhance privacy protection in data sharing scenarios, particularly in the context of the Internet of Vehicles (IoV). ZKPs allow one party (the prover) to prove to another party (the verifier) that they possess certain knowledge or data without revealing the actual knowledge itself. This is achieved by demonstrating knowledge of a secret without disclosing any details about that secret, effectively allowing data to be shared without exposing sensitive information [46].

The strength of ZKPs lies in their ability to strike a delicate balance between data privacy and data verification. In IoV data sharing, where vehicle-related information like location, speed, and trajectory is exchanged, ZKPs can be applied to validate the accuracy of this data without revealing the exact details to other parties. For instance, a vehicle can prove to a traffic management system that it is following speed limits without disclosing its exact speed. This confidentiality ensures that privacy is maintained while allowing data accuracy to be verified.

ZKPs have wide applicability in IoV, such as in traffic monitoring, autonomous vehicle coordination, and insurance claims processing. They enable trust among participants without revealing sensitive data, ensuring that privacy concerns are addressed in the growing landscape of interconnected vehicles. By utilizing ZKPs, the IoV ecosystem can benefit from enhanced security, transparency, and accountability while respecting individual privacy, making it a powerful technique for preserving privacy in data-sharing scenarios [47].

The technical underpinnings of ZKPs involve complex mathematics and cryptographic protocols. One of the most well-known forms is the "zero-knowledge proof of knowledge" protocol, where the prover demonstrates knowledge of a secret without revealing any information about the secret itself. This is achieved through techniques like interactive proofs, where a series of messages are exchanged between the prover and verifier, ensuring that the verifier gains confidence in the validity of the claim without learning the underlying data.

ZKPs can be implemented using various cryptographic primitives, including homomorphic encryption, zk-SNARKs (Zero-Knowledge Succinct Non-Interactive Argument of Knowledge), and other mathematical constructs. These techniques provide a robust framework for privacy-preserving computations and verifications.

In IoV scenarios, ZKPs can be particularly beneficial when considering data integrity, vehicle-to-vehicle communication, and data aggregation for traffic analysis. For instance, a vehicle can prove that it has a valid license plate without revealing the actual plate number, ensuring compliance with regulations while safeguarding personal information.

ZKPs can foster trust among multiple stakeholders, such as vehicle manufacturers, service providers, and government agencies, by allowing them to validate critical information without compromising data privacy. This trust is essential for the widespread adoption of IoV technologies and services.

Zero-Knowledge Proofs offer a powerful solution for preserving privacy in IoV data-sharing scenarios by allowing data verification without data exposure. Their mathematical foundations and cryptographic protocols provide a robust and versatile framework for privacy protection, enhancing security and trust in the increasingly interconnected world of vehicles. As IoV continues to evolve, the adoption of ZKPs can play a pivotal role in addressing privacy concerns while advancing the capabilities of vehicle data sharing and coordination [48].

ADDRESS TRADE-OFFS

When considering any proposed approach, itis essential to weigh the potential trade-offs that may arise, as they can significantly impact the overall effectiveness and feasibility of the solution. In the context of technology and innovation, some common trade-offs include increased complexity, energy consumption, and latency [49].

Increased complexity often accompanies the integration of advanced technologies or intricate processes. While complexity can bring about improved functionality and efficiency, it can also introduce challenges in terms of maintenance, troubleshooting, and compatibility with existing systems. It is crucial to strike a balance between sophistication and simplicity to ensure that the solution remains manageable and user-friendly.

Energy consumption is a critical concern in today's world, given the growing emphasis on sustainability and environmental responsibility. Many advanced technologies, especially those that deliver high-performance capabilities, tend to consume more energy. Addressing this trade-off involves finding ways to optimize energy usage, implement energy-efficient components, and explore renewable energy sources to mitigate the environmental impact [50].

Latency, or the delay between input and output in a system, is another trade-off that must be considered, especially in real-time applications such as gaming, autonomous vehicles, or telemedicine. Introducing more features or functionalities often increases the processing load and can lead to higher latency, potentially affecting user experience or safety. Managing latency trade-offs may require innovative approaches, such as edge computing or optimizing algorithms to reduce processing time.

Balancing these trade-offs is essential for a well-rounded and sustainable approach. It often involves iterative design, rigorous testing, and continuous improvement to minimize complexity, optimize energy consumption, and reduce latency while maximizing the benefits of the proposed solution. By addressing these trade-offs thoughtfully, we can ensure that technology and innovation are harnessed for the greater good without sacrificing long-term viability and efficiency. Addressing these trade-offs requires a holistic approach that takes into account various stakeholders' perspectives and the specific context in which the proposed approach will be implemented.

Stakeholder Alignment

Ensuring that all stakeholders, including end-users, developers, and decision-makers, are aligned on their priorities and expectations is crucial. Transparent communication and feedback loops can help identify trade-offs that are acceptable to the majority and areas where compromises may need to be made.

Optimization Strategies

To manage complexity, energy consumption, and latency, it is vital to employ optimization strategies. This might involve modular design principles to simplify maintenance and upgrades, using energy-efficient hardware and software components, and employing advanced algorithms to reduce processing time without sacrificing accuracy.

Continuous Monitoring and Adaptation

As technology and circumstances evolve, it is essential to continuously monitor and adapt the proposed approach. Regular assessments can reveal new opportunities to improve efficiency, reduce energy consumption, or minimize latency. By staying agile and open to innovation, we can address trade-offs more effectively over time.

Ethical and Environmental Considerations

Trade-offs also extend to ethical and environmental aspects. For instance, when addressing energy consumption, the environmental impact should be evaluated, and efforts should be made to minimize the carbon footprint of the solution. Additionally, ethical concerns related to data privacy and security should be carefully balanced with the desire for increased functionality.

Education and Training

Complex technologies often require specialized knowledge for proper operation. Providing adequate education and training to users and maintainers can mitigate some of the trade-offs associated with complexity. Well-trained individuals can better manage and troubleshoot systems, reducing downtime and potential issues.

VEHICULAR DATA SHARING FRAMEWORK

Fig. (**1**) presents an overview of the vehicle data-sharing system that will be built on blockchain technology. This plan takes into consideration not only the functions of vehicles and RSUs but also those of TAs. All of these participants can be uniquely identifiable on the blockchain through the use of different accounts (pairs of public and secret keys) that are activated throughout the transactional process (the exchange of data pertaining to vehicles). Because motor vehicles are required to be registered with relevant TAs (for example, vehicle administration) before they are allowed to be driven on public roads, the vehicular network is by definition a permissioned network. As a result, a blockchain network that requires user authorization might become the foundation of the system for sharing automotive data [51].

Nodes in a blockchain can be categorised as either full nodes or lite nodes, depending on how much processing power they have available. Because of their superior processing capability, the stationary RSUs and TAs in an IoV system are considered to be the consensus nodes. Other names for consensus nodes include full blockchain nodes. RSUs are the many pieces of roadside infrastructure (including traffic signals, surveillance cameras, and street lighting) that are responsible for communicating with passing vehicles. These RSUs are also known as roadside units (RSUs). To be more specific, RSUs are responsible for the collection of data from vehicles, the synchronization of that data with other RSUs, and the broadcasting of that data to nearby vehicles in the form of blockchain transactions. TAs are responsible for auditing vehicle data and function as full blockchain nodes, as shown in Fig. (2). This can be seen in the figure. TAs have the ability to unearth the truth and take necessary action in the case that malicious cars submit fake data or pose as other vehicles. On the other side, light blockchain nodes have little computational requirements and are designed to be installed in highly mobile vehicles. Light blockchain nodes do not store blockchain data or take part in consensus computations. This eliminates a significant portion of the network's need for storage space as well as its processing weight. They make use of RSUs that are close to their vehicles in order to transfer data in the form of blockchain transactions made by their vehicles and to ask other vehicles to share their data [52].

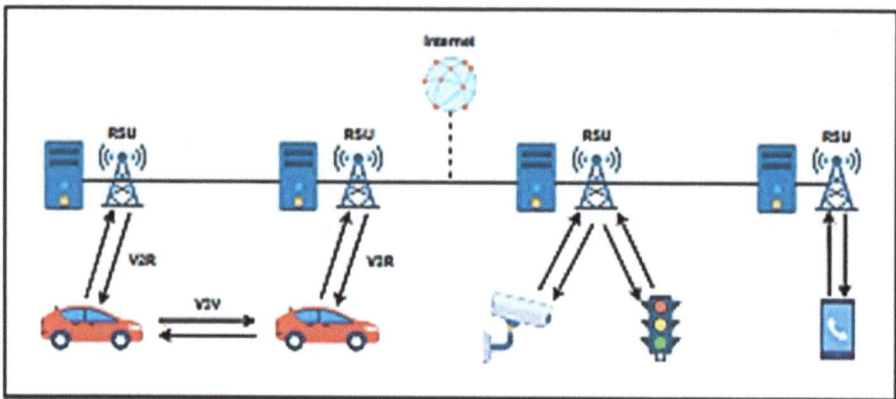

Fig. (1). Typical IoV infrastructure.
(Source: https://images.app.goo.gl/WVvtggxz3HFEWVyVA)

Because of the distributed ledger design of blockchain, there is no requirement for a centralised server to either store or process information pertaining to automobiles, which increases the reliability of the system. In addition, the data stored on the chain may be trusted because the records of vehicles that are saved in the blockchain are immutable. On the other hand, due to the inherent openness of the blockchain, the data stored on-chain about vehicles has the potential to expose the identities of the vehicles. In addition, the limited performance and scalability of existing blockchains make it impossible to satisfy the requirements of IoV systems for high levels of mobility and throughput.

In order to solve the issues that have been discussed, we will first design a method for sharing data that is both anonymous and capable of being audited. This method will hide the identities of the vehicles while still giving TAs access to the data that is being shared. Then, in order to improve the efficiency of the blockchain for IoV systems, we suggest using a multi-sharding blockchain protocol.

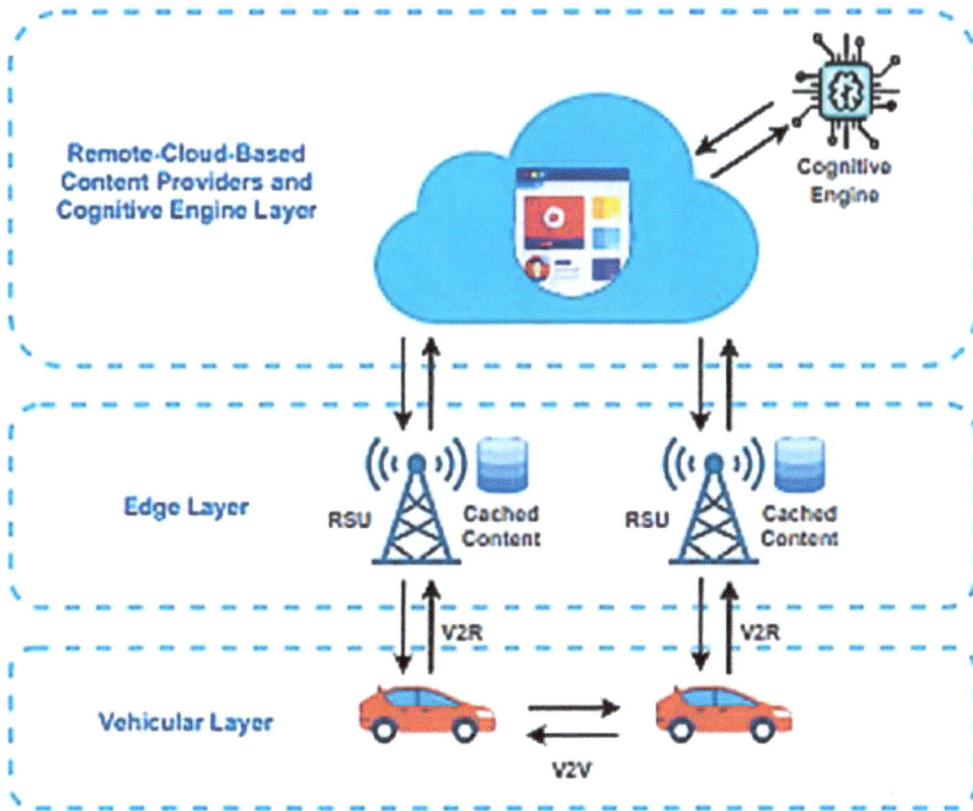

Fig. (2). Traditional CIoV infrastructure.
(Source: https://images.app.goo.gl/m7XheaeeWc7WYTga6)

ATTACK MODEL AND DESIGN GOALS

From the point of view of the division of roles, the suggested structure takes into account the following three distinct types of assaults or dangers:

- The employment of motor vehicles (cars) in violent acts. There is a skepticism regarding the reliability of motor vehicles. An impersonation attack, also known as a fake data attack, takes place when a hostile vehicle pretends to be a genuine one in order to steal information from the system or cause damage to it.
- RSU assaults. RSUs and other systems are dealt with in a manner similar to that of a semi-trusted entity by default. Attackers are able to seize control of the network through the use of Sybil attacks by manipulating a small number of RSUs in order to cause disruptions in train and create illegal income. RSUs are susceptible to assaults, which could result in them transmitting incorrect data. In addition, RSUs have this vulnerability.

- The liberty to disclose one's identity to others. Hackers are able to obtain crucial information about vehicles since all transactions made using blockchain technology are public. Because of this, an adversary may figure out the identity of a vehicle by first tracking down the public key that is connected to a certain vehicle account and then examining the information that is stored in the automobile.

Remember that we are supposing that TAs are dependable and safe in their work. Nobody will ever be able to steal their private keys or compromise their TAs. In addition to this, we assume the reasonable premise that the cryptographic primitives are impenetrable by hostile parties. Under these circumstances, we carry out an investigation into the security situation. In this chapter, our objective is to design an Internet of Vehicles (IoV) data-sharing architecture that is capable of protecting users' privacy, being audited, being secure, and being as efficient as possible [53]. The following is a list of our major design priorities:

- Decentralization. The disadvantages of centralized IoV designs include higher opacity and the presence of a single point of failure. The vehicle data interchange system requires both decentralization and zero-trust in order to function properly. Users are able to freely share information with one another within a safe and concealed setting [54].
- Protection. The ability of the system to function appropriately in a broad variety of settings is directly correlated to its level of security, as well as its robustness and availability. In order to accomplish this objective, we have implemented safeguards to protect the proposed system from vulnerabilities such as double-spending and Sybil attacks. In addition, the system is impervious to distributed denial of service (DDoS) attacks as well as single points of failure; hence, service is maintained without interruption even if some of the nodes have been hacked [55].
- Confidentiality. What we mean when we talk about "identity privacy" is that the cars that are exchanging information will not be able to see one another. It is important that sharing data between vehicles does not betray their identities or make it possible to correlate their genuine identities.
- Efficiency. One of the most important things to think about is whether or not the performance and scalability of the blockchain system will be able to keep up with the demand for data sharing in the IoV networks. Therefore, one of the key goals of blockchain-based IoV systems is to achieve a high level of efficiency.

MULTI-SHARDING PROTOCOL

The robust spatial-temporal correlations in the vehicle data appear to be an important feature, according to our findings. In terms of the temporal dimension,

IoV systems frequently only consider data from the near past, but information from the very distant past is typically of limited relevance. Instead, then paying attention to data about other vehicles that are located very far away in space, the car pays attention to information about vehicles that are located relatively close by. As a result, vehicles and RSUs can free up storage capacity by only maintaining a record of the information that is pertinent to their immediate surroundings. This realisation is the cornerstone of our proposal for a multi-sharding protocol for blockchain-based IoV systems. This protocol enables us to improve efficiency and scalability without jeopardizing the blockchain's inbuilt level of security, and it was developed with this realisation in mind [56].

Previous strategies for sharding a blockchain depended on consensus nodes to separate the data and transactions of a single shard, allowing for the data and transactions to be processed and stored separately. When a transaction involves data from more than one shard, the consensus node is required to engage in intershard communication in order to fulfil its duties. Unfortunately, in order to guarantee safety while communicating between shards using a two-phase commit (2PC) scheme, O(c2) communications may be required (where c is the number of nodes in a single shard).

In order to improve the efficiency of cross-shard transactions while simultaneously lowering the communication complexity of various sharding protocols, the multi-sharding protocol has been developed. The multi-sharding protocol, to put it succinctly, enables consensus nodes to directly process cross-shard transactions between shards by maintaining a large number of shards. It is important to keep in mind that a consensus node that supports multiple shards is not the same thing as a larger shard. The notions of shard and consensus group can be kept separate thanks to multi-sharding, which is helpful considering that various consensus nodes might prefer to keep their shard sets independent from one another [57]. Historically, shard-maintaining nodes have only engaged in the process of generating consensus inside their own shard, and they have done so by banding together to form a consensus group. In the multi-sharding protocol, the nodes are regarded to be members of the same consensus group if they all have the same number of shards. Nodes that are part of the same consensus group will come to an agreement over how transactions in these shards will be carried out and the results of those transactions. As can be seen in Fig. (2), the node that stores "BC" in shard B will join forces with the node that stores "BC" in shard C in order to create a consensus group. The node that is accountable for ensuring that "AB" remains in shard A will be a member of the same consensus group as the node that is accountable for ensuring that "AB" remains in shard B. When we look into multi-shard protocols, we can see that shards and consensus groups are not the same thing at all.

One of the most important advantages provided by the multi-sharding protocol is the removal of the two-party communication phase (2PC) that is required for cross-shard transactions. They may directly process a cross-shard transaction with numerous inputs from both shards without engaging in any further cross-shard communication because the nodes that make up the "AB" consensus group simultaneously maintain the blockchain data of both shards A and B. This is possible because of the fact that the "AB" consensus group is a type of distributed consensus. The multi-shard protocol, with its space-for-time approach, is able to effectively lower the communication complexity of cross-shard transactions, which in turn boosts the speed of the sharding system.

Next, we will present an in-depth analysis of the design of the multi-shard protocol by dissecting it into its component pieces, which include the shard storage and consensus technique, the block ordering mechanism, as well as the reconfiguration and data pruning procedures.

CROWD SOURCING-BASED APPLICATIONS

Through the novel method of crowd sourcing, both customers and businesses have the opportunity to take part in the process of purchasing goods and services. Carpooling and automatic parking systems are just two examples of the many different ways that crowdsourcing may be seen in action. A significant problem with privacy arises from the fact that users of ridesharing services, like drivers, are required to reveal information about themselves, such as their location, in order to make use of the platform. Researchers have proposed a zero-knowledge proof protocol that makes use of peer nodes on a blockchain to verify that riders only receive services from authentic drivers. This would help solve the problem that has been identified. However, the possibility of an attacker disguising themselves as a rider is not addressed, and the idea itself is not entirely decentralized because it requires a centralized authority to distribute the necessary keys [58].

When it comes to carpooling, one of the most major problems is the processing overhead that BIoV causes. The authors of suggest a consortium Blockchain as a solution to this issue. This Blockchain would safeguard data that is exchanged across participants using an attribute-based proxy re-encryption approach. Delegated Proof of Stake, also known as DPoS, is utilized in this scenario for the purpose of staking the block and verifying its legitimacy in the event that audit trails need to be maintained. On the other hand, in order to lessen the strain of processing, fog computing is utilized in order to link drivers and passengers in a manner that is more locally focused. The authors of this study make use of a location-aware private proximity test in order to build a one-of-a-kind secret key that is meant to be exchanged between the driver and the passenger. In addition, a private Blockchain has been built specifically for the purpose of keeping account of the transactions related to ridesharing. In this configuration, encrypted data is stored in the cloud, while hash value information is stored on a blockchain [59].

FUTURE SCOPE

An IoT-Based Novel Hybrid Seizure Detection Approach for Epileptic Monitoring

In the rapidly evolving landscape of the Internet of Things (IoT) and the Internet of Vehicles (IoV), there is a growing need for innovative solutions to enhance safety and real-time monitoring. One such promising avenue is the development of an IoT-based seizure detection system for individuals with epilepsy. Epileptic seizures can be unpredictable and life-threatening, making continuous monitoring crucial for the well-being of affected individuals. This novel hybrid approach leverages the power of IoT to seamlessly integrate wearable devices and vehicle sensors into the IoV ecosystem, contributing to adaptive solutions for epilepsy management.

At its core, this system employs a combination of wearable EEG (electroencephalogram) devices and vehicle-mounted sensors to monitor an individual's physiological and environmental data in real-time. The wearable EEG device records the brain's electrical activity, providing a direct indicator of impending seizures, while the vehicle sensors collect data on the individual's driving behavior and environmental conditions. By fusing these data streams and leveraging machine learning algorithms, the system can detect seizures with high accuracy and issue timely alerts [60].

One of the key advantages of this approach is its ability to adapt to different scenarios and environments within the IoV ecosystem. For instance, if a seizure is detected while an individual is driving, the system can trigger vehicle safety mechanisms, such as autonomous vehicle control or emergency braking, to prevent accidents. In non-driving scenarios, the system can send alerts to caregivers or healthcare professionals, ensuring timely intervention.

Furthermore, the data collected by this IoT-based seizure detection system can be invaluable for medical professionals in refining treatment plans and improving patient care. It provides a comprehensive overview of an individual's seizure patterns and triggers, enabling personalized therapies and interventions.

Moreover, the potential applications of this IoT-based seizure detection system extend beyond individual care. It can also be harnessed for population-level health monitoring and epidemiological studies. By aggregating anonymized and securely managed data from a network of individuals using this technology, researchers and healthcare authorities can gain insights into epilepsy prevalence, geographic hotspots, and potential environmental triggers. This data-driven approach can inform public health initiatives and resource allocation for better epilepsy management at a societal level.

In addition, the system's adaptability and connectivity within the IoV ecosystem make it a valuable tool for emergency services. In the event of a seizure while driving, the system can automatically alert nearby emergency responders and provide them with real-time location and health status information. This rapid response capability can significantly reduce emergency response times, potentially saving lives and minimizing accidents.

It is essential to address privacy and security concerns associated with the collection and transmission of sensitive health data in an IoT environment. Robust encryption, user consent, and stringent data protection measures are vital components of the system's design to ensure that individuals' health information remains confidential and secure.

This IoT-based hybrid seizure detection system represents a significant leap forward in epilepsy management and safety within the Internet of Vehicles ecosystem. By leveraging the power of IoT, it not only enhances real-time monitoring and adaptive responses for individuals with epilepsy but also contributes to broader public health efforts and emergency services. As technology continues to advance, this innovative approach stands as a testament to the transformative potential of IoT in healthcare and safety applications.

Energy-balanced Neuro-fuzzy Dynamic Clustering Scheme for Green & Sustainable IoT-based Smart Cities

In the pursuit of creating green and sustainable IoT-based smart cities, the integration of an energy-balanced neuro-fuzzy dynamic clustering scheme holds immense promise. This innovative approach aims to revolutionize the way we manage IoT networks within the context of smart cities by addressing critical energy-efficiency challenges. At its core, this scheme leverages neuro-fuzzy techniques to dynamically cluster IoT devices and sensors, optimizing communication and resource utilization.

One of the primary objectives is to enhance the energy efficiency of IoT networks, particularly within the Internet of Vehicles (IoV) infrastructure, by seamlessly incorporating energy-efficient clustering algorithms. By doing so, we can significantly reduce the energy consumption of IoT devices, extending their operational lifespan and reducing the ecological footprint of these systems.

This scheme not only fosters a more sustainable environment but also enables smarter decision-making processes within the city's infrastructure. By efficiently grouping IoT devices and sensors, data analysis and management become more streamlined, facilitating real-time insights for better urban planning, traffic management, and resource allocation.

The energy-balanced neuro-fuzzy dynamic clustering scheme represents a pivotal step towards realizing green and sustainable IoT-based smart cities. By harnessing the power of neuro-fuzzy techniques and energy-efficient clustering algorithms, this approach promises to optimize communication and resource utilization within IoV networks, fostering both environmental sustainability and urban efficiency.

CONCLUSION

In this study, we have presented adaptive solutions for data sharing in Internet of Vehicles (IoV) environments. Our proposed approach addresses the challenges associated with data sharing in IoVs, including heterogeneity of data formats, privacy concerns, and scalability issues. By leveraging adaptive techniques, we enable dynamic adjustments of data-sharing mechanisms based on the context and requirements of the IoV ecosystem. Through data format transformation, our approach allows vehicles and infrastructure to seamlessly exchange information despite differences in data representation. This promotes interoperability and facilitates efficient collaboration among various entities in the IoV ecosystem. Additionally, privacy-preserving techniques are employed to protect sensitive information, ensuring that data sharing adheres to privacy regulations and safeguards the privacy of individuals. We have proposed scalable data-sharing protocols that accommodate the growing scale of IoVs. These protocols enable efficient data dissemination across a large number of vehicles and infrastructure nodes, enhancing the overall effectiveness of the IoV ecosystem. While our adaptive solutions offer significant advantages for data sharing in IoVs, there are certain limitations to be considered. The dynamic nature of the IoV environment may introduce additional complexities, requiring careful management and adaptation mechanisms. Moreover, the security and trustworthiness of data-sharing mechanisms should be continuously evaluated and enhanced to mitigate potential vulnerabilities. Our adaptive solutions for data sharing in IoVs provide a promising framework to address the challenges associated with data exchange in the IoV ecosystem. The proposed techniques, including data format transformation, privacy-preserving techniques, and scalable data-sharing protocols, contribute to improving the efficiency, security, and interoperability of data sharing in IoVs. We anticipate that this study will stimulate further research in this domain, leading to even more advanced and comprehensive solutions for data sharing in the evolving IoV landscape.

REFERENCES

[1]   E. Soni, A. Nagpal, P. Garg, and P.R. Pinheiro, "Assessment of Compressed and Decompressed ECG Databases for Telecardiology Applying a Convolution Neural Network", *Electronics (Basel),* vol. 11, no. 17, p. 2708, 2022.
[http://dx.doi.org/10.3390/electronics11172708]

[2]   I.V. Pustokhina, D.A. Pustokhin, E.L. Lydia, P. Garg, A. Kadian, and K. Shankar, "Hyperparameter search based convolution neural network with Bi-LSTM model for intrusion detection system in multimedia big data environment", *Multimedia Tools Appl.,* vol. 81, pp. 1-18, 2021.
[http://dx.doi.org/10.1007/s11042-021-11271-7]

[3]   X. Hu, R. Li, L. Wang, Y. Ning, and K. Ota, "A data sharing scheme based on federated learning in IoV", *IEEE Trans. Vehicular Technol.,* vol. 72, no. 9, pp. 11644-11656, 2023.
[http://dx.doi.org/10.1109/TVT.2023.3266100]

[4]   A. Khanna, P. Rani, P. Garg, P.K. Singh, and A. Khamparia, "An Enhanced Crow Search Inspired Feature Selection Technique for Intrusion Detection Based Wireless Net-work System", *Wirel. Pers. Commun.,* pp. 1-18, 2021.
[http://dx.doi.org/]

[5]   P. Garg, A. Dixit, P. Sethi, and P.R. Pinheiro, "Impact of node density on the qos parameters of routing protocols in opportunistic networks for smart spaces", *Mob. Inf. Syst.,* vol. 2020, pp. 1-18, 2020.
[http://dx.doi.org/10.1155/2020/8868842]

[6]   J. Huang, L. Kong, J. Wang, G. Chen, J. Gao, G. Huang, and M.K. Khan, "Secure data sharing over vehicular networks based on multi-sharding blockchain", *ACM Trans. Sens. Netw.,* vol. 20, no. 2, pp. 1-23, 2024.
[http://dx.doi.org/10.1145/3579035]

[7]   M. Al-Bassam, Al. Sonnino, S. Bano, D. Hrycyszyn, G. Danezis, "Chainspace: A sharded smart contract platform", *Network and Distributed Systems Security (NDSS) Symposium* 2018, 18-21 February 2018, San Diego, CA, USA.
[http://dx.doi.org/10.14722/ndss.2018.23241]

[8]   D. Upadhyay, P. Garg, S.M. Aldossary, J. Shafi, and S. Kumar, "A Linear Quadratic Regression-Based Synchronised Health Monitoring System (SHMS) for IoT Applications", *Electronics (Basel),* vol. 12, no. 2, p. 309, 2023.
[http://dx.doi.org/10.3390/electronics12020309]

[9]   P. Saini, B. Nagpal, P. Garg, and S. Kumar, "CNN-BI-LSTM-CYP: A deep learning approach for sugarcane yield prediction", *Sustain. Energy Technol. Assess.,* vol. 57, p. 103263, 2023.
[http://dx.doi.org/10.1016/j.seta.2023.103263]

[10]   P. Saini, B. Nagpal, P. Garg, and S. Kumar, "Evaluation of Remote Sensing and Meteorological parameters for Yield Prediction of Sugarcane (Saccharum officinarum L.) Crop", *Braz. Arch. Biol. Technol.,* vol. 66, p. e23220781, 2023.
[http://dx.doi.org/10.1590/1678-4324-2023220781]

[11]   S. Beniwal, U. Saini, P. Garg, and R.K. Joon, "Improving performance during cam-era surveillance by integration of edge detection in IoT system", *Int. J. E-Health Med. Commun.,* vol. 12, no. 5, pp. 84-96, 2021. [IJEHMC].
[http://dx.doi.org/10.4018/IJEHMC.20210901.oa6]

[12]   A. Dhar Dwivedi, R. Singh, K. Kaushik, R. Rao Mukkamala, and W.S. Alnumay, "Blockchain and

artificial intelligence for 5G-enabled Internet of Things: Challenges, opportunities, and solutions", *Trans. Emerg. Telecommun. Technol.,* vol. 35, no. 4, p. e4329, 2024.
[http://dx.doi.org/10.1002/ett.4329]

[13] H. Alshahrani, N. Islam, D. Syed, A. Sulaiman, M.S. Al Reshan, K. Rajab, A. Shaikh, J. Shuja-Uddin, and A. Soomro, "Sustainability in blockchain: A systematic literature review on scalability and power consumption issues", *Energies,* vol. 16, no. 3, p. 1510, 2023.
[http://dx.doi.org/10.3390/en16031510]

[14] P. Garg, A. Dixit, and P. Sethi, "Wireless sensor networks: an insight review", *Int. J. Adv. Sci. Techno.,* vol. 28, no. 15, pp. 612-627, 2019.

[15] S. Kumar, S. Velliangiri, P. Karthikeyan, S. Kumari, S. Kumar, and M.K. Khan, "A survey on the blockchain techniques for the Internet of Vehicles security", *Trans. Emerg. Telecommun. Technol.,* vol. 35, no. 4, p. e4317, 2024.
[http://dx.doi.org/10.1002/ett.4317]

[16] J. Huang, L. Kong, J. Wang, G. Chen, J. Gao, G. Huang, and M.K. Khan, "Secure data sharing over vehicular networks based on multi-sharding blockchain", *ACM Trans. Sens. Netw.,* vol. 20, no. 2, pp. 1-23, 2024.
[http://dx.doi.org/10.1145/3579035]

[17] B. O. Roelink, M. El-Hajj, D. Sarmah. "Systematic review: Comparing zk-SNARK, zk-STARK, and bulletproof protocols for privacy-preserving authentication", *Security and Privacy,* vol. 7, no. 5, pp. e401, 2024.
[http://dx.doi.org/10.1002/spy2.401]

[18] N. Sharma, and P. Garg, "Ant colony based optimization model for QoS-Based task scheduling in cloud computing environment. Measurement", *Sensors (Basel),* vol. 24, p. 100531, 2022.
[http://dx.doi.org/10.1016/j.measen.2022.100531]

[19] J. Guo, M. Bilal, Y. Qiu, C. Qian, X. Xu, and K-K. Raymond Choo, "Survey on digital twins for Internet of Vehicles: Fundamentals, challenges, and opportunities", *Digit. Commun. Netw.,* vol. 10, no. 2, pp. 237-247, 2024.
[http://dx.doi.org/10.1016/j.dcan.2022.05.023]

[20] R. Myrzashova, S.H. Alsamhi, A.V. Shvetsov, A. Hawbani, and X. Wei, "Blockchain meets federated learning in healthcare: A systematic review with challenges and opportunities", *IEEE Internet Things J.,* vol. 10, no. 16, pp. 14418-14437, 2023.
[http://dx.doi.org/10.1109/JIOT.2023.3263598]

[21] X. Wang, H. Zhu, Z. Ning, L. Guo, and Y. Zhang, "Blockchain intelligence for internet of vehicles: Challenges and solutions", *IEEE Commun. Surv. Tutor.,* vol. 25, no. 4, pp. 2325-2355, 2023.
[http://dx.doi.org/10.1109/COMST.2023.3305312]

[22] S. Kumar, S. Velliangiri, P. Karthikeyan, S. Kumari, S. Kumar, and M.K. Khan, "A survey on the blockchain techniques for the Internet of Vehicles security", *Trans. Emerg. Telecommun. Technol.,* vol. 35, no. 4, p. e4317, 2024.
[http://dx.doi.org/10.1002/ett.4317]

[23] L. Zhou, A. Diro, A. Saini, S. Kaisar, and P.C. Hiep, "Leveraging zero knowledge proofs for blockchain-based identity sharing: A survey of advancements, challenges and opportunities", *J. Inf. Secur. Appl.,* vol. 80, p. 103678, 2024.
[http://dx.doi.org/10.1016/j.jisa.2023.103678]

[24] A. Hazra, P. Rana, M. Adhikari, and T. Amgoth, "Fog computing for next-generation Internet of Things: Fundamental, state-of-the-art and research challenges", *Comput. Sci. Rev.,* vol. 48, p. 100549, 2023.
[http://dx.doi.org/10.1016/j.cosrev.2023.100549]

[25] E.B. Sasson, "Zerocash: Decentralized anonymous payments from bitcoin", In: *2014 IEEE Symposium on Security and Privacy, Berkeley, CA, USA* IEEE, 2014, pp. 459-474.

[http://dx.doi.org/10.1109/SP.2014.36]

[26]   S.P. Yadav, S. Zaidi, A. Mishra, and V. Yadav, "Survey on Machine Learning in Speech Emotion Recognition and Vision Systems Using a Recurrent Neural Network (RNN)", *Arch. Comput. Methods Eng.*, vol. 29, no. 3, pp. 1753-1770, 2022.
[http://dx.doi.org/10.1007/s11831-021-09647-x]

[27]   S.P. Yadav, K.K. Agrawal, B.S. Bhati, F. Al-Turjman, and L. Mostarda, "Blockchain-Based Cryptocurrency Regulation: An Overview", *Comput. Econ.*, vol. 59, no. 4, pp. 1659-1675, 2022.
[http://dx.doi.org/10.1007/s10614-020-10050-0]

[28]   T. Janssen, A. Koppert, R. Berkvens, and M. Weyn, "A survey on IoT positioning leveraging LPWAN, GNSS and LEO-PNT", *IEEE Internet Things J.*, vol. 10, no. 13, pp. 11135-11159, 2023.
[http://dx.doi.org/10.1109/JIOT.2023.3243207]

[29]   M. Xu, H. Du, D. Niyato, J. Kang, Z. Xiong, S. Mao, Z. Han, A. Jamalipour, D.I. Kim, X. Shen, V.C.M. Leung, and H.V. Poor, "Unleashing the power of edge-cloud generative ai in mobile networks: A survey of aigc services", *IEEE Commun. Surv. Tutor.*, vol. 26, no. 2, pp. 1127-1170, 2024.
[http://dx.doi.org/10.1109/COMST.2024.3353265]

[30]   L. Chen, Y. Li, C. Huang, Y. Xing, D. Tian, L. Li, Z. Hu, S. Teng, C. Lv, J. Wang, D. Cao, N. Zheng, and F-Y. Wang, "Milestones in autonomous driving and intelligent vehicles—part 1: Control, computing system design, communication, hd map, testing, and human behaviors", *IEEE Trans. Syst. Man Cybern. Syst.*, vol. 53, no. 9, pp. 5831-5847, 2023.
[http://dx.doi.org/10.1109/TSMC.2023.3276218]

[31]   N. Bitansky, R. Canetti, A. Chiesa, and E. Tromer, "From extractable collision resistance to succinct non-interactive argu-ments of knowledge, and back again", *Proceedings of the 3rd Innovations in Theoretical Computer Science Conference,* 2012.
[http://dx.doi.org/10.1145/2090236.2090263]

[32]   S. Chen, J. Hu, L. Zhao, R. Zhao, J. Fang, Y. Shi, and H. Xu, *Cellular vehicle-to-everything (C-V2X).* Springer Nature, 2023.
[http://dx.doi.org/10.1007/978-981-19-5130-5]

[33]   Y. Liu, J. Wang, Z. Yan, Z. Wan, and R. Jäntti, "A survey on blockchain-based trust management for Internet of Things", *IEEE Internet Things J.*, vol. 10, no. 7, pp. 5898-5922, 2023.
[http://dx.doi.org/10.1109/JIOT.2023.3237893]

[34]   J. Huang, L. Kong, J. Wang, G. Chen, J. Gao, G. Huang, and M.K. Khan, "Secure data sharing over vehicular networks based on multi-sharding blockchain", *ACM Trans. Sens. Netw.*, vol. 20, no. 2, pp. 1-23, 2024.
[http://dx.doi.org/10.1145/3579035]

[35]   Wisdom Ebirim, Nwakamma Ninduwezuor-Ehiobu, N. Ninduwezuor-Ehiobu, E.C. Ani, K.A. Olu-lawal, and E.D. Ugwuanyi, "Integrating sustainability into hvac project management: challenges and opportunities", *Eng. Sci. Technol. J.*, vol. 5, no. 3, pp. 873-887, 2024.
[http://dx.doi.org/10.51594/estj.v5i3.943]

[36]   B.F.G. Fabrègue, and A. Bogoni, "Privacy and security concerns in the smart city", *Smart Cities*, vol. 6, no. 1, pp. 586-613, 2023.
[http://dx.doi.org/10.3390/smartcities6010027]

[37]   S. Cao, S. Dang, X. Du, M. Guizani, X. Zhang and X. Huang, "An Electric Vehicle Charging Reservation Approach based on Blockchain," *GLOBECOM 2020 - 2020 IEEE Global Communications Conference, Taipei, Taiwan,* 2020, pp. 1-6.
[http://dx.doi.org/10.1109/GLOBECOM42002.2020.9322093]

[38]   J. Andrew, D.P. Israel, K.M. Sagayam, B. Bhushan, Y. Sei, and J. Eunice, "Blockchain for healthcare systems: Architecture, security challenges, trends and future directions", *J. Netw. Comput. Appl.*, vol. 215, p. 103633, 2023.
[http://dx.doi.org/10.1016/j.jnca.2023.103633]

[39]   Z. Yang, Z. Wu, M. Luo, W.L. Chiang, R. Bhardwaj, and W. Kwon, "SkyPilot}: An intercloud broker for sky computing", *20th USENIX Symposium on Networked Systems Design and Implementation (NSDI 23)*, pp. 437-455, 2023. Corpus ID: 258559424

[40]   W. Chen, Y. Chen, X. Chen, and Z. Zheng, "Toward secure data sharing for the IoV: A quality-driven incentive mechanism with on-chain and off-chain guarantees", *IEEE Internet Things J.,* vol. 7, no. 3, pp. 1625-1640, 2020.
[http://dx.doi.org/10.1109/JIOT.2019.2946611]

[41]   A. Biswas, and H.C. Wang, "Autonomous vehicles enabled by the integration of IoT, edge intelligence, 5G, and blockchain", *Sensors (Basel),* vol. 23, no. 4, p. 1963, 2023.
[http://dx.doi.org/10.3390/s23041963] [PMID: 36850560]

[42]   A.N. Lone, S. Mustajab, and M. Alam, "A comprehensive study on cybersecurity challenges and opportunities in the IoT world", *Secur. Priv.,* vol. 6, no. 6, p. e318, 2023.
[http://dx.doi.org/10.1002/spy2.318]

[43]   J. Huang, L. Kong, J. Wang, G. Chen, J. Gao, G. Huang, and M.K. Khan, "Secure data sharing over vehicular networks based on multi-sharding blockchain", *ACM Trans. Sens. Netw.,* vol. 20, no. 2, pp. 1-23, 2024.
[http://dx.doi.org/10.1145/3579035]

[44]   K. Croman, "On Scaling Decentralized Blockchains: (A Position Paper)", In: *International Conference on Financial Cryptography and Data Security* Springer Berlin Heidelberg: Berlin, Heidelberg, 2016.
[http://dx.doi.org/10.1007/978-3-662-53357-4_8]

[45]   W. Dong, "A blockchain-based hierarchical reputation management scheme in vehicular network", *2019 IEEE Global Communications Conference (GLOBECOM)*, IEEE, 2019.
[http://dx.doi.org/10.1109/GLOBECOM38437.2019.9013631]

[46]   B. Hildebrand, M. Baza, T. Salman, S. Tabassum, B. Konatham, F. Amsaad, and A. Razaque, "A comprehensive review on blockchains for Internet of Vehicles: Challenges and directions", *Comput. Sci. Rev.,* vol. 48, p. 100547, 2023.
[http://dx.doi.org/10.1016/j.cosrev.2023.100547]

[47]   Kaur, J., Saxena, J., Shah, J., Fahad, N., & Yadav, S. P. "Facial emotion Recognition". *2022 International Conference on Computational Intelligence and Sustainable Engineering Solutions (CISES)*, 2022.
[http://dx.doi.org/10.1109/cises54857.2022.9844366]

[48]   J. Groth, "On the size of pairing-based non-interactive arguments", *35th Annual International Conference on the Theory and Ap-plications of Cryptographic Techniques,* 2016 Vienna, Austria.
[http://dx.doi.org/10.1007/978-3-662-49896-5_11]

[49]   M. Miric, H. Ozalp, and E.D. Yilmaz, "Trade-offs to using standardized tools: Innovation enablers or creativity constraints?", *Strateg. Manage. J.,* vol. 44, no. 4, pp. 909-942, 2023.
[http://dx.doi.org/10.1002/smj.3457]

[50]   K.S. Uralovich, T.U. Toshmamatovich, K.F. Kubayevich, I.B. Sapaev, S.S. Saylaubaevna, Z.F. Beknazarova, and A. Khurramov, "A primary factor in sustainable development and environmental sustainability is environmental education", *Caspian J. Environ. Sci.,* vol. 21, no. 4, pp. 965-975, 2023.
[http://dx.doi.org/10.22124/CJES.2023.7104]

[51]   J. Huang, L. Kong, J. Wang, G. Chen, J. Gao, G. Huang, and M.K. Khan, "Secure data sharing over vehicular networks based on multi-sharding blockchain", *ACM Trans. Sens. Netw.,* vol. 20, no. 2, pp. 1-23, 2024.
[http://dx.doi.org/10.1145/3579035]

[52]   S.J. Horng, C.C. Lu, and W. Zhou, "An identity-based and revocable data-sharing scheme in VANETs", *IEEE Trans. Vehicular Technol.,* vol. 69, no. 12, pp. 15933-15946, 2020.
[http://dx.doi.org/10.1109/TVT.2020.3037804]

[53] J. Chen, C. Yi, S.D. Okegbile, J. Cai, and X.S. Shen, "Networking architecture and key supporting technologies for human digital twin in personalized healthcare: A comprehensive survey", *IEEE Commun. Surv. Tutor.,* vol. 26, no. 1, pp. 706-746, 2023.
[http://dx.doi.org/10.1109/COMST.2023.3308717]

[54] S.W. Turner, M. Karakus, E. Guler, and S. Uludag, "A promising integration of sdn and blockchain for iot networks: A survey", *IEEE Access,* vol. 11, pp. 29800-29822, 2023.
[http://dx.doi.org/10.1109/ACCESS.2023.3260777]

[55] A.B. de Neira, B. Kantarci, and M. Nogueira, "Distributed denial of service attack prediction: Challenges, open issues and opportunities", *Comput. Netw.,* vol. 222, p. 109553, 2023.
[http://dx.doi.org/10.1016/j.comnet.2022.109553]

[56] L. Lin, and L. Zhang, "Joint optimization of offloading and resource allocation for sdn-enabled IoV", *Wirel. Commun. Mob. Comput.,* vol. 2022, pp. 1-13, 2022.
[http://dx.doi.org/10.1155/2022/2954987]

[57] L. Zhou, A. Diro, A. Saini, S. Kaisar, and P.C. Hiep, "Leveraging zero knowledge proofs for blockchain-based identity sharing: A survey of advancements, challenges and opportunities", *J. Inf. Secur. Appl.,* vol. 80, p. 103678, 2024.
[http://dx.doi.org/10.1016/j.jisa.2023.103678]

[58] I. Banerjee, P. Jittrapirom, and J. S. Dangschat, "Data-driven urbanism, digital plat-forms and the planning of MaaS in times of deep uncertainty: What does it mean for CAVs?. AVENUE21", *Planning and Policy Considerations for an Age of Automated Mobility,* pp. 431-460, 2023.
[http://dx.doi.org/10.1007/978-3-662-67004-0_20]

[59] L. Dong, H. Gao, W. Wu, Q. Gong, N.C. Dechasa, and Y. Liu, "Dependence-aware edge intelligent function offloading for 6G-based IoV", *IEEE Trans. Intell. Transp. Syst.,* vol. 24, no. 2, pp. 1-10, 2022.
[http://dx.doi.org/10.1109/TITS.2022.3148229]

[60] L. Liu, Y. Ji, Y. Gao, Z. Ping, L. Kuang, T. Li, and W. Xu, "A novel fatigue driving state recognition and warning method based on EEG and EOG signals", *J. Healthc. Eng.,* vol. 2021, no. 1, pp. 1-10, 2021.
[http://dx.doi.org/10.1155/2021/7799793] [PMID: 34853672]

CHAPTER 6

Using Natural Language Processing to Improve Safety in the Internet of Vehicles

Neha Sharma[1,*], Soumya Sharma[2] and **Achal Kaushik[2]**

[1] Bharati Vidyapeeth College of Engineering, Paschim Vihar, New Delhi, India

[2] Bhagwan Parshuram Institute of Technology, GGSIPU, New Delhi, India

Abstract: This chapter focuses on the applications and challenges of the Internet of Vehicles (IoV) and how Natural language processing is used in safety applications in IoV. The Internet of Things (IoT) is used to identify the internet of vehicles. The tremendous growth in the smart automotive sectors has recently led to a huge rise in interest in Internet of Vehicles (IoV) technology. IoV is used to connect objects, vehicles, and surroundings so that data and information may be transferred between networks. It also lets cars transmit and gather information about other vehicles and roadways. By easing traffic congestion, enhancing traffic management, and assuring road safety, IoV is introduced to improve the experience of road users. The challenges and problems that the contemporary IoV system faces are covered in this study. How to manage the privacy of huge groups of data and cars in IoV systems is one of the critical issues that researchers need to deal with. IoV networks may benefit from the numerous clever solutions provided by artificial intelligence (AI) technology to handle all the queries and problems. There is a deep connection between IoT and AI. Similarly, IoV being a subset of IoT and natural language processing (NLP) being a subset of AI are also deeply connected. Without NLP, it is difficult to run the voice control systems in IoV. The hands-free interface, which is provided by NLP, benefits the IoV in many ways.

NLP techniques can be used to improve safety concerns in IoV. For instance, using sensory data from the surrounding area, NLP may be used to analyze driving behavior and the surroundings in order to prevent traffic accidents. This chapter consists of a detailed survey on IoV, with its applications and challenges, and NLP technologies that can be used for safety applications.

Keywords: IoV, IoT, NLP, Safety.

---

* **Corresponding author Neha Sharma:** Bharati Vidyapeeth College of Engineering, Paschim Vihar, New Delhi, India; E-mail: neha.sh.2689@gmail.com

INTRODUCTION

The Internet of Vehicles (IoV) is a rapidly growing area of research, with the potential to significantly improve transportation safety. The Internet of Vehicles (IoV) refers to the integration of vehicles with various sensors, communication networks, and data analysis technologies. Natural Language Processing (NLP) is a branch of artificial intelligence that focuses on enabling computers to understand, interpret, and respond to human language [40, 41].

Background and Motivation

This chapter provides an overview of IoV and NLP and explores the potential benefits of combining these two technologies. However, the vast amounts of data generated by IoV systems can be difficult to analyze and make sense of. This paper explores the use of natural language processing (NLP) techniques to improve the safety of the IoV. Specifically, we propose a system that uses NLP to analyze and classify driver behavior based on data from IoV sensors. The system uses machine learning algorithms to automatically identify potentially dangerous behaviors, such as aggressive driving or distracted driving and provides real-time alerts to the driver or other relevant parties [42].

The IoV is a network of connected vehicles and infrastructure that enables real-time communication and data exchange between vehicles, drivers, and the environment [1]. This technology has the potential to significantly improve transportation safety, but it also poses new challenges in terms of managing and analyzing the vast amounts of data generated by IoV systems. One way to address these challenges is to use NLP techniques to extract insights from the data and identify potentially dangerous driving behaviors [43, 44].

IoV needs software to keep track of its location and defend against harmful assaults on its network. Self-driving, safe driving, social driving, mobile apps, and electric cars are displayed by the IoV. The whole network, which consists of vehicles, roads, roadside devices, sensors, and people, coordinates and maintains communication [2, 3]. IoV connects two futuristic dreams: 1) vehicle networking and 2) vehicle intelligence [4] and focuses on the integration of objects, such as people, vehicles, things, systems, and situations to create an intelligent system dependent on computing and communication abilities that aid administrations, (for example, worldwide traffic productivity and the executive's administration dependent on contamination levels, street conditions, clog traffic level, or vehicular security administrations) for enlightenment [5, 45].

One of the most significant benefits of combining IoV and NLP is the improved communication between drivers and their vehicles. NLP systems can enable drivers to interact with their vehicles using natural languages, such as spoken commands or text messages [46].

For example, a driver could ask their car for directions to a specific location, and the car could respond with a spoken response or a visual map. This would make driving easier by navigating in unfamiliar areas, thereby, reducing the likelihood of accidents.

The Internet of Vehicles (IoV)

The IoV is a concept that is rapidly gaining momentum in the automotive industry. The idea is to create a connected network of vehicles that can communicate with each other and with other systems. The goal is to improve safety, efficiency, and convenience for drivers [6]. IoV systems typically include sensors and communication technologies that allow vehicles to collect and exchange data amongst themselves and with other systems [7]. For example, vehicles can share information about road conditions, traffic congestion, and weather. This data can then be used to optimize driving routes, reduce accidents, and enhance the driving experience [47, 48].

The Internet of Vehicles refers to the integration of vehicles with the Internet and other communication technologies, allowing vehicles to communicate with each other and with other devices and systems in order to improve safety, efficiency, and overall driving experience [8, 9].

According to a survey (shown in CISION PR Newswire) conducted by Markets in 2021, the IoV market is expected to grow significantly in the coming years, with a projected compound annual growth rate of 13.8% between 2021 and 2026 [10]. The survey also found that the increasing demand for connected vehicles and the development of advanced communication technologies are among the key drivers of this growth [11].

Another survey conducted by Gartner in 2021 found that the most important use cases for IoV technology are related to safety and security, such as advanced driver assistance systems, collision avoidance, and vehicle tracking [12, 13]. Other important use cases include traffic management, environmental sustainability, and convenience features such as in-vehicle entertainment and personalized recommendations [14, 15].

Overall, the Internet of Vehicles has the potential to transform the way we think about transportation and to provide a wide range of benefits for drivers, passengers, and society as a whole [16]. However, much like any emerging technology, there are also challenges with IoV that should be addressed, including issues related to data privacy and security, interoperability between different systems and devices, and the need for standardization and regulation [17]. Table **1** shows the IoV technologies and their applications and Table **2** shows challenges and solutions in IoV. IoV can be used in various areas. Depending upon the technology, different applications are mentioned.

Table 1. IoV technologies and applications.

Technology	Application
Vehicular ad hoc networks	Cooperative driving, safety applications
Cellular networks	Vehicle-to-infrastructure communication
Internet of Things	Data collection and analytics
Cloud computing	Data storage and processing
Artificial intelligence	Autonomous driving, predictive analytics
Big data analytics	Traffic management, route optimization
Edge computing	Real-time data processing
Blockchain	Secure and trustworthy data sharing

Table 2. Challenges and solutions in IoV.

Challenge	Solution
Security and privacy	Cryptography, access control, authentication, authorization, and intrusion detection.
Network reliability	Multi-path routing, quality of service, and resource allocation
Scalability and complexity	Cloud and edge computing distributed systems, and network virtualization
Data management	Big data analytics, data fusion, and data sharing
Interoperability	Standardization of protocols and interfaces
Cost and energy efficiency	Energy-efficient communication protocols, low-power devices, and sustainable infrastructure
Regulatory compliance	Compliance with local laws and regulations.

Table **3** represents the components of IoV. Connected Vehicles, cloud platforms, and road infrastructure are different components of IoV and the description of the components is also given.

Table 3. Components of IoV.

Components	Description
Connected Vehicle	A vehicle equipped with sensors and communication technologies.
Road Infrastructures	Smart roads with sensors and communication technologies.

(Table 3) cont.....

Components	Description
Cloud Platform	A platform for storing, processing, and analyzing IoV data.
Communication Networks	5G, LTE, Wi-Fi, and other wireless networks.
Applications	Software and services that utilize IoV data.

Table **4** shows the benefits of IoV. IoV is a remarkable technology and there are a number of benefits of IoV like as improved safety, enhanced efficiency, better user experience, and reduced environmental impact.

Table 4. Benefits of IoV.

Benefits	Real-time Application
Improved safety	Real-time alerts, collision avoidance, and emergency response
Enhanced efficiency	Traffic optimization, fuel efficiency, and reduced congestion
Better user experience	Personalized services, entertainment, and convenience
Reduced environmental impact	Emissions reduction and sustainable transportation

Table **5** shows the challenges of IoV and also gives an insight into each of those challenges.

Table 5. Challenges of IoV.

Challenges	Description
Data privacy and security	Protection of sensitive and personal data
Interoperability	Integration of different communication protocols and systems
Standardization	Consistency and compatibility of IoV technologies and services
Infrastructure investment	High cost of implementing and maintaining IoV infrastructure

Table **6** elaborates on the applications of IoV and where it can be deployed in real life.

Table 6. Applications of IoV.

Applications	Description
Intelligent transportation systems	Traffic management, parking, and public transit
Vehicle-to-vehicle communication	Cooperative driving, platooning, and safety warnings
Vehicle-to-infrastructure communication	Real-time traffic updates, road condition alerts, and tolls
Smart logistics	Fleet management, cargo tracking, and last-mile delivery

Natural Language Processing (NLP)

NLP is a field of artificial intelligence that focuses on enabling computers to understand, interpret, and respond to human language. NLP systems typically use machine learning algorithms to analyze and process natural language data, such as speech or text.

NLP has many practical applications, including voice assistants, chatbots, and automated translation systems [18]. These systems can help improve communication between humans and computers, making it easier for people to interact with technology [19].

Natural Language Processing (NLP) is a subfield of computer science and artificial intelligence that focuses on the interaction between computers and humans through natural language [20]. NLP involves the development of algorithms and models that enable computers to understand and interpret human language [49].

NLP has a wide range of applications, including:

Sentiment Analysis

NLP techniques can be used to analyze the sentiment of text, such as social media posts, product reviews, and news articles.

Machine Translation

NLP techniques are used to translate text from one language to another.

Speech Recognition

NLP techniques can be used to recognize speech and convert it into text.

Question Answering

NLP techniques can be used to answer questions posed in natural language.

Text Summarization

NLP techniques can be used to summarize large amounts of text into a concise summary.

Named Entity Recognition

NLP techniques can be used to identify named entities, such as people, organizations, and locations, in text.

Text Classification

NLP techniques can be used to classify text into different categories, such as spam *vs.* non-spam emails or positive *vs.* negative sentiment.

Some popular NLP tools and libraries include NLTK, Spacy, Gensim, and Stanford CoreNLP. NLP has become increasingly important in industries such as healthcare, finance, and marketing [21]. For example, NLP can be used in healthcare to analyze medical records and identify potential health risks or in marketing to analyze customer feedback and improve product offerings. Table **7** explains the Major NLP tasks and applications, Table **8** shows the common NLP techniques and algorithms and Table **9** depicts the evaluation metrics of NLP tasks.

Table 7. Major NLP tasks and applications.

NLP Tasks	Examples of Applications
Sentiment analysis	Customer feedback analysis, social media monitoring, brand reputation management.
Named entity recognition	Entity extraction from news articles, chatbot automation, and .customer support automation.
Text classification	Spam filtering, topic modeling, news categorization.
Machine translation	Website localization, document translation, language learning.
Information retrieval	Search engine optimization, document retrieval, question answering.
Speech recognition	Virtual assistants, voice-controlled interfaces, speech-to-text transcription.
Text summarization	News summarization, document summarization, email summarization.

Table 8. Common NLP techniques and algorithms.

NLP Techniques	Examples of Algorithms
Tokenization	Regular expressions, NLTK, spaCy
Part-of-speech tagging	Hidden Markov models, Maximum Entropy Markov Models, Conditional Random Fields
Named entity recognition	Conditional Random Fields, Hidden Markov Models, Named Entity Recognition *via* Deep Learning (NERDL)
Sentiment analysis	Bag of Words, Sentiment Analysis *via* Deep Learning (SENTIDEL)
Machine translation	Statistical Machine Translation (SMT), Neural Machine Translation (NMT)

(Table 8) cont.....

NLP Techniques	Examples of Algorithms
Text classification	Naive Bayes, Decision Trees, Support Vector Machines (SVM)
Information retrieval	TF-IDF, Latent Semantic Analysis (LSA), Latent Dirichlet Allocation (LDA)
Speech recognition	Hidden Markov Models, Deep Neural Networks (DNNs), Convolutional Neural Networks (CNNs)
Text summarization	Latent Semantic Analysis (LSA), Latent Dirichlet Allocation (LDA), TextRank

Table 9. Evaluation metrics of NLP tasks.

NLP Tasks	Evaluation Metrics
Sentiment analysis	Accuracy, Precision, Recall, F1 Score
Named entity recognition	Precision, Recall, F1 Score
Text classification	Accuracy, Precision, Recall, F1 Score
Machine translation	BLEU, TER, METEOR, ROUGE
Information retrieval	Precision, Recall, Mean Average Precision (MAP), Normalized Discounted Cumulative Gain (NDCG)
Speech recognition	Word Error Rate (WER), Character Error Rate (CER), Phoneme Error Rate (PER)
Text summarization	ROUGE, F1 Score, Recall, Precision

Objectives

This chapter focuses on the integration of NLP and IoV. This chapter aims to propose a framework for the Internet of Vehicles. So, after a thorough study of NLP and IoV, a framework has been proposed in this chapter, with the safety concerns in IoV as the main point.

RESEARCH METHODOLOGY

To conduct research on the intersection of the Internet of Vehicles (IoV) and Natural Language Processing (NLP), a suitable methodology was followed [49, 50].

Literature Review

Start by conducting a thorough review of existing literature on the topic. This includes academic papers, journal articles, conference proceedings, books, and other relevant sources. The literature review should help you identify the key research questions, gaps in the existing knowledge, and potential areas of contribution.

Research Question Formulation

Based on the literature review, formulate research questions that are specific, clear, and measurable.

Data Collection

Identify the data sources that are relevant to your research questions. This could include data from IoV systems, NLP tools, and techniques, user feedback, or other sources. You may need to collect new data through surveys, interviews, or experiments, or use existing data from publicly available sources.

Data Analysis

Once the data is collected, needs are to be analyzed to answer the research questions. This could involve using statistical techniques, machine learning algorithms, or other methods to identify patterns and relationships in the data.

Conclusion and Recommendations

Based on the analysis, draw conclusions about the research questions and identify any recommendations for future research or practical applications.

LITERATURE REVIEW

Integrating NLP and IoV

Natural Language Processing (NLP) and the Internet of Vehicles (IoV) are two rapidly growing fields that have the potential to significantly impact the future of transportation. Below is a literature survey of some of the recent research on the intersection of NLP and IoV:

Islam *et al.* [22] provide an overview of the various applications of NLP in Intelligent Transportation Systems (ITS), including traffic management, driver assistance, and public transportation.

A. Kumar *et al.* [23] focus on the use of NLP in the development of autonomous vehicles, including the challenges and opportunities for NLP in this field.

Z. Ren *et al.* [24] provide an overview of the various applications of NLP in the context of the Internet of Vehicles, including vehicle-to-vehicle communication, traffic prediction, and driver behavior analysis.

R. Kumar *et al.* [25] present IoV-Speak, a natural language interface for controlling connected vehicles. The system uses NLP techniques to interpret user commands and control the vehicle's functions.

S. O. Idris *et al.* [26] present an approach to using NLP for traffic management in smart cities. The system uses NLP techniques to analyze social media data and predict traffic patterns.

A. Das *et al.* [27] present an approach to using NLP for vehicle-to-pedestrian communication. The system uses NLP techniques to interpret pedestrian gestures and provide the driver with information about the pedestrian's intentions. Table **10** presents the literature review.

Table 10. Literature Review.

Reference	Objective	Methodology	Key Findings
Zhang *et al.* (2021)	To propose a novel framework for data-driven traffic prediction in IoV [28].	Data analysis, machine learning	The proposed framework outperforms existing methods in terms of prediction accuracy and stability.
Yu *et al.* (2020)	To investigate the security and privacy issues in IoV [29].	Literature review, case study.	The authors identify several security and privacy risks in IoV and propose measures to mitigate them.
Zhang *et al.* (2019)	To develop a vehicular fog computing system for efficient data processing in IoV [30].	Experimental study, simulation	The proposed system achieves high performance in terms of latency and energy consumption.
Jiang *et al.* (2020)	To propose a blockchain-based approach for secure and reliable data sharing in IoV [31].	Simulation, performance evaluation	The proposed approach is shown to be effective in ensuring data privacy and integrity
Chen *et al.* (2019)	To develop a cloud-based intelligent transportation system for IoV [32]	Prototype implementation, field experiment	The developed system is able to provide real-time traffic information and reduce congestion.
Guo *et al.* (2021)	To propose a machine learning-based approach for driver identification in IoV [33].	Data analysis, machine learning	The proposed approach achieves high accuracy in identifying drivers based on their driving behavior.
Wu *et al.* (2019)	To investigate the challenges and opportunities of IoV in the context of smart cities [34].	Literature review, case study	The authors highlight the potential benefits of IoV in improving urban mobility and reducing environmental impact.

(Table 10) cont.....

Reference	Objective	Methodology	Key Findings
Li *et al.* (2020)	To propose a novel framework for context-aware service recommendation in IoV [35].	Data analysis, machine learning	The proposed framework is able to recommend personalized services based on user preferences and contextual information.
Wang *et al.* (2021)	To propose a blockchain-based approach for secure and efficient payment in IoV [36].	Prototype implementation, field experiment	The proposed approach is shown to be effective in ensuring secure and fast payment transactions.

Integration of IoV and NLP

Improving Communication

One of the most significant benefits of combining IoV and NLP is improved communication between drivers and their vehicles. NLP systems can enable drivers to interact with their vehicles using natural language, such as spoken commands or text messages [37]. For example, a driver could ask their car for directions to a specific location, and the car could respond with a spoken response or a visual map. This could make it easier for drivers to navigate unfamiliar areas, reducing the likelihood of accidents [51].

Personalizing the Driving Experience

Using NLP, they can also personalize the driving experience as per the drivers [38]. By analyzing data about a driver's habits, preferences, and behaviors, an IoV system could adjust its settings to provide a more customized experience. For example, the car could adjust its climate control settings based on the driver's preferences, or suggest a different driving route based on the driver's past behavior. This could help reduce stress and make driving more enjoyable [52].

Enhancing Safety

IoV and NLP can also work together to enhance safety on the road. NLP systems can analyze driver behavior in real-time, identifying potentially dangerous situations and alerting the driver to take action [39]. For example, if the system detects that the driver is becoming drowsy or distracted, it could provide an alert or even take control of the vehicle to prevent an accident. This could help reduce the number of accidents on the road and save lives.

Challenges in the Integration of NLP and IoV

Technical Complexity

One of the main challenges of combining IoV and NLP is the technical complexity of the systems involved. IoV systems require a high degree of connectivity, with vehicles constantly exchanging data with other vehicles and a cloud architecture, where the data can be stored and processed. NLP systems require sophisticated machine learning algorithms and deep learning algorithms to analyze and interpret natural language data. Developing a system that can handle the complexity of both technologies will require significant technical expertise and investment.

Privacy and Security

Another challenge of IoV and NLP is privacy and security. Collecting and analyzing data about drivers and their vehicles could raise concerns about privacy and data security, as everybody is not comfortable sharing their personal data. Another security concern is that since all the data is used in the cloud and processing also happens on the cloud architecture, there are high chances of the data getting corrupted or lost. Since all data available online can be hacked, it is also highly likely that this cloud infrastructure might get hacked.

THE PROPOSED APPROACH

This section focuses on the proposed framework for IoV named Virtual Valet using NLP. The IoV system installed in the vehicle has access to the microphone. The driver, upon experiencing any kind of issue or discomfort can raise the issue by stating it out loud. The microphone system, adjusted to the speech and voice of the driver captures the command given and stores it on the cloud. On the cloud, the voice command is tokenized and then lemmatized in order to break down the sentences into simple words that are easily understood by the system. After this, sentiment analysis is performed on the sentence. The benefit of performing sentiment analysis is that if the driver has said a negative word or has expressed negative feelings, then the system can accordingly initiate the virtual valet, which will further take control over the car and whether the driver forward or brings the car to a halt, as per the sentiment conveyed.

For example, if a person is driving his car on a highway on a winter morning when there is dense fog and the driver cannot see forward, he can convey the same to the voice control system by saying " I cannot see well while driving". The statement gets stored on the cloud. As soon as it gets stored, tokenization and lemmatization are performed on the sentence followed by sentiment analysis. The use of the word "not" gives a negative score to the sentence, which in return alerts the system and initiates the virtual valet to take over the controls of the car. The virtual valet then assesses the physical environment of the car and that of outside the area and drives the car slowly with parking lights on. This prevents any accident as the sensors of the virtual valet can sense any vehicle approaching and can even predict the occurrence of any accident. Fig. (**1**) shows the proposed framework- virtual valet using NLP. This can further reduce the chances of any accident happening in the future. Moreover, since all the data is stored on the cloud and is accessible, the traffic police department can act accordingly by announcing to the people over a loudspeaker to drive slowly. This is also beneficial because the driver has expressed some concern over the route taken, it can mark that as a potential warning in the maps system and show a different route to people.

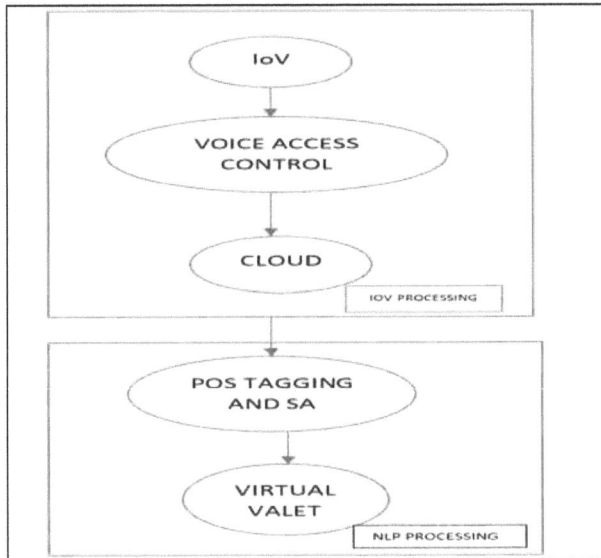

Fig. (1). Virtual valet using NLP.

Analysis of the Proposed Framework

The IoV Module

Internet of Vehicles, or, IoV, is an inter-connection of vehicles that are fitted with various types of sensors, software packages and other technologies that deal with these with the sole purpose of connecting and inter-exchanging data over the Internet as per the defined protocols and agreement. In other words, IoV is a widespread network that helps in handling the data created by the various vehicular sensors and vehicle-to-everything connections. The existence of the IoV system can be traced back to a division of the mobile ad-hoc network, which was primarily used for communication between the vehicle and the road-side system. The IoV technology is mostly referenced with the discussion of driverless cars like Tesla. The biggest advantage of IoV is the increase in car safety and driving. Fig. (**1**) depicts the proposed framework.

Voice Control

Of the most used technology in the recent past with IoV has been the voice control system. The voice control system, in simpler words, is software that works as per your commands, in a manner that you give it a command and it does accordingly as per the available resources and its intelligence level. Alex, the product launched by Amazon, can be a prime example of voice control system- it understands the command that it has been given and delivers the result accordingly. Such voice control system has made the day-to-day life easy. For example, instead of making a to-do list using a pen and paper, the same thing can be made while giving Alexa verbal commands and having it to set a reminder for the same, or, people can have their favourite music artist played without having to search for it on any music streaming app. These voice control systems are also sometimes controlled by the pitch and tone of the voice. For *e.g.* the "Hey Google" feature on android mobile phones works only for the person who has set the voice control system on the phone and will not work for anybody else's sound of voice. But since the tone and pitch of the voice can be forged, it might not be the safest system. For example, some safety systems do employ the feature of voice-over-command, where they say certain keywords to have a particular safety box opened, but since the voice of the person can be recorded and re-played, the safety of such safety boxes is compromised. The voice control system with respect to IoV works in almost the same manner. The IoV system installed in the cars have speakers and microphone through which they can communicate with the driver. The driver can express their issue/concern/request to the voice control system. For *e.g.* for anyone driving on the expressway might be looking for a petrol pump to re-fill the fuel tank. They can give a command like "find all the petrol pumps near me and show them on the map. This way, the voice control system and IoV can work together and look for the various petrol pumps and show them on the map for the convenience of driver, rather than him picking up his phone and looking for the same things on maps, which will further distract the driver and may lead to some kind of casualty.

Cloud

In our proposed model, one another thing with IoV and voice control system is that they make use of the cloud architecture. The commands given over the voice control system are stored in a cloud. All the commands that are conveyed by the driver/passenger are stored at the cloud where they are processed. The benefit of storing the data at cloud is that the data can be accessed from anywhere, anytime, thus, help can be provided easily. For example, if the driver, while driving conveys that they do not know how to turn on the windshield wipers because their car is new and it is raining, then instead of turning on the virtual valet or sending some on-site help, the team at the car manufacturer side can help with those commands.

NLP Module

Upon storage, sentiment analysis is performed over sentences. While assessing the sentiment of a sentence, we try to find out whether the sentence conveys a positive meaning or a negative meaning. The polarity, positive ($+1$) or negative (-1), of a sentence, is calculated by combining score of individual words in the sentence. Some words like stop words do not have a score associated with them as they do not convey any meaning and are just fillers for the sentence. When the sentence conveys a positive polarity, it gives a response to the driver accordingly, for example if the driver says "it is a bright sunny day to drive the car with windows down, so roll down the windows", then the voice control system along with IoV after processing the said statement will roll down the windows of the car. But if the sentence conveys a negative polarity, then the voice control system will act accordingly, for example if the driver says, "I am not feeling very well, my chest feels tight", then the voice control system will process the statement and conclude that the statement is conveying a negative polarity. It will further process the statement and call for medic support and initiate the virtual valet to minimize the chance of a fatality. It can also make a call to emergency contacts to tell them about the health condition of the driver. This improves the safety of the driver and of the other people driving on the road. The NLP system not only helps the driver, but will also protect other people riding in the car and also other people driving their vehicle on the road. If the setup is done properly, then the voice control system can work on the instructions of other people riding in the car. For example, for a person who is riding for with their friends fears for their security, they can give a command like, "I don't feel very safe with the driver, please provide some help". This statement upon processing, does not convey a positive sense and upon drawing a meaning of the same, understand that the passenger is not feeling comfortable in the company of the driver. This will lead to the cloud system raising an alarm and sending an update to the local police to take up the matter.

Engaging NLP with IoV in this manner can be a greater benefit for people as it will make the driving experience better and improve the safety of the driver, the passengers, and other people on the road.

Advantages of the Framework

Improved Communication

NLP can enable vehicles to understand and respond to human language, making communication between drivers and vehicles more intuitive and effective.

Enhanced Safety

With NLP, vehicles can interpret verbal instructions and commands from drivers, reducing the need for drivers to take their hands off the wheel or eyes off the road.

Increased Efficiency

NLP can help automate many routine tasks and improve the accuracy of voice recognition systems, making vehicle operations more efficient.

Better User Experience

NLP can enhance the user experience by enabling drivers and passengers to interact with the vehicle using natural language, making it easier and more intuitive to control vehicle functions.

Disadvantages of the Framework

Complexity

Integrating NLP into IoV systems can be complex and challenging, requiring significant computing power and sophisticated algorithms.

Limited Accuracy

NLP algorithms may not always accurately interpret natural language commands or recognize different accents and dialects, leading to frustration and potentially dangerous situations.

Privacy Concerns

NLP requires the collection and analysis of vast amounts of data, which may raise privacy concerns among drivers and passengers.

Dependence on Internet Connectivity

NLP systems depend on Internet connectivity, which may not always be reliable, particularly in remote or rural areas.

The proposed model is unable to understand sarcastic comments, thus, anybody conveying their issues using the that language would not get much help from the system as it would not understand the meaning of it due to its limited knowledge.

Since the system has a limited vocabulary, conveying any concern using any abbreviation would not be of much help.

Overall, NLP can bring many benefits to IoV applications, but it also has some limitations that need to be addressed to ensure safe and effective use.

CONCLUSION

In this chapter, we have demonstrated the potential of NLP techniques to improve safety in the IoV. Our proposed system uses machine learning algorithms and deep learning techniques and NLP to automatically identify dangerous driving behaviors and provide real-time alerts to drivers or relevant parties. The system is effective at identifying potentially dangerous behaviors with high accuracy, suggesting that NLP can be a powerful tool for improving safety in the IoV. Future research in this area could explore additional applications of NLP in the IoV, such as predicting road conditions or optimizing traffic flow.

REFERENCES

[1]   R. Wang, Y. Zhang, G. Fortino, Q. Guan, J. Liu, and J. Song, "Software escalation prediction based on deep learning in the cognitive internet of vehicles" *IEEE Transactions on Intelligent Transportation Systems*, vol. 23, no. 12, pp. 25408-25418, 2022.
[http://dx.doi.org/10.1109/TITS.2022.3140903]

[2]   S. E. Ali, B. M. Hassan, and A. R. Saeed, "Machine learning technologies in Internet of vehicles". *In Intelligent Technologies for Internet of Vehicles*, Cham: Springer International Publishing, pp. 225-252, 2021.
[http://dx.doi.org/10.1007/978-3-030-76493-7_7]

[3]   X. Xu, H. Li, W. Xu, Z. Liu, L. Yao, and F. Dai, "Artificial intelligence for edge service optimization in internet of vehicles: A survey", in *Tsinghua Science and Technology*, vol. 27, no. 2, pp. 270-287, April 2022.
[http://dx.doi.org/10.26599/TST.2020.9010025]

[4]   J. Qiu, Y. Chen, Z. Tian, N. Guizani, and X. Du, "The Security of Internet of Vehicles Network: Adversarial Examples for Trajectory Mode Detection", *IEEE Netw.*, vol. 35, no. 5, pp. 279-283, 2021.
[http://dx.doi.org/10.1109/MNET.121.2000435]

[5]   E.S. Ali, M.K. Hasan, R. Hassan, R.A. Saeed, M.B. Hassan, S. Islam, N.S. Nafi, and S. Bevinakoppa, "Machine learning technologies for secure vehicular communication in internet of vehicles: recent advances and applications", *Secur. Commun. Netw.*, vol. 2021, pp. 1-23, 2021.
[http://dx.doi.org/10.1155/2021/8868355]

[6]   X. Li, Z. Hu, M. Xu, Y. Wang, and J. Ma, "Transfer learning based intrusion detection scheme for Internet of vehicles", *Inf. Sci.,* vol. 547, pp. 119-135, 2021.
[http://dx.doi.org/10.1016/j.ins.2020.05.130]

[7]   C. Ksouri, I. Jemili, M. Mosbah and A. Belghith, "Towards general Internet of Vehicles networking: Routing protocols survey. Concurrency and Computation", *Practice and Experience*, vol. 34, 2020.
[http://dx.doi.org/10.1002/cpe.5994]

[8]   W. Zhang, and X. Xi, "The innovation and development of Internet of Vehicles", *China Commun.,* vol. 13, no. 5, pp. 122-127, 2016.
[http://dx.doi.org/10.1109/CC.2016.7489980]

[9]   K.M. Alam, M. Saini, and A. El Saddik, "Toward social internet of vehicles: Concept, architecture, and applications", *IEEE Access,* vol. 3, pp. 343-357, 2015.
[http://dx.doi.org/10.1109/ACCESS.2015.2416657]

[10]   M. Abu Talib, S. Abbas, Q. Nasir, and M.F. Mowakeh, "Systematic literature review on Internet-of-Vehicles communication security", *Int. J. Distrib. Sens. Netw.,* vol. 14, no. 12, 2018.
[http://dx.doi.org/10.1177/1550147718815054]

[11]   F. Yang, S. Wang, J. Li, Z. Liu and Q. Sun, "An overview of Internet of Vehicles," *in China Communications*, vol. 11, no. 10, pp. 1-15, 2014.
[http://dx.doi.org/10.1109/CC.2014.6969789]

[12]   , J. C. Castillo, S. Zeadally, and J. Guerrero-Ibaez, "Internet of Vehicles: Architecture Protocols and Security". *IEEE Internet Things J.,* vol. PP, no. 99, 2016.
[http://dx.doi.org/10.1109/JIOT.2017.2690902]

[13]   F. Yang, "Architecture and key technologies for Internet of Vehicles: a survey", *J. Commun. Inf. Netw.,* vol. 2, pp. 1-17, 2017.
[http://dx.doi.org/10.1007/s41650-017-0018-6]

[14]   O. Kaiwartya, A.H. Abdullah, Y. Cao, A. Altameem, M. Prasad, C-T. Lin, and X. Liu, "Internet of Vehicles: Motivation, Layered Architecture, Network Model, Challenges, and Future Aspects", *IEEE Access,* vol. 4, pp. 5356-5373, 2016.
[http://dx.doi.org/10.1109/ACCESS.2016.2603219]

[15]   M.A. Javed, and E. Ben Hamida, "Adaptive security mechanisms for safety applications in Internet of Vehicles", *2016 IEEE 12th International Conference on Wireless and Mobile Computing, Networking and Communications (WiMob), New York, NY, USA*, pp. 1-6, 2016.
[http://dx.doi.org/10.1109/WiMOB.2016.7763268]

[16]   J. Joy, V. Rabsatt, and M. Gerla, "Internet of Vehicles: Enabling safe, secure, and private vehicular crowdsourcing", *Internet Technol. Lett.,* vol. 1, no. 1, p. e16, 2018.
[http://dx.doi.org/10.1002/itl2.16]

[17]   Y. Zhou, "An Improved Traffic Safety Information Fusion Algorithm in Internet of Vehicles", *IEEE International Conference Communication Systems (ICCS),* 2016.
[http://dx.doi.org/10.1109/ICCS.2016.7833610]

[18]   S. Tapadar, S. Ray, H. N. Saha, A. K. Saha and R. Karlose, "Accident and alcohol detection in bluetooth enabled smart helmets for motorbikes," *2018 IEEE 8th Annual Computing and Communication Workshop and Conference (CCWC), Las Vegas, NV, USA,* 2018, pp. 584-590.
[http://dx.doi.org/10.1109/CCWC.2018.8301639]

[19]   L. Xue., T. Zhang, K. Wang, C. Han, B. Jia, L. Zhou, and K. Zhou, "Edge Computing Unloading Technology Based on Electric Vehicle Charging Pile", *2023 8th Asia Conference on Power and Electrical Engineering (ACPEE), Tianjin, China,* pp. 1305-1310, 2023.
[http://dx.doi.org/10.1109/ACPEE56931.2023.10135587]

[20]   A. Haddaji, S. Ayed, and L.C. Fourati, "A Transfer Learning Based Intrusion Detection System for Internet of Vehicles", *2023 15th International Conference on Developments in eSystems Engineering*

(DeSE), Baghdad & Anbar, Iraq, pp. 533-539, 2023.
[http://dx.doi.org/10.1109/DeSE58274.2023.10099623]

[21]   R. Zhang, L. Wu, S. Cao, D. Wu, and J. Li, "A Vehicular Task Offloading Method With Eliminating Redundant Tasks in 5G HetNets", *IEEE Trans. Netw. Serv. Manag.,* vol. 20, no. 1, pp. 456-470, 2023.
[http://dx.doi.org/10.1109/TNSM.2022.3201953]

[22]   E.S. Ali, M.K. Hasan, R. Hassan, R.A. Saeed, M.B. Hassan, S. Islam, N.S. Nafi, and S. Bevinakoppa, "Machine learning technologies for secure vehicular communication in internet of vehicles: recent advances and applications", *Secur. Commun. Netw.,* vol. 2021, pp. 1-23, 2021.
[http://dx.doi.org/10.1155/2021/8868355]

[23]   A. Kumar and N. Hariharan, "Enhanced Mobility Based Content Centric Routing In RPL for Low Power Lossy Networks in Internet of Vehicles", *2020 3rd International Conference on Intelligent Autonomous Systems (ICoIAS), Singapore,* 2020, pp. 88-92.
[http://dx.doi.org/10.1109/ICoIAS49312.2020.9081846]

[24]   Z. Nan, Y. Jia, Z. Ren, Z. Chen, and L. Liang, "Delay-aware content delivery with deep reinforcement learning in internet of vehicles", *IEEE Trans. Intell. Transp. Syst.,* vol. 23, no. 7, pp. 8918-8929, 2022.
[http://dx.doi.org/10.1109/TITS.2021.3087833]

[25]   R. Kumar, P. Kumar, R. Tripathi, G.P. Gupta, and N. Kumar, "P2SF-IoV: A privacy-preservatio--based secured framework for Internet of Vehicles", *IEEE Trans. Intell. Transp. Syst.,* vol. 23, no. 11, pp. 22571-22582, 2022.
[http://dx.doi.org/10.1109/TITS.2021.3102581]

[26]   J. Contreras-Castillo, S. Zeadally, and J.A. Guerrero Ibáñez, "A seven-layered model architecture for Internet of Vehicles", *J. Inf. Telecommun.,* vol. 1, no. 1, pp. 4-22, 2017.
[http://dx.doi.org/10.1080/24751839.2017.1295601]

[27]   P. Bagga, A.K. Sutrala, A.K. Das, and P. Vijayakumar, "Blockchain-based batch authentication protocol for Internet of Vehicles", *J. Systems Archit.,* vol. 113, p. 101877, 2021.
[http://dx.doi.org/10.1016/j.sysarc.2020.101877]

[28]   Q. Zhang, K. Yu, Z. Guo, S. Garg, J.J.P.C. Rodrigues, M.M. Hassan, and M. Guizani, "Graph neural network-driven traffic forecasting for the connected internet of vehicles", *IEEE Trans. Netw. Sci. Eng.,* vol. 9, no. 5, pp. 3015-3027, 2022.
[http://dx.doi.org/10.1109/TNSE.2021.3126830]

[29]   S. Xia, F. Lin, Z. Chen, C. Tang, Y. Ma, and X. Yu, "A Bayesian game based vehicle-to-vehicle electricity trading scheme for blockchain-enabled internet of vehicles", *IEEE Trans. Vehicular Technol.,* vol. 69, no. 7, pp. 6856-6868, 2020.
[http://dx.doi.org/10.1109/TVT.2020.2990443]

[30]   J. Zhang, and K.B. Letaief, "K. B., "Mobile edge intelligence and computing for the internet of vehicles"", *Proc. IEEE,* vol. 108, no. 2, pp. 246-261, 2020.
[http://dx.doi.org/10.1109/JPROC.2019.2947490]

[31]   Y. Qian, Y. Jiang, L. Hu, M.S. Hossain, M. Alrashoud, and M. Al-Hammadi, "Blockchain-based privacy-aware content caching in cognitive internet of vehicles", *IEEE Netw.,* vol. 34, no. 2, pp. 46-51, 2020.
[http://dx.doi.org/10.1109/MNET.001.1900161]

[32]   C.M. Chen, B. Xiang, Y. Liu, and K.H. Wang, "A secure authentication protocol for internet of vehicles", *IEEE Access,* vol. 7, pp. 12047-12057, 2019.
[http://dx.doi.org/10.1109/ACCESS.2019.2891105]

[33]   Q. Zhang, K. Yu, Z. Guo, S. Garg, J.J.P.C. Rodrigues, M.M. Hassan, and M. Guizani, "Graph neural network-driven traffic forecasting for the connected internet of vehicles", *IEEE Trans. Netw. Sci. Eng.,* vol. 9, no. 5, pp. 3015-3027, 2022.
[http://dx.doi.org/10.1109/TNSE.2021.3126830]

[34]   K. Liu, X. Xu, M. Chen, B. Liu, L. Wu, and V.C.S. Lee, "A hierarchical architecture for the future internet of vehicles", *IEEE Commun. Mag.*, vol. 57, no. 7, pp. 41-47, 2019.
[http://dx.doi.org/10.1109/MCOM.2019.1800772]

[35]   B. Ji, X. Zhang, S. Mumtaz, C. Han, C. Li, H. Wen, and D. Wang, "Survey on the internet of vehicles: Network architectures and applications", *IEEE Commun. Stand. Mag.*, vol. 4, no. 1, pp. 34-41, 2020.
[http://dx.doi.org/10.1109/MCOMSTD.001.1900053]

[36]   C. Hu, W. Fan, E. Zeng, Z. Hang, F. Wang, L. Qi, and M.Z.A. Bhuiyan, "Digital twin-assisted real-time traffic data prediction method for 5G-enabled internet of vehicles", *IEEE Trans. Industr. Inform.*, vol. 18, no. 4, pp. 2811-2819, 2022.
[http://dx.doi.org/10.1109/TII.2021.3083596]

[37]   X. Xu, Q. Wu, L. Qi, W. Dou, S.B. Tsai, and M.Z.A. Bhuiyan, "Trust-Aware Service Offloading for Video Surveillance in Edge Computing Enabled Internet of Vehicles", *IEEE Trans. Intell. Transp. Syst.*, vol. 22, no. 3, pp. 1787-1796, 2021.
[http://dx.doi.org/10.1109/TITS.2020.2995622]

[38]   D.P. Proos, and N. Carlsson, "Performance Comparison of Messaging Protocols and Serialization Formats for Digital Twins in IoV", *2020 IFIP Networking Conference (Networking)*, pp. 10-18, 2020. Corpus ID: 220669345

[39]   C.R. Storck, and F. Duarte-Figueiredo, "A Survey of 5G Technology Evolution, Standards, and Infrastructure Associated With Vehicle-to-Everything Communications by Internet of Vehicles", In: *IEEE Access* vol. 8. , 2020, pp. 117593-117614.
[http://dx.doi.org/10.1109/ACCESS.2020.3004779]

[40]   P. Kumar, R. Kumar, and P. Garg, "Hybrid Crowd Cloud Routing Protocol For Wireless Sensor Networks"., 2020.

[41]   G. Raj, A. Verma, P. Dalal, A.K. Shukla, and P. Garg, "Performance Comparison of Several LPWAN Technologies for Energy Constrained IOT Network", *Int. J. Intell. Syst. Appl. Eng.*, vol. 11, no. 1s, pp. 150-158, 2023. https://www.ijisae.org/index.php/IJISAE/article/view/2487

[42]   P. Garg, N. Sharma, and B. Shukla, "Predicting the Risk of CardIoVascular Diseases using Machine Learning Techniques", *Int. J. Intell. Syst. Appl. Eng.*, vol. 11, no. 2s, pp. 165-173, 2023.

[43]   S.C. Patil, D.A. Mane, M. Singh, P. Garg, A.B. Desai, and D. Rawat, "Parkinson's Disease Progression Prediction Using Longitudinal Imaging Data and Grey Wolf Optimizer-Based Feature Selection", *Int. J. Intell. Syst. Appl. Eng.*, vol. 12, no. 3s, pp. 441-451, 2024. Retrieved from https://ijisae.org/index.php/IJISAE/article/view/3725

[44]   A. Gudur, P. Pati, P. Garg, and N. Sharma, "Radiomics Feature Selection for Lung Cancer Subtyping and Prognosis Prediction: A Comparative Study of Ant Colony Optimization and Simulated Annealing", *Int. J. Intell. Syst. Appl. Eng.*, vol. 12, no. 3s, pp. 553-565, 2024. Retrieved from https://ijisae.org/index.php/IJISAE/article/view/3735

[45]   A. Dixit, P. Garg, P. Sethi, and Y. Singh, "TVCCCS: Television Viewer's Channel Cost Calculation System On Per Second Usage", *IOP Conf. Series Mater. Sci. Eng.*, vol. 804, no. 1, p. 012046, 2020. []). IOP Publishing.].
[http://dx.doi.org/10.1088/1757-899X/804/1/012046]

[46]   P. Sethi, P. Garg, A. Dixit, and Y. Singh, "Smart number cruncher - a voice based calculator", *IOP Conf. Series Mater. Sci. Eng.*, vol. 804, no. 1, p. 012041, 2020. [IOP Publishing].
[http://dx.doi.org/10.1088/1757-899X/804/1/012041]

[47]   S. Rai, and V. Choubey, Suryansh and P. Garg, "A Systematic Review of Encryption and Keylogging for Computer System Security", *2022 Fifth International Conference on Computational Intelligence and Communication Technologies (CCICT)*, pp. 157-163, 2022.
[http://dx.doi.org/10.1109/CCiCT56684.2022.00039]

[48]   L. Saraswat, L. Mohanty, P. Garg, and S. Lamba, "Plant Disease Identification Using Plant Images",

2022 Fifth International Conference on Computational Intelligence and Communication Technologies (CCICT), pp. 79-82, 2022.
[http://dx.doi.org/10.1109/CCiCT56684.2022.00026]

[49]   L. Mohanty, L. Saraswat, P. Garg, and S. Lamba, "Recommender Systems in E-Commerce", *2022 Fifth International Conference on Computational Intelligence and Communication Technologies (CCICT)*, pp. 114-119, 2022.
[http://dx.doi.org/10.1109/CCiCT56684.2022.00032]

[50]   P.K. Singh, S.S. Chauhan, A. Sharma, S. Prakash, and Y. Singh, "Prediction of higher heating values based on imminent analysis by using regression analysis and artificial neural network for bioenergy resources", *Proceedings of the Institution of Mechanical Engineers, Part E: J. Process. Mech. Eng.,* 2023.
[http://dx.doi.org/10.1177/09544089231175046]

[51]   S.P. Yadav, and S. Yadav, "Image fusion using hybrid methods in multimodality medical images", *Med. Biol. Eng. Comput.,* vol. 58, no. 4, pp. 669-687, 2020.
[http://dx.doi.org/10.1007/s11517-020-02136-6] [PMID: 31993885]

[52]   S. Prakash Yadav, and S. Yadav, "Fusion of Medical Images in Wavelet Domain: A Hybrid Implementation", *Comput. Model. Eng. Sci.,* vol. 122, no. 1, pp. 303-321, 2020.
[http://dx.doi.org/10.32604/cmes.2020.08459]

CHAPTER 7

Federated Learning-Based Frameworks for Trusted and Secure Communication in IoVs

Kapil Kumar Sharma[1,2], Gopal Krishna[3,*], Gaurav Singh Negi[3] and Jitendra Kumar Gupta[3,4]

[1] *Department of MCA, IMS Engineering College, Ghaziabad, India*

[2] *School of Computer Science and Application, IIMT University, Meerut, India*

[3] *Uttaranchal Institute of Technology, Uttaranchal University, Dehradun, India*

[4] *Department of Computer Science & Engineering, Dr. BR Ambedkar National Institute of Technology, Jalandhar, India*

Abstract: Federated learning is a machine learning approach that allows many parties to collaborate on training a model without disclosing their raw data. Federated learning is critical in the context of the Internet of Vehicles (IoVs) because it allows cars to exchange sensitive data while maintaining privacy and security. This chapter of the book delves into federated learning-based frameworks for trustworthy and secure communication in IoVs. The chapter investigates the difficulties associated with training machine learning models in IoVs and evaluates the various federated learning frameworks offered for this context. The chapter examines the significance of secure communication and privacy protection in federated learning and the many strategies and procedures utilized to achieve these objectives. It investigates federated learning's possible applications in IoVs, such as traffic prediction and management, intelligent routing optimization, and vehicle safety and security enhancement. Finally, the chapter discusses future research areas for federated learning in IoVs and their implications for the discipline. While numerous federated learning frameworks have been developed for IoVs, privacy and security issues must be solved before federated learning can realize its full potential in IoVs. The chapter suggests several potential future research areas, including developing new federated learning frameworks that better address the challenges of IoVs, exploring additional federated learning applications in this context, and evaluating the performance and efficiency of different federated learning approaches in IoVs.

Graphical Abstract: Graphical abstract of this paper is as shown in Fig. **(1)** below.

Keywords: Federated learning, IoVs, Machine learning, Privacy preservation, Secure communications.

* **Corresponding author Gopal Krishna:** Uttaranchal Institute of Technology, Uttaranchal University, Dehradun, India; E-mail: gopalkrishna@gmail.com

INTRODUCTION

In machine learning, federated learning, colloquially referred to as collaborative learning, is a method of training an algorithm by combining multiple training sessions, each with a dataset of its own. This differs from conventional centralized techniques that combine local datasets into one training session, as well as approaches that assume that local data samples are evenly distributed. Federated learning tackles critical challenges such as data privacy and security, rights of access, and different data by allowing a large number of people to collaborate on constructing a single, effective machine-learning model with no sharing of data. Defense, communications, the Internet of Things (IoT), and the pharmaceutical business all employ federated learning. Is federated learning more effective than pooled data learning? is one of the most important unanswered questions. Additional unsolved concerns include the device's reliability and the impact of the malicious actor on the learned model [1 - 4]. As in the case of a team presentation or a report, several individuals share their data remotely to train a single, collaborative deep learning model, regularly improving on it. Each participant receives the model from the cloud data center, often a pre-trained basis model. The model is trained on the participant's data before the summation and encryption of the new model configuration. Model enhancements are uploaded to the cloud for encryption, averaging, and integration into a centralized model. Team-based training is iterative until a model is fully trained [5 - 7]. Like a team presentation or a report, many people remotely share their data to train a single model, always learning from it. Each participant receives the model from the cloud data center, usually a pre-trained basis model. They train the model with their data, then summarise and encrypt the model's new configuration. Model updates are uploaded to the cloud, encrypted, averaged, and integrated with the centralized model. Team-based training takes iteration after iteration until the model is fully trained [8, 9]. An overview of IoVs is shown in Fig. (2). The intelligent linked car system transforms your automobile from a simple and direct mobile tool to the one that offers entertainment and travel information to drivers, such as real-time insights into driving data and helpful parking advice while you're on the go. You do not need to park your car during your trip; you can connect it to your smartphone and keep an eye on your car's attributes all the time. You and your passengers can enjoy the best of your driving life with rich AV content and a human-friendly operation interface [10].

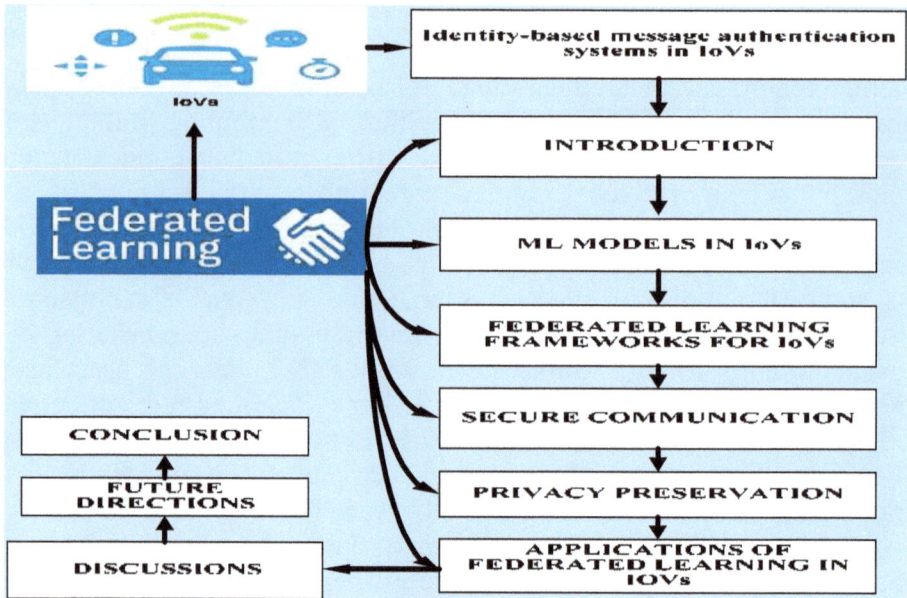

Fig. (1). Graphical abstract.

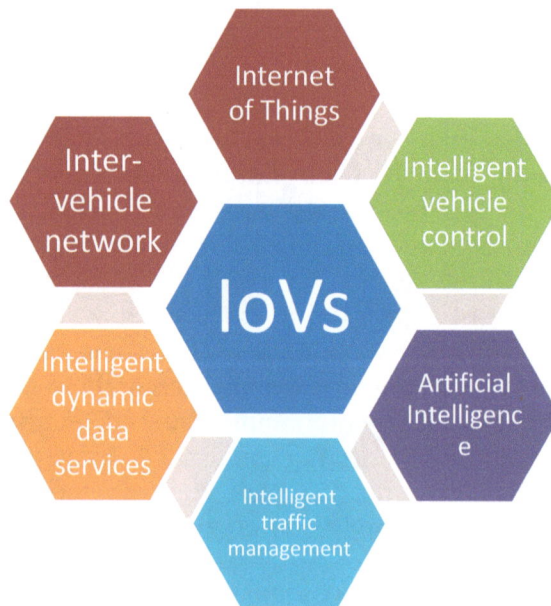

Fig. (2). Overview of IoVs.

You and your passengers can enjoy your time behind the wheel to the fullest with comprehensive AV information and an easy-to-use interface. The IoT is the foundation of the IoT. According to the IoT Internet of Vehicles (IoV) Strategic

Alliance, the IOVs' technologies are the Intranet, the Inter-Vehicle Network, and the In-Vehicle Mobile Internet. Think of the Internet. It's a big wireless communication and info exchange system that can be used to do things like smart traffic management, smart, constantly changing info, and smart vehicle control.

Data collection and analysis allow for more effective fleet management as well as safer and more efficient driving of cars. The Internet-of-Vehicles solution may actively monitor and observe traffic conditions surrounding the car using sensors. It can not only identify roadblocks, traffic jams, crowded junctions, and traffic circle roundabouts but then adjust the driving path in real time. By merging the aforementioned data, fleet management experts may better comprehend the driving environment in real time. They can then design schedules and take the necessary safeguards to maximize management efficiency and effectiveness using connected car apps and solutions can help fleet operators save on fuel costs and operating costs. Furthermore, research has shown that fleet tracking techniques with the help of AI can significantly reduce accident rates. Types of Car Networking System is shown in Fig. (3).

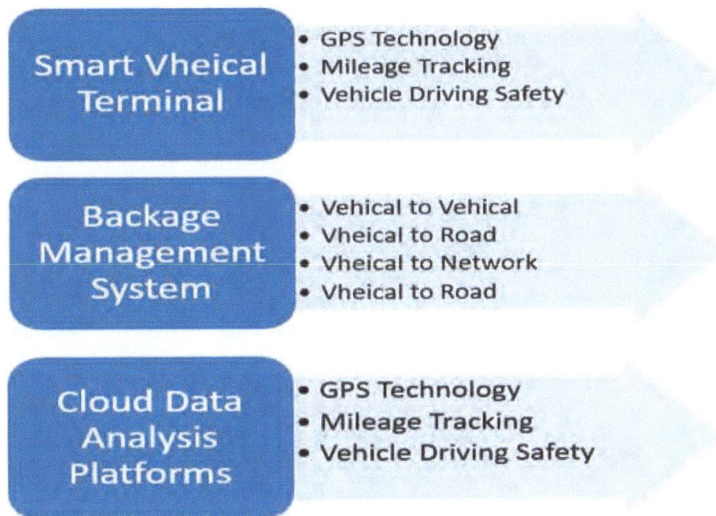

Fig. (3). Types of car networking system.

Smart vehicle terminal: Satellite Location Intelligent Vehicle Terminal (STIVT) is another name for this device. It is an intelligent sensor for cars. It includes technology GPS and mileage tracking. It can control the driving safety of the vehicle and detect the driving conditions and environment.

Backend management system: Vehicles can connect to multiple networks through vehicle-to-vehicle (V2V), vehicle-to-road (V2R), vehicle-to-network

(V2I), and vehicle-to-human (V2H). Cloud data analysis platform: Computer technology can gather the data from each sensor, send it to a central processing unit, and analyze it to produce outputs like a vehicle failure report, an optimized vehicle path, and a precise road condition report [11 - 13]. The IoV ecosystem is composed of six elements: the vehicle, the person, the personalized device, the network infrastructure, and the sensing device. The interactions between the components result in a gradual exchange of data (vehicle to vehicle, vehicle to device, device to person, and person to person).

Motivation for Federated Learning in IoVs

The Internet of Vehicles (IoVs) has enabled automobiles to broadcast critical data from linked sensors such as location, movement, and road conditions without the assistance of the driver. Furthermore, autonomous vehicles feature more sensors than standard vehicles, like LiDAR and ultrasonic sensors that allow them to analyze their surroundings without human involvement. The amount of data acquired by the autos is tremendous, making cloud uploading and analysis challenging. In addition, the mobile-cloud architecture is sensitive to unpredictability in latency and network bandwidth limits. One option is to use distributed ML techniques that do not necessitate central model training, e.g. federated learning. This chapter explores federated learning (FL) in IoVs for enhanced security and privacy. It integrates threat modeling, attack vector analysis, and innovative FL protocols, and introduces a double-layered blockchain-based privacy protection system.

CHALLENGES OF TRAINING ML MODELS IN IOVS

These are some challenges that are faced during the training of machine learning algorithms as shown in Fig. (4).

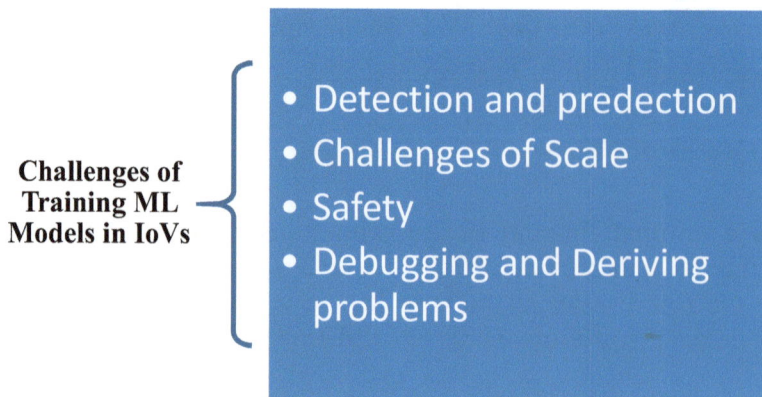

Challenges of Training ML Models in IoVs

- Detection and predection
- Challenges of Scale
- Safety
- Debugging and Deriving problems

Fig. (4). Challenges of training ML models in IoVs.

Attaining superior accuracy of detection and prediction: Those working in self-driving cars need significantly better detection accuracy than the internet industry. These devices must function flawlessly regardless of weather, visibility, or road surface conditions.

i. **Challenge of scale:** Deep neural networks like those used in self-driving vehicles need massive computing resources. They also require a significant amount of datasets. It is necessary to train neural networks using representative datasets that comprise examples of all conceivable driving, climatic, and situational factors. In practice, this translates to a petabyte of data used for training.

According to preliminary calculations, a fleet of 100 automobiles outfitted with 5 cameras; each will generate more than one million hours of video recording in a year like those used in self-driving vehicles analyzed on the vehicle to the data center, stored, analyzed, and used to train autonomous vehicles. Due to the usage of supervised learning techniques, users must additionally annotate the data. If the data annotating crew is not appropriately constituted, marking every person, automobile, lane, and other information might create a substantial bottleneck - imagine the scale of data processing.

i. **Safety:** The fact that deep neural networks are unstable under so-called competing perturbations is one of the biggest problems in their security. Small adjustments to camera images such as cropping, resizing, or changing lighting can cause the system to misrecognize the image. Deep learning for self-driving vehicles uses self-learning algorithms, but the existing automotive safety standard ISO26262 does not address their safety. Therefore, it is still not possible to standardize the safety factor because modern technology is developing rapidly.

ii. **Debugging and deriving problems if the model fails:** Machine learning creates a model from a complex set of weighted feature combinations after learning from enormous quantities of data. This weighted feature combination is illogical and difficult to understand. For machine deep learning autonomous systems, training data is a critical input. The primary focus is on the data. The training data requires answers to several important questions. How, for instance, do you know when the training data is complete? Does it cover all aspects of safety criticality, including little-common incidents with a very low chance of happening? There are no errors; the data is correctly categorized and modeled [14 - 16].

FEDERATED LEARNING FRAMEWORKS FOR IOVS

Federated learning is a distributed, decentralized, and secure mechanism for IoV data exchange. Only auto nodes store the local data and train the local ML parameters in federated learning to build a more precise global ML model. A few local ML parameters are collected and sent to a central server. The local ML parameter sharing preserves data privacy and reduces data transmission costs. But data sharing is a hot topic. The IoV generates a lot of extra real-time data. Different road conditions (*i.e.*, urban, suburban, uphill, *etc.*) influence the statistics.

One of the main objectives of the study was to successfully include all cars in the global ML model training and to integrate incremental data into the current ML model to enhance the response to the IoV DRAS, or safety alerts. There is a problem with incremental data. The answer to the problem of "instant learning" is "incremental learning". In other words, incremental learning is the ability of a learning system to keep extracting new information from new data while still retaining most of the information that was previously understood. If you want to reduce the accuracy and bias of global ML models, you can use the standard ensemble learning method, which relies too much on repeating the learning process and does not take into account the weight of extra data. The more different the parameters of different local ML models, the better the outcome, because the goal of combined learning *vs.* incremental learning is to get more accurate predictions using the parameters of different cars. If all the local ML models are very similar and not complementary, then you do not need to train the global ML models - you just copy them, which adds to your computational cost. Our architecture combines the benefits of lots of local ML models with lots of IoV models to make up for each other's weaknesses and handle data diversity better [17, 18].

SECURE COMMUNICATION IN FEDERATED LEARNING

The newest communication standards (5G and 6G) provide a wide range of communication technology prospects, including widespread connections, increased capacity, rapid speed, and more. But because it is a primitive technology, it has many of the same problems and restrictions as terrestrial networks. On the other hand, satellite communication networks provide a vast range of coverage, including practically all cities, towns, isolated rural regions, seas, and roadways. As a result, the integration of space networks with terrestrial networks is crucial for the future of information networks. This type of integration is known as satellite-territorial integrated networks (STIN) or "integrated space and terrestrial networks" (ISTN). This results in a massive amount of transfers across two networks that have very different resource allocation, security, and other configurations, like privacy, processing capabilities, *etc.* More important and sensitive data is transmitted through satellites than through terrestrial networks, which means strict privacy and security regulations. The proliferation of satellite network connections in recent years, connecting billions of devices *via* satellites, has led to an urgent need for increased security and privacy measures.

Territorial networks have a range of privacy and security measures in place, but they are not effective. Since terrestrial networks have no resource limitations, it is hard to update hardware and other resources once a satellite has been deployed. Space networks are not necessarily strong enough to withstand today's increasingly sophisticated attacks, despite intrusion detection systems, firewalls, and other security measures. In the event of an attack on a satellite network, all of the satellite network's resources are lost. Another major issue is the availability of normal and abnormal data for satellite-to-ground networks to train and validate a strong defense system. FL's privacy-protective and decentralized nature makes it quite attractive in this situation [19, 20].

Threat Models and Attack Vectors

A modern car can have more than 100 ECUs, which can connect to third-party networks and interact with internal vehicle networks, making them vulnerable to cyberattacks. Threat modeling can be used by manufacturers to identify potential security threats early and support the development of more secure vehicles to enhance the security of connected cars. Threat modeling can also create quantitative security indicators, which have been successful in other industries but have not yet been widely adopted when combined with probable threat simulations. Threat Models and Attack Vectors are shown in Fig. (5) According to an examination of the literature on the topic, connected cars, threat modeling, and assault simulations as a whole have gotten relatively little attention. We constructed and ran assault simulations on two vehicle threat models using the technology. Our work serves as a proof of concept for the approach's value. Particularly if more investigation is conducted on vehicle-specific flaws, vulnerabilities, and defenses for a more thorough study, combine it into a more specialized, vehicle-specific model [55].

Federated Learning Security Protocols

Numerous contexts, including the troublesome mobile environment, have successfully implemented federated learning. Federated learning has many advantages, but the idea also presents certain privacy and security issues. Federated learning offers certain privacy benefits over sending individual data between data centers. One advantage is the possibility to construct machine learning algorithms in large quantities based on user input while minimizing bandwidth constraints for sending sensitive data across the network. Federating learning networks are exposed to two major security threats: model and data poisoning, both of which are exacerbated by the vulnerability of wireless connections in communication networks. Furthermore, updates to federated systems can be manipulated or hijacked through these vulnerable connections. These targeted attacks, which are conducted under the supervision of a complex model, seek to exploit low sensitivity in machine learning algorithms of some data poisoning risk groups. The internet connection and the Edge Device (ED) of a linked learning paradigm are two of the distributional learning attack surfaces susceptible to these attacks, making them two of the most significant security risks for connected learning networks [21 - 23].

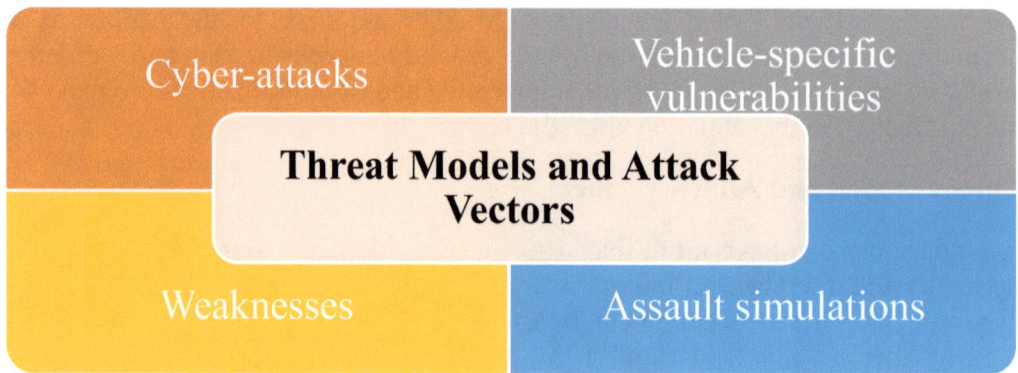

Fig. (5). Threat models and attack vectors.

Trust Evaluation Mechanisms

One of the most important components of intelligent transportation systems is the Internet of Vehicles (IoV). Real-time traffic data sharing is possible between vehicle nodes. Even while IoV can increase travel efficiency, there are still safety issues. Safety management studies have frequently used the trust-value-based technique. However, in the Internet of Vehicles, car nodes travel at high speeds, the period for car node communication and message inspection is incredibly short, and network architecture is continually evolving, which puts further load on trust evaluation techniques. How to effectively assess, keep up, and manage the trust of vehicle nodes is a serious concern. The process of evaluating nodes and messages for reliability using the concept of trust is known as trust assessment. At now, the message-based trust evaluation technique must assess each message received and concentrate on the message's credibility. According to the node and message evaluation technique, the measure must consider both the node and message components. The majority of the aforementioned techniques either concentrate on determining the dependability of incoming signals or assess nodes using expertise, advice from nearby vehicles, and ideas from centralized organizations. Even the assessment technique that considers both message trust and node behavior avoids the issue of untrustworthy messages delivered by nodes that have shown good behavior. A unique trust assessment technique was presented to swiftly carry out dynamic trust evaluation, precisely identify dangerous vehicle nodes, and address the problem of unreliable signals supplied by behavioral trusted nodes. This method assumed that the comprehensive trust value was the foundation for trust and that the message trust value obtained through instant messaging was a result of the comprehensive trust value. To maintain and retain the trust value data of car nodes, a distributed vehicle node trust database was constructed using blockchain technology, and the proof of trust technique was employed in place of the proof of work approach [24 - 27].

PRIVACY PRESERVATION IN FEDERATED LEARNING

Federated learning enables the training of collaborative models without the need to exchange raw data. However, recent attacks have shown that local storage of data during training may not provide sufficient privacy protection [56, 57].

What we want is a federated learning architecture that can provide a high enough degree of model prediction accuracy to prevent inference on both the training messages and the completed trained model. Currently, federated learning architectures either use differential privacy (which can lead to accuracy issues when there are multiple participants and a limited amount of data) or use secure multiparty computing (SMC) which adds inference. In this paper, we present a novel approach to balance these tradeoffs: differential privacy using SMC. We can reduce the increase in noise output as the number of participants increases while maintaining a pre-set level of trust by combining different privacy tiers with private multiparty computing.

Data Privacy and Confidentiality in IoVs

As the Internet of Vehicles (IOV) becomes more and more integrated into our daily lives, the privacy of each car's data is becoming a hot concern. A double-layered link-based privacy safety system is created to address this issue and reduce the security risk associated with exchanging vehicle data. In addition, the immutability of the blockchain enables rational arbitration in disputes over auto insurance claims, traffic accidents, and other matters. We develop an IOV double-layered chain model to simulate a semi-centralized system that is easy for the government to monitor. We also created an RSA protocol based on zero KPI to bring security and zero KPI features to the system. The possibility of widespread adoption of our double-layered chain-based IOV privacy protection solution in the vehicle-sharing sector is the last thing we consider. We compare the communication expenses of the single-layer chain framework with the double-layer chain framework to show how cost-effective the double-layer structure is. This offers an IOV privacy method that is more cost-effective and safe [28 - 30].

Differential Privacy Techniques: A sound, mathematical definition of privacy in the context of statistical and machine-learning analysis is differential privacy (DP). DP is a privacy protection criterion that has led to the development of numerous strategies for the inspection of sensitive personal information because of its mathematical reason [31 - 34].

Data input for ML algorithms typically refers to private databases containing sensitive data. Computer scientists often use anonymization techniques to ensure the confidentiality of the data used for training ML systems. However, these anonymization techniques are far from perfect. Numerous studies have demonstrated that ML models that employ anonymization methods are susceptible to a wide range of privacy attacks designed to expose sensitive information. To protect sensitive data within private data within machine learning, we provide a unique task-specific adaptive differential privacy approach (DP) for structured data.

There are two main types of data protection strategies used in ML research: DP techniques for different private model modifications and DP strategies for different private data publications. Differential private model modification strategies look at how to share the ML model securely between different people while keeping attackers from spying on the hyperparameters. Differential private model modification protects the hyperparameters of the ML model, not the data itself, from different types of privacy risks like model inversion and model theft. Differential private data publishing strategies look at how the affected data can be produced to spread the private data around different organizations for ML, which we focus on because we care about the details of the data for ML [35 - 38].

Federated Learning Privacy-preserving Mechanisms

Many users train the same model through federated learning, where the raw training data is shared. Typically, federated learning requires multi-party computing solutions to ensure privacy by preventing an unauthenticated or curious aggregator from collecting isolated responses from participants during the training process. Some of these secure aggregation methods were once thought to be sufficient to protect against inference attacks from an interested aggregator. However, a curious aggregator may launch a distributed attack to discover a target's model changes, according to a new study. DeTrust-FL is the framework for privacy-friendly federated learning. By making parties' model updates private and safe to be included in the aggregated model, it solves the transparency issue that allows isolation attacks (such as breakdown attacks) to occur in the context of secure aggregation. To increase control and trust in the decentralized, secure aggregating process, it includes a new decentralized functional encryption (FE) scheme in which everyone agrees on the participation matrix, and then collaboratively generates decrypted key fragments. According to our tests, in terms of the training time and the amount of data transmitted, deTrust-FL outperforms the current FE-based, secure, multi-party aggregation systems. Unlike previous approaches, this strategy accomplishes the same objective without anyone being involved [39, 40].

APPLICATIONS OF FEDERATED LEARNING IN IOVS

Traffic Prediction and Management

Wireless traffic forecasting is super important for mobile networks to be able to do advanced things like use load-aware resources and control traffic. Current prediction systems usually use centralized training systems and require a lot of traffic data to be transferred, which can sometimes cause delays and privacy problems. In this article, we're going to talk about FedDA, which is a new way of looking at wireless traffic prediction. It's a way of looking at it where a bunch of edge clients all work together to make a really good prediction model. Instead of just recording all the different types of wireless traffic and saving the data in one place, FedDA divides the clients into different clusters using a tiny augmentation dataset. To tackle the challenge of statistical heterogeneity posed by federated learning, we create a semi-global model and share it with clients. We do not just average the weights of the local models, we use a double attention technique to create a global model by combining the weights of the inside and outside clusters. We run lots of tests on two wireless traffic datasets and the results show that FedDA outperforms the current approaches. On both datasets, we see an average squared error performance increase of up to 10-30% [41, 42].

Intelligent Routing Optimization

It is challenging to extend basic physical equipment since network traffic is always changing. It is challenging to offer improved network connection and quality of service at an affordable price since it requires a lot of resources to keep up with the traffic and it takes a while to refresh them. By distributing traffic among several devices, network traffic routing control may ease the burden on available network resources and help users make the most of them [43 - 45]. Traditional networks employ several routing algorithms that operate on various routers. Although distributed routing algorithms often use the best-effort concept to compute routing, due to the limited accuracy of traffic control, they are unable to provide good network quality of service (QoS). On the other hand, with a software-defined network (SDN), the traffic control approach is based on a centralized network perspective, and after collecting data from the entire network, the network strategy is developed based on macro control information from the network status to provide a more specific service plan for the entire network. Finding the best routing strategy based on knowing the entire network is NP-hard work. Most of the current routing optimization techniques rely on heuristic AI algorithms, which cannot guarantee the accuracy of the routing plan. To solve this problem, the industry will be focused on the rapid development of AI technologies in the last few years. The advantages of AI routing strategies based on ANNs and DRLs are starting to become clear. Compared to other machine learning schemes, the smart routing scheme based on DRL has the advantages of autonomous training, high flexibility, and the lack of the need to manually label large amounts of data, which makes it stand out from many machine learning-based schemes. However, today's intelligent routing techniques based on DRLs are mostly based on FNNs, RNNs, and other NN topologies. The inflexible nature of the network topology and low generalization ability make it hard to adjust to dynamic changes in network topology [46 - 48].

Vehicle Safety and Security Enhancement

We all want to drive safely, but as there are more cars on the road, it is getting more and more difficult to do so since accidents are more common. There are two things you may do to lessen the likelihood of an accident occurring or worsening. To prevent chain collisions, you might first warn the vehicles behind you. However, even if you can see a collision, you would not be able to identify it until it is too late if you are driving in poor conditions, like fog. To reduce traffic, you may also warn other vehicles that may be passing by the scene of the collision [49 - 52]. Unfortunately, the present radio-based method of reporting accidents necessitates that someone must be sitting in a vehicle when it occurs. Therefore, to identify a collision in real-time and to share vehicle status information with adjacent vehicles, the vehicle safety improvement system needs two subsystems:

Vehicle Information Acquisition Systems (VIAS): This subsystem is responsible for identifying the accident information (such as position, *etc.*), classifying the severity level of the accident (such as slight bumping or rolling over), detecting some dangerous driving behaviors (such as sudden slowing or S-shape driving), current additive sensor technologies (such as GPS, accelerometer, or angle sensors), onboard vehicular signals (such as airbag deployment signal or brake pedal signal or vehicle speed signal, *etc.*). The second subsystem is the Intervehicle Wireless Communication System (IVWCS) which is responsible for transferring information between vehicles. In recent years, wireless technology has made it possible to enable vehicle-to-vehicle (V2W) and vehicle-to-infrastructure communication for ITS *via* mobile ad hoc networks (MANETs). Given the unique characteristics of the automotive environment, vehicle ad hoc networks (VANETs) offer apparent advantages; that is, VANETs not only increase the general security of the vehicular system but also smooth the traffic flow [53, 54].

DISCUSSION

Key Outcomes

- Federated Learning is a collaborative approach to machine learning models that prioritize data security and privacy, especially in the Internet of Vehicles.
- The Internet of Vehicles (IoV) transforms vehicles into intelligent systems that provide real-time information to drivers.
- Developing machine learning models for IoVs is challenging due to accuracy, data volume, safety, and debugging complexity.
- Differential privacy is crucial in machine learning, especially in the IoV space.
- Federated learning frameworks can help protect data privacy by only sharing model updates.
- Trust assessment and Blockchain and trust databases are suggested as trust management tools for IoVs to mitigate security threats.
- Double layer chain privacy protection system using Blockchain technology is introduced to address privacy and security concerns in IoVs.

Limitations

- Implementing and managing federated learning in IoVs can be a huge problem, necessitating significant resources and experience.
- While the article mentions collaborative learning without data sharing, it does not go into detail about the possible data privacy issues that come with sharing sensitive IoV data among numerous parties.
- Securing federated learning processes in the context of IoVs is a significant challenge, and the paper does not give complete insights into tackling these security challenges.
- The introduction covers federated learning applications in IoVs briefly, such as traffic prediction and vehicle safety, but fails to offer actual examples or case studies to demonstrate their usefulness and limits.
- The essay raises concerns regarding the efficacy of federated learning in IoVs, but it lacks the facts and analysis to back up or dispute these statements.
- Although worries concerning the dependability of federated learning devices are briefly discussed, there is a lack of extensive investigation into how these problems might influence the overall efficacy and security of the communication system in IoVs.

- Despite their crucial importance in the handling of sensitive IoV data, ethical concerns such as data bias, fairness, and openness are conspicuously absent from the conversation.
- Future research fields are mentioned briefly, but the text does not go into detail on the obstacles and potential solutions related to these areas, providing readers with an inadequate picture of the research landscape.

FUTURE DIRECTIONS

Future Research Directions for Federated Learning in IoVs.

While challenges have been addressed in recent federated learning projects, there are still open issues to be addressed. Federated learning necessitates the use of extreme communication techniques, yet it is still essential to comprehend one-shot and few-shot techniques in huge, heterogeneous networks. It is common to use bulk synchronous and asynchronous communication for distributed optimization. Devices in federated networks are not active on certain iterations or assigned to a job. We require a new communication paradigm that incorporates device decision-making. Recent research attempts to measure statistical heterogeneity using training-time measurements, however, these metrics must be computed beforehand. This begs the question of whether straightforward diagnostics for assessing systems and statistical heterogeneity might enhance the convergence of federated optimization techniques. Contextual challenges including idea drift, diurnal changes, and cold start issues with federated learning in production necessitate solutions to successfully handle these problem.

CONCLUSION

In conclusion, federated learning is a revolutionary method of machine learning that tackles important issues like data security and privacy, enabling numerous parties to work together on creating powerful models without disclosing sensitive information. Its use in the Internet of Vehicles (IoVs) shows significant promise for improving a number of areas, such as traffic forecasting, intelligent routing optimization, vehicle safety, and security. Achieving greater accuracy in detection and prediction, managing huge datasets, assuring safety, and tackling the complexity of model debugging are still issues. Secure communication is also essential, particularly when connecting satellite networks with terrestrial networks. Federated learning makes use of measures that protect privacy, such as differential privacy, yet problems like model and data poisoning still exist.

REFERENCES

[1]   https://en.wikipedia.org/wiki/Federated_learning n.d.

[2]   https://research.ibm.com/blog/what-is-federated-learning n.d.

[3]   Www.Market-Prospects.Comhttps://www.market-prospects.com/articles/the-internet-of-vehicles

[4]   https://www.iiot-world.com/artificial-intelligence-ml/autonomous-vehicles/challenges-in-tr-ining-algorithms-for-autonomous-cars/

[5]   Y. Lei, S.L. Wang, M. Zhong, M. Wang, and T.F. Ng, "A Federated Learning Framework Based on Incremental Weighting and Diversity Selection for Internet of Vehicles", *Electronics (Basel)*, vol. 11, no. 22, p. 3668, 2022.
[http://dx.doi.org/10.3390/electronics11223668]

[6]   W. Xiong, F. Krantz, and R. Lagerström, "Threat Modeling and Attack Simulations of Connected Vehicles: Proof of Concept", *Commun. Comput. Inf. Sci.*, vol. 1221, pp. 272-287, 2020.
[http://dx.doi.org/10.1007/978-3-030-49443-8_13]

[7]   H.M. Asif, M.A. Karim, and F. Kausar, "Federated Learning and its Applications for Security and Communication", *Int. J. Adv. Comput. Sci. Appl.*, vol. 13, no. 8, 2022.
[http://dx.doi.org/10.14569/IJACSA.2022.0130838]

[8]   P.S. Xie, X.Q. Wang, X.J. Pan, Y.F. Wang, T. Feng, and Y. Yan, "Blockchain-based Trust Evaluation Mechanism for Internet of Vehicles Nodes", *Int. J. Netw. Secur.*, vol. 23, pp. 1065-1073, 2021.
[http://dx.doi.org/10.6633/IJNS.202111 23(6).13]

[9]   S. Truex, N. Baracaldo, A. Anwar, T. Steinke, H. Ludwig, R. Zhang, and Y. Zhou, "A Hybrid Approach to Privacy-Preserving Federated Learning", *Informatik Spektrum*, vol. 42, no. 5, pp. 356-357, 2019.
[http://dx.doi.org/10.1007/s00287-019-01205-x]

[10]   Y.R. Chen, J.R. Sha, and Z.H. Zhou, "IOV Privacy Protection System Based on Double-Layered Chains", *Wirel. Commun. Mob. Comput.*, vol. 2019, pp. 1-11, 2019.
[http://dx.doi.org/10.1155/2019/3013562]

[11]   A. Nguyen, *Understanding Differential Privacy.*, 2022. https://towardsdatascience.com/understanding-differential-privacy-85ce191e198a

[12]   A. Utaliyeva, J. Shin, and Y.H. Choi, "Task-Specific Adaptive Differential Privacy Method for Structured Data", *Sensors (Basel)*, vol. 23, no. 4, p. 1980, 2023.
[http://dx.doi.org/10.3390/s23041980] [PMID: 36850576]

[13]   S. Truex, N. Baracaldo, A. Anwar, T. Steinke, H. Ludwig, R. Zhang, and Y. Zhou, "A Hybrid Approach to Privacy-Preserving Federated Learning", *Informatik Spektrum*, vol. 42, no. 5, pp. 356-357, 2019.
[http://dx.doi.org/10.1007/s00287-019-01205-x]

[14]   C. Zhang, S. Dang, B. Shihada, and M.S. Alouini, "Dual Attention-Based Federated Learning for Wireless Traffic Prediction", *IEEE INFOCOM 2021 - IEEE Conference on Computer Communications, Vancouver, BC, Canada*, pp. 1-10, 2021.
[http://dx.doi.org/10.1109/INFOCOM42981.2021.9488883]

[15]   P. Garg, A. Dixit, and P. Sethi, "Ml-fresh: novel routing protocol in opportunistic networks using machine learning", *Comput. Syst. Sci. Eng.*, vol. 40, no. 2, pp. 703-717, 2022.
[http://dx.doi.org/10.32604/csse.2022.019557]

[16]   P.S. Yadav, S. Khan, Y.V. Singh, P. Garg, and R.S. Singh, "A Lightweight Deep Learning-Based Approach for Jazz Music Generation in MIDI Format", *Comput. Intell. Neurosci.*, vol. 2022, pp. 1-7, 2022.
[http://dx.doi.org/10.1155/2022/2140895] [PMID: 36035841]

[17]   E. Soni, A. Nagpal, P. Garg, and P.R. Pinheiro, "Assessment of Compressed and Decompressed ECG Databases for Telecardiology Applying a Convolution Neural Network", *Electronics (Basel)*, vol. 11, no. 17, p. 2708, 2022.
[http://dx.doi.org/10.3390/electronics11172708]

[18]   I.V. Pustokhina, D.A. Pustokhin, E.L. Lydia, P. Garg, A. Kadian, and K. Shankar, "Hyperparameter search based convolution neural network with Bi-LSTM model for intrusion detection system in multimedia big data environment", *Multimedia Tools Appl.,* vol. 81, pp. 1-18, 2021. [http://dx.doi.org/10.1007/s11042-021-11271-7]

[19]   A. Khanna, P. Rani, P. Garg, P.K. Singh, and A. Khamparia, "An Enhanced Crow Search Inspired Feature Selection Technique for Intrusion Detection Based Wireless Network System", *Wirel. Pers. Commun.,* vol. 127, pp. 1-18, 2021. [http://dx.doi.org/10.1007/s11277-021-08766-9]

[20]   P. Garg, A. Dixit, P. Sethi, and P.R. Pinheiro, "Impact of node density on the qos parameters of routing protocols in opportunistic networks for smart spaces", *Mob. Inf. Syst.,* vol. 2020, pp. 1-18, 2020. [http://dx.doi.org/10.1155/2020/8868842]

[21]   D. Upadhyay, P. Garg, S.M. Aldossary, J. Shafi, and S. Kumar, "A Linear Quadratic Regression-Based Synchronised Health Monitoring System (SHMS) for IoT Applications", *Electronics (Basel),* vol. 12, no. 2, p. 309, 2023. [http://dx.doi.org/10.3390/electronics12020309]

[22]   P. Saini, B. Nagpal, P. Garg, and S. Kumar, "CNN-BI-LSTM-CYP: A deep learning approach for sugarcane yield prediction", *Sustain. Energy Technol. Assess.,* vol. 57, p. 103263, 2023. [http://dx.doi.org/10.1016/j.seta.2023.103263]

[23]   P. Saini, B. Nagpal, P. Garg, and S. Kumar, "Evaluation of Remote Sensing and Meteorological parameters for Yield Prediction of Sugarcane (Saccharum officinarum L.) Crop", *Braz. Arch. Biol. Technol.,* vol. 66, p. e23220781, 2023. [http://dx.doi.org/10.1590/1678-4324-2023220781]

[24]   S. Beniwal, U. Saini, P. Garg, and R.K. Joon, "Improving performance during camera surveillance by integration of edge detection in IoT system", *Int. J. E-Health Med. Commun.,* vol. 12, no. 5, pp. 84-96, 2021. [IJEHMC]. [http://dx.doi.org/10.4018/IJEHMC.20210901.oa6]

[25]   P. Garg, A. Dixit, and P. Sethi, "Wireless sensor networks: an insight review", *Int. J. Adv. Sci. Techno,* vol. 28, no. 15, pp. 612-627, 2019.

[26]   N. Sharma, and P. Garg, "Ant colony based optimization model for QoS-Based task scheduling in cloud computing environment. Measurement", *Sensors (Basel),* vol. 24, p. 100531, 2022. [http://dx.doi.org/10.1016/j.measen.2022.100531]

[27]   P. Kumar, R. Kumar, and P. Garg, *Hybrid Crowd Cloud Routing Protocol For Wireless Sensor Networks.,* 2020.

[28]   G. Raj, A. Verma, P. Dalal, A.K. Shukla, and P. Garg, "Performance Comparison of Several LPWAN Technologies for Energy Constrained IOT Network", *Int. J. Intell. Syst. Appl. Eng.,* vol. 11, no. 1s, pp. 150-158, 2023. Retrieved from: https://www.ijisae.org/index.php/IJISAE/article/view/2487

[29]   P. Garg, N. Sharma, and B. Shukla, "Predicting the Risk of Cardiovascular Diseases using Machine Learning Techniques", *Int. J. Intell. Syst. Appl. Eng.,* vol. 11, no. 2s, pp. 165-173, 2023. Retrieved from https://www.ijisae.org/index.php/IJISAE/article/view/2487

[30]   A. Dixit, P. Garg, P. Sethi, and Y. Singh, "TVCCCS: Television Viewer's Channel Cost Calculation System On Per Second Usage", *IOP Conf. Series Mater. Sci. Eng.,* vol. 804, no. 1, p. 012046, 2020. []. IOP Publishing.]. [http://dx.doi.org/10.1088/1757-899X/804/1/012046]

[31]   P. Sethi, P. Garg, A. Dixit, and Y. Singh, "Smart number cruncher – a voice based calculator", *IOP Conf. Series Mater. Sci. Eng.,* vol. 804, no. 1, p. 012041, 2020. []. IOP Publishing.]. [http://dx.doi.org/10.1088/1757-899X/804/1/012041]

[32]   S. Rai, and V. Choubey, "Suryansh and P. Garg, "A Systematic Review of Encryption and Keylogging

for Computer System Security", *2022 Fifth International Conference on Computational Intelligence and Communication Technologies (CCICT)*, pp. 157-163, 2022.
[http://dx.doi.org/10.1109/CCiCT56684.2022.00039]

[33]   L. Saraswat, L. Mohanty, P. Garg, and S. Lamba, "Plant Disease Identification Using Plant Images", *2022 Fifth International Conference on Computational Intelligence and Communication Technologies (CCICT)*, pp. 79-82, 2022.
[http://dx.doi.org/10.1109/CCiCT56684.2022.00026]

[34]   L. Mohanty, L. Saraswat, P. Garg, and S. Lamba, "Recommender Systems in E-Commerce", *2022 Fifth International Conference on Computational Intelligence and Communication Technologies (CCICT)*, pp. 114-119, 2022.
[http://dx.doi.org/10.1109/CCiCT56684.2022.00032]

[35]   C. Maggo, and P. Garg, "From linguistic features to their extractions: Understanding the semantics of a concept", *2022 Fifth International Conference on Computational Intelligence and Communication Technologies (CCICT)*, pp. 427-431, 2022.
[http://dx.doi.org/10.1109/CCiCT56684.2022.00082]

[36]   N. Puri, P. Saggar, A. Kaur, and P. Garg, "Application of ensemble Machine Learning models for phishing detection on web networks", *2022 Fifth International Conference on Computational Intelligence and Communication Technologies (CCICT)*, pp. 296-303, 2022.
[http://dx.doi.org/10.1109/CCiCT56684.2022.00062]

[37]   R. Sharma, S. Gupta, and P. Garg, "Model for Predicting Cardiac Health using Deep Learning Classifier", *2022 Fifth International Conference on Computational Intelligence and Communication Technologies (CCICT)*, pp. 25-30, 2022.
[http://dx.doi.org/10.1109/CCiCT56684.2022.00017]

[38]   S.L. Varshney, and P. Garg, "A Comprehensive Survey on Event Analysis Using Deep Learning", *2022 Fifth International Conference on Computational Intelligence and Communication Technologies (CCICT)*, pp. 146-150, 2022.
[http://dx.doi.org/10.1109/CCiCT56684.2022.00037]

[39]   A. Dixit, P. Sethi, P. Garg, and J. Pruthi, "Speech Difficulties and Clarification: A Systematic Review", *2022 11th International Conference on System Modeling & Advancement in Research Trends (SMART), Moradabad, India*, pp. 52-56, 20222022.
[http://dx.doi.org/10.1109/SMART55829.2022.10047048]

[40]   S Chauhan., M. Singh., and; P. Garg., "Rapid Forecasting of Pandemic Outbreak Using Machine Learning". Enabling Healthcare 4.0 for Pandemics: A Roadmap Using AI, Machine Learning, IoT and Cognitive Technologies, pp. 59-73 , 2021.

[41]   S. Gupta, and P. Garg, "An insight review on multimedia forensics technology", *Cyber Crime and Forensic Computing: Modern Principles, Practices, and Algorithms*, vol. 11, pp. 27-48, 2021.
[http://dx.doi.org/10.1515/9783110677478-002]

[42]   P. Shrivastava, P. Agarwal, K. Sharma, and P. Garg, "Data leakage detection in Wi-Fi networks", *Cyber Crime and Forensic Computing: Modern Principles, Practices, and Algorithms*, vol. 11, pp. 215-228, 2021.
[http://dx.doi.org/10.1515/9783110677478-010]

[43]   P.G. Meenakshi, P. Garg, and P. Shrivastava, "Machine learning for mobile malware analysis", *Cyber Crime and Forensic Computing: Modern Principles, Practices, and Algorithms*, vol. 11, pp. 151-178, 2021.
[http://dx.doi.org/10.1515/9783110677478-008]

[44]   P. Shrivastava, P. Agarwal, K. Sharma,and P. Garg, P. "Data leakage detection in Wi-Fi networks". In: Cyber Crime and Forensic Computing: Modern Principles, Practices, and Algorithms, vol.11, pp. 215, 2021.,
[http://dx.doi.org/10.1515/9783110677478-010]

[45]   J. Nanwal, P. Garg, P. Sethi, and A. Dixit. "Green IoT and Big Data: Succeeding towards Building Smart Cities". In: Green Internet of Things for Smart Cities, pp. 83-98, CRC Press, 2021., [http://dx.doi.org/10.1201/9781003032397-5"10.1201/9781003032397-5]

[46]   M. Gupta, P. Garg, and P. Agarwal, "Ant Colony Optimization Technique in Soft Computational Data Research for NP-Hard Problems", In: *Artificial Intelligence for a Sustainable Industry 4.0.* Springer: Cham, 2021, pp. 197-211. [http://dx.doi.org/10.1007/978-3-030-77070-9_12]

[47]   C. Maggo and P. Garg, "From linguistic features to their extractions: Understanding the semantics of a concept" *2022 Fifth International Conference on Computational Intelligence and Communication Technologies (CCICT)* 2022, pp. 427-431. [http://dx.doi.org/10.1109/CCiCT56684.2022.00082]

[48]   P. Garg, A.K. Srivastava, A. Anas, B. Gupta, and C. Mishra, "Pneumonia Detection Through X-Ray Images Using Convolution Neural Network", In: *Advancements in Bio-Medical Image Processing and Authentication in Telemedicine.* IGI Global, 2023, pp. 201-218. [http://dx.doi.org/10.4018/978-1-6684-6957-6.ch011]

[49]   A. Chaudhary, and P. Garg, "Detecting and diagnosing a disease by patient monitoring system", *Int. J. Mech. Eng. Inform, technol.,* vol. 2, no. 6, pp. 493-499, 2014.

[50]   X. Zhou, and H. Guo, "An intelligent routing optimization strategy based on deep reinforcement learning", *J. Phys. Conf. Ser.,* vol. 2010, no. 1, p. 012046, 2021. [http://dx.doi.org/10.1088/1742-6596/2010/1/012046]

[51]   G. Krishna, R. Singh, and A. Gehlot, "Cloud-based Monitoring of the Health of Battery using IoT", *2022 5th International Conference on Contemporary Computing and Informatics (IC3I), Uttar Pradesh, India,* pp. 2232-2235, 2022. [http://dx.doi.org/10.1109/IC3I56241.2022.10072860]

[52]   G. Krishna, R. Singh, A. Gehlot, N. Yamsani, S. Kathuria, and S.V. Akram, "Enhancing the Cyber-Security of Battery Management Systems for Energy Storage", *2023 IEEE World Conference on Applied Intelligence and Computing (AIC),* pp. 959-964, 2023. Sonbhadra, India. [http://dx.doi.org/10.1109/AIC57670.2023.10263843]

[53]   G. Krishna , R. Singh , A. Gehlot , P. Singh , S. Rana, S. V. Akram and K. Joshi, "An imperative role of studying existing battery datasets and algorithms for battery management system", *Rev. Comput. Eng. Res.,* vol. 10, no. 2, 2023. [http://dx.doi.org/10.18488/76.v10i2.3413]

[54]   H. Qian, Y. Chen, Y. Sun, N. Liu, N. Ding, Y. Xu, G. Xu, Y. Tang, and J. Yan, "Vehicle Safety Enhancement System: Sensing and Communication", *Int. J. Distrib. Sens. Netw.,* vol. 9, no. 12, p. 542891, 2013. [http://dx.doi.org/10.1155/2013/542891]

[55]   P.K. Singh, S.S. Chauhan, A. Sharma, S. Prakash, and Y. Singh, "Prediction of higher heating values based on imminent analysis by using regression analysis and artificial neural network for bioenergy resources", *Proceedings of the Institution of Mechanical Engineers Part EJ. Process Mech. Eng.,* 2023. [http://dx.doi.org/10.1177/09544089231175046]

[56]   S.P. Yadav, and S. Yadav, "Image fusion using hybrid methods in multimodality medical images", *Med. Biol. Eng. Comput.,* vol. 58, no. 4, pp. 669-687, 2020. [http://dx.doi.org/10.1007/s11517-020-02136-6] [PMID: 31993885]

[57]   S. Prakash Yadav, and S. Yadav, "Fusion of Medical Images in Wavelet Domain: A Hybrid Implementation", *Comput. Model. Eng. Sci.,* vol. 122, no. 1, pp. 303-321, 2020. [http://dx.doi.org/10.32604/cmes.2020.08459]

SUBJECT INDEX